God's Not Forgotten Me

God's Not Forgotten Me
Experiencing Faith in Dementia

'TRICIA WILLIAMS

Foreword by John Swinton

CASCADE *Books* · Eugene, Oregon

GOD'S NOT FORGOTTEN ME
Experiencing Faith in Dementia

Copyright © 2022 'Tricia Williams. All rights reserved. Except for brief quotations in critical publications or reviews, no part of this book may be reproduced in any manner without prior written permission from the publisher. Write: Permissions, Wipf and Stock Publishers, 199 W. 8th Ave., Suite 3, Eugene, OR 97401.

Cascade Books
An Imprint of Wipf and Stock Publishers
199 W. 8th Ave., Suite 3
Eugene, OR 97401

www.wipfandstock.com

PAPERBACK ISBN: 978-1-7252-7216-3
HARDCOVER ISBN: 978-1-7252-7217-0
EBOOK ISBN: 978-1-7252-7218-7

Cataloguing-in-Publication data:

Names: Williams, 'Tricia, author. | Swinton, John, foreword.

Title: God's not forgotten me : experiencing faith in dementia / 'Tricia Williams; foreword by John Swinton.

Description: Eugene, OR: Cascade Books, 2022 | Includes bibliographical references and index.

Identifiers: ISBN 978-1-7252-7216-3 (paperback) | ISBN 978-1-7252-7217-0 (hardcover) | ISBN 978-1-7252-7218-7 (ebook)

Subjects: LCSH: Dementia. | Dementia—Patients—Biography. | Dementia—Religious aspects—Christianity. | Pastoral care.

Classification: BV4435.5 W50 2022 (paperback) | BV4435 (ebook)

05/09/22

Unless otherwise indicated, Scripture quotations are from New Revised Standard Version Bible: Anglicized Edition, copyright © 1989, 1995 National Council of the Churches of Christ in the United States of America. Used by permission. All rights reserved worldwide. http://nrsvbibles.org
Scripture quotations marked ESV® are from the ESV® Bible (The Holy Bible, English Standard Version®), copyright © 2001 by Crossway Bibles, a publishing ministry of Good News Publishers. Used by permission. All rights reserved.
Scripture quotations marked (NIVUK) are from Holy Bible, New International Version® Anglicized, NIV® Copyright © 1979, 1984, 2011 by Biblica, Inc.® Used by permission. All rights reserved worldwide.
Scripture quotations marked (NLT) are taken from the Holy Bible, New Living Translation, copyright © 1996, 2004, 2007, 2013, 2015 by Tyndale House Foundation. Used by permission of Tyndale House Publishers, Inc., Carol Stream, Illinois 60188. All rights reserved.

Participants in the research have given consent for their words to be used. Their names and those of other private individuals referred to in this book have been anonymized.

For all those whose words and stories are remembered in this book.

"I will not forget you! See, I have engraved you on the palms of my hands."
(Isaiah 49:15–16 NIVUK)

Contents

Foreword by John Swinton		ix
Acknowledgments		xi
Scripture Abbreviations		xiii
Introduction		xv
1	Faith in Dementia?	1
2	Seeking Understanding	17
3	Who I Am	32
4	Knowing God: The Experience of Faith	51
5	Being Not Doing: The Experience of Practice	66
6	Walking through Shadow	82
7	Memory Funding Faith	100
8	Growing Faith	117
9	Present-Future Hope	133
10	Walking Together	150
Bibliography		165
Index		175

Foreword

It's interesting to notice the kinds of language that we use around age care and dementia. As the paradigms of business continue to be applied to the aged care enterprise—now being described as a "market," an "industry," a "sector," with elderly people viewed as consumers whose choice should sit at the center of the system—there is a difficult tension between the need for safety, professionalism, clinical compliance, and financial governance and the "soft," "dangerous," and "risky" language of spirituality and love. And yet, there is a strange irony in the fact that some argue that "the consumer" should be at the heart of the system, whilst at the same time often avoiding the language of the heart. The idea that love and the enablement of love might be a key indicator for success within an organization is not something that is easily assimilated into standard business models. However, as Christians we are called to offer care that is marked by the core practices of love: joy, peace, forbearance, kindness, goodness, faithfulness. Care without love may be "safe" and "efficient" but it is inevitably lacking. There is a need for a new language and perhaps a new paradigm.

In order to engage in love-filled spiritual care, we need to listen to people; to begin to see that the stories of their lives are not determined by their ages or the state of their neurons. There is a need for a different story, a story that places God at the center and holds on to the fullness of life for elderly people even in difficult times. In this book 'Tricia Williams gently helps us to listen carefully to the voices of people living with dementia and to allow that listening to transform our understanding of dementia, care, and indeed humanness. Through the sensitive use of qualitative research she lets people give voice to their hopes, their fears, their theologies, and their loves. As we as individuals and as members of Jesus' church listen to such stories, we are offered a challenge. We are challenged to ensure that we continue to recognize people's discipleship and to strive with innovation and faithful imagination to enable people to continue to experience love, joy, peace, forbearance, kindness, goodness, faithfulness, and gentleness in the midst of the challenges of dementia. How do we do this? It's remarkably simple: we offer people Christlike friendship. In offering radical hospitality through friendship Jesus cuts through cultural stigma and draws people into a journey that follows the way of the heart. If each member of Jesus' body were to find the time to offer friendship to someone with dementia, life in all of its fullness would become a real possibility for all of us. Such love involves care, but it is care that is immersed in love.

We are challenged to *notice* people. One of the heartbreaking experiences for people with dementia is not only that they have forgotten things, but that they are often forgotten. Friends abandon them, we stop using their names and begin to call them patients, consumers, clients, units, sufferers. When this happens people as people begin to disappear. The task of the church is to notice the things that others often do not or cannot see: the value of people, their lovability, the hopefulness of their lives, the possibilities for development even in the midst of change. Love notices pain and loneliness and steps out in faith to counter it. Noticing means renewing our minds and allowing the Spirit of love to draw us close to those with whom others are distant. A ministry of friendship and noticing is a powerful countercultural manifestation of God's love in the time of dementia. 'Tricia's book offers us the perspective and the understanding that can enable such an aspiration to become a lived reality.

John Swinton
University of Aberdeen
December 17, 2021

Acknowledgments

I am especially thankful to Alice, Bill, David, Jess, Jill, Matthew, Ron, and Rosemary (the participants in my research project), who were living with dementia during the time of my study, and to their families and friends—all of whom made this book possible. Thank you for your grace and courage in being willing to take part. It has been a privilege to walk with you, and you have taught me much.

I am indebted to Professor John Swinton, my PhD supervisor,[1] whose guidance and profound thinking in the areas of faith and dementia have contributed greatly to my own curiosity and search for understanding. I am grateful also to the University of Aberdeen for their support in enabling me to carry out my study from which this book arises, and to the Bible Society, who partially funded my study.[2] I am thankful too to the many scholars, pastoral carers, writers, and theologians on whose work I have drawn, and which has inspired my own reflection.

A number of dear friends have kindly read the manuscript during the book's writing, and I have deeply appreciated their support, helpful insights, and feedback. I am very grateful too for the skillful support of the Cascade Books publishing team, especially that of my editor Rodney Clapp, who has brought this book to publication.

My thanks also to my dear family (including "my cat Jeoffrey"!) and friends, whose loving support has upheld me as always in this work. Especial

---

1. This book arises from my PhD research: "What Happens to Faith when Christians get Dementia? A Critical Exploration of how Dementia affects the Faith Experience and Practice of Christians from the Evangelical Tradition Living with Mild to Moderate Symptoms of Dementia" (University of Aberdeen, 2018). My author name on the thesis appears as Patricia S. Williams. It has subsequently been published in lightly edited form by Pickwick Publications, January 2021 under the author name 'Tricia Williams.

2. Bible Society, Stonehill Green, Westlea, Swindon, SN5 7DG, https://www.biblesociety.org.uk.

thanks to my husband for his ongoing patience, critical faithfulness, and willing endurance throughout the writing of this book.

Above all I am thankful to God who brought me to this work. His love sustains me, and particularly those disciples of Jesus I have met who were living with dementia.

Scripture Abbreviations

All Scripture quotations are taken from the New Revised Standard Version, Anglicized Edition, unless another version is indicated, as follows:

ESV English Standard Version
NIVUK New International Version
NLT New Living Translation

Introduction

"God is always with me . . . and I know that there's nothing that can ever separate me from him . . . But now, even when my brain falls apart . . . it doesn't matter."

Alice is living with dementia. She has done so for several years. Yet, her words quoted above express her continuing sense of God's presence. You might notice that her trust in God is resourced by memory of Scripture ("nothing can separate me"),[1] as well as the conviction that her identity and faith are not threatened by the cognitive losses that dementia is bringing. Astonishingly, she asserts of her dementia, "even when my brain falls apart . . . it doesn't matter." Why? What sense can we possibly make of such words?

For those who experience it, or who observe and care—perhaps especially those living in the Western world—the coming of this illness raises troubling questions. What does it mean to be human? For the Christian believer, dementia then brings a further question: Is my faith "safe" if I can't remember? Such questions are not only of relevance to those who are in the advanced stages of this illness. They have profound importance for those who are newly diagnosed or who are in the early years of their journey with this disease—those who find themselves *beginning* to struggle with loss of words, concentration, and short-term memory. They are also those who are aware of troubling, stereotypical views about dementia and, in the light of these, able to consider their own future stories. How are they experiencing God's love? How can they *grow* in relationship with him as the dementia progresses? How will they share their gifts in the body of Christ? What might others learn from them? The illness inevitably prompts hard questions about theological underpinnings of certainty of relationship with God,

---

1. See Romans 8:39: ". . . nor anything else in all creation, will be able to separate us from the love of God that is in Christ Jesus our Lord" (NIVUK).

the nature of saving faith, and what it means to be part of the community of faith—whether or not we live with developing dementia.

This book explores questions such as these—drawing on the words of people of committed faith who are living with this disease. It reflects on their experience in the light of writing about Christian spirituality, theological tradition, and, especially, in conversation with the Bible. In reflecting on these voices, deeper understanding of the experience of faith in dementia begins to emerge. Questions for discussion and further reflection follow each chapter to help readers to talk and think further individually or with others.

The book arises from research undertaken as part of my doctoral studies at the University of Aberdeen.[2] It is written in the hope that it will contribute to a growing awareness of the crucial importance of faith for those who live with this illness, to nurturing that faith, and to the transforming ministry practice of those who walk alongside them. The words and lives of the Christians who have contributed to this book have moved, challenged, and encouraged me. I hope that they will challenge and encourage you too.

"We're not *dying from* dementia; we're *living with* dementia."

—Andrew, Jess's husband

---

2. The thesis has been published in lightly edited form by Pickwick Publications: see Williams, *What Happens to Faith When Christians Get Dementia?*

1

Faith in Dementia?

". . . even when my brain falls apart . . ."

The phone rang. It was Tom, a friend and former colleague, who was hunting for an appropriate Bible reading guide for his wife who was living with developing dementia. Cathy had been a teacher, a highly capable professional, deeply involved in leading activities for Christian young people, and in leadership roles in her church. But now regular Bible reading and prayer, which had always been an important part of her life, were becoming difficult as concentration and memory began to diminish. Could I help?

At the time of that phone call, I was working as a developer of Bible resources with a Christian publisher, focusing on faith nurture and discipleship through Bible engagement and prayer. Hence, my friend's question. So, what about the increasing numbers of believers who were beginning to encounter the cognitive difficulties being brought by dementia? What was their experience of faith as this illness began to develop? How could they continue to meet with God and grow as Christians? Were we listening to *their* voices? How was the community of faith responding to such questions? Were they—in some ways—being *marginalized* by the church because of the advent of dementia in their lives? And do we as Christians truly believe, like Alice, that *"nothing"* can separate me—whoever I am, whatever my situation—from the love of God in Christ Jesus our Lord?

The conversation began for me a journey, bringing questions about the nature of dementia, and questions which this illness raises for faith—perhaps especially for Christians of an evangelical tradition. Seeking understanding, I began to talk with experts and those working in care homes. In due course, this led to the development and publication of resources that have been used widely by individuals and in ministry,[1] and then to my own involvement with volunteer chaplaincy teams in care homes, with a focus on those living with dementia.

These were the beginnings of my inquiries and reflections on the faith experience of those who were living with dementia, which led to my PhD research in the field of practical theology—and to the writing of this book. In doing this I have sought to listen to and learn from Christians who were living with dementia, with the goals of deepening understanding of faith and enabling better care for one another. Who better to ask about this experience than those with an insider's perspective?

First, some background information, definitions, and context of the original research, looking at dementia and faith, evangelicalism, and understandings of practical theology (the field of my study), and at the structure of this book.

DEMENTIA AND FAITH?

Research suggests that dementia is one of today's most feared diseases.[2] Currently, there are an estimated 850,000 people living with dementia in the UK. By 2050 that figure is projected to rise to over 2 million.[3] In the US, there are around 6 million people living with the disease.[4] And in Australia, there are an estimated 472,000 people with dementia.[5] Globally, the figures are heading towards 152 million in 2050.[6] Almost certainly, you will know someone with dementia—and in the future, with increasing life expectancy, we may also find ourselves included in the statistics. Perhaps even now, you are someone at the beginning of this journey.

The term "dementia" covers a range of illnesses, for example, Alzheimer's disease, Lewy bodies disease, or vascular dementia.[7] Each one affects a different part of the brain and consequently has impacts on different capacities, although bringing a range of characteristic symptoms. In the early

1. Williams, *Words of Faith*; *Words of Hope*; *Words of Peace*.
2. SAGA, "Dementia more feared than Cancer."
3. Alzheimer's Research UK, "Facts and Stats."
4. Alzheimer's Association, "Alzheimer's Disease Facts and Figures."
5. Dementia Australia, "Dementia Statistics."
6. Alzheimer's Disease International, "Numbers of People with Dementia."
7. Alzheimer's Society, "Types of Dementia."

stages, many types of dementia begin with memory loss. Cognitive function is progressively severely affected, eventually bringing loss of ability to think rationally, and loss of a sense of time and place. To the observer, the person in advanced dementia may appear to have lost both rational and relational capacities, and with these, some would suggest controversially, their personhood.[8] I explore this question further in later chapters.[9]

There are different definitions of the "stages" of dementia and the course of one person's dementia illness will vary from another's.[10] In this book I use the terms "early" to describe the symptoms of those who are recently diagnosed and are beginning to notice cognitive difficulties, and "moderate" to describe those who have lived with dementia for a number of years and for whom conversation is possible but is becoming more challenging. The journey with this illness may last many years. Christine Bryden, a Christian writer who lives with dementia, has provocatively asked: "The question is, where does this journey begin, and at what stage can you deny me my self-hood and my spirituality?"[11] So what about faith?

For Christians from an evangelical tradition, questions raised by dementia are significant for the assumptions involved in having such faith. These particularly concern the emphases on cognitive assent to propositional truths, and on having a personal, responsive relationship with God, both of which seem to be dependent on the idea of personhood. Where evangelical faith is presumed (or assumed) to be *dependent* on the cognitive aspects of belief and relationality, such faith is threatened by the advent of dementia. For those beginning this journey, such prognoses are frightening, bringing threat to self and faith. Elizabeth MacKinlay, writing about her friend Christine Bryden in the early stages of her dementia, reflected on this:

> As she struggled with these factors that went to the core of who she was, this question of "would she lose God?" became a crucial one for her. From the Christian perspective, God would still be there, but the other question, "would she still have a sense of God being there?" was a different matter.[12]

---

8. Keck, *Forgetting Whose We Are*, 22–24. See also Post, *Moral Challenge of Alzheimer Disease*, 136.

9. See chapter 2, 20–21, 25–28; chapter 3, 33–45.

10. Shamy, *Guide to the Spiritual Dimension of Care*, 50. See also Alzheimer's Association, "Stages of Alzheimer's."

11. Bryden and MacKinlay, "Dementia: A Spiritual Journey Towards the Divine," 71.

12. MacKinlay, "Walking with a Person into Dementia," 43.

Such questions as these prompted my own concern to discover a deeper understanding of the faith experience and practice of Christians living with dementia from the evangelical tradition.

Some have suggested that addressing spiritual needs of those with dementia is as important as early engagement with other aspects of their care,[13] and that to neglect the spiritual dimension of care seriously impoverishes the quality of their lives—just as surely as neglect of the physical dimension.[14] How might we respond?

AN EVANGELICAL TRADITION . . .

A key definition of evangelicalism has sometimes been found in David Bebbington's[15] historical account of this tradition. He describes four main attributes (conversionism, activism, biblicism, crucicentrism) which have been thought of as static, transcending cultural and historical context. Today, however, whilst these aspects are still important, many evangelical theologians recognize that theology and practice are inevitably integrated and shaped by social context.[16] As David Congdon and Travis McMaken wrote in *Christianity Today*: "There is no single right way to be an evangelical. In truth, evangelicalism is always 'on the way.'"[17] New challenges arise, and new contexts repeatedly challenge us to think again about how we understand and interpret Christian truth in these new situations. The experience of dementia is a context that is prompting new understandings and bringing fresh insights.

The word "evangelical" has, in fact, as Tom Greggs describes, "a rainbow-like variety of meanings."[18] It transcends denominational boundaries, including the spectrum of emphases from Protestant Reformed, through to open evangelicalism in the Church of England and free churches, to the charismatic emphases found, for example, in today's network of New Wine churches in the UK.[19] Despite the different perspectives and understandings, there seems to be agreement in key areas: faith in the evangelical

---

13. Kevern, "I Pray that I Will Not Fall," 293.
14. Shamy, *Guide to the Spiritual Dimension of Care*, 60.
15. Bebbington, *Evangelicalism in Modern Britain*, 2–3.
16. Harris, "Beyond Bebbington."
17. Congdon and McMaken, "Ten Reasons Why Theology Matters." See also Greggs, "Introduction."
18. Greggs, *New Perspectives for Evangelical Theology*, 5.
19. Bebbington, "Evangelical Trends, 1959–2009"; New Wine, https://www.newwine.org.

tradition is Christ-centered and "in the light of the Word."[20] In the light of these, dementia brings its challenges.

The voices of the participants involved in my research reflected this range, yet there were essential characteristics in common (and some will be shared by Christians of other faith traditions too). Theirs was not simply an "extrinsic religiousness" dependent on churchgoing and religious practices.[21] Rather it was an "intrinsic faith," where a sense of relationship with God was part of who they were, shaping values and moment-by-moment living. And it was this experience of relationship with God that seemed to be sustaining them in the face of dementia. Rowan Williams adds another perspective. Being a disciple of Jesus is not just about how we live; not just the decisions we make, not just the things we believe, but "a state of being."[22] *Being* in the context of dementia makes us ask new questions of faith and our faith practice.

In the following, I highlight four key aspects of evangelicalism and emphases that were evident in the research participants' words: *relationship with Christ, relationship with others, mission,* and *the Bible*. Keeping aware of these may be helpful in understanding their accounts of experience of faith in dementia—and it is these which have prompted my own reflections on their words and on theology.

Relationship with Christ

A sense of transcendent relationship with God through Christ is a key characteristic of faith of the evangelical tradition. David (one of the research participants) would say: "I know Jesus—that's the core of everything." Ron would emphasize, "I was 'born again.'" Biblically, such relationships with Christ are brought about by Spirit-mediated rebirth into God's family.[23] For David, Ron, and the other research participants, it became clear that this was an unchangeable state which was enduring in spite of dementia.

For many evangelicals, like Ron, the starting point of this relationship has been understood as a life-changing event akin to Paul's conversion experience on the road to Damascus when he met the risen Jesus (see

---

20. Gutiérrez, *Theology of Liberation*, 13.
21. Swinton, *Spirituality and Mental Health Care*, 31.
22. Williams, *Being Disciples*, 1.
23. See John 3:1–8: "You must be born again" (v. 7); and Romans 8:15–17: ". . . you received the Spirit of sonship. And by him we cry, 'Abba, Father.' The Spirit himself testifies with our spirit that we are God's children." See also Zahl, "Reformation Pessimism or Pietist Personalism," 80–81.

Acts 9:1–19). But others have a gentler understanding of conversion "as a journey towards the cross and an embrace of its message."[24] For example, Alice had always had a sense of relationship with God that seemed to have grown from childhood onwards: "Always, always. Even when I was little." Both these "coming-into-relationship-with-God" experiences were evident in the stories of the individuals I met with for this research.

However, in spite of evangelicalism's emphasis on grace (Eph 2:8), some traditions have also—perhaps subtly—stressed the importance of rational capacity to affirm faith and commitment in intentional, responsive relationship with God.[25] For Christians living with developing dementia and declining cognitive capacity this brings the crucial and painful question: "What will happen to my faith when I can no longer remember?"[26]

Relationship with Others

An individualistic emphasis on personal relationship is increasingly balanced today with more attention being focused on belonging to the believing community.[27] Biblical faith is, of course, inherently relational. In the New Testament, the church is typified in Paul's writing as "the body of Christ" (for example, see 1 Corinthians 12). In this understanding, the whole and every part is significant. Recognition of mutuality of faith in relationship with others in the body of Christ is profoundly important for those living with developing dementia. This perspective both challenges and motivates the quest for understanding about how the belongingness of those with dementia can be expressed and affirmed within our communities of faith. For those learning to live with dementia this sometimes may not be easy. Rosemary (another of the research group) said: "The difficulty sometimes is church itself."

---

24. Harris, "Beyond Bebbington," 205; Peace, *Conversion in the New Testament*, 4–5. Peace considers the Pauline conversion alongside "the unfolding conversion of the Twelve" in the Gospel of Mark, as their understanding of Christ and his mission grew.

25. This has arisen from some evangelical interpretations of Romans 10:9: "If you confess with your mouth, 'Jesus is Lord,' and believe in your heart that God raised him from the dead, you will be saved." On this see the reflections in Gaventa, "Which Human?"

26. Shamy, *Guide to the Spiritual Dimension of Care*, 21.

27. See for example, Harris, "Beyond Bebbington": "missional communities of invitation, welcome and embrace," 213.

Mission

Spreading the good news of Jesus Christ has been a priority for evangelicals in response to scriptural passages such as Matthew 28:19: "Go and make disciples of all nations." This has often been thought of as the church's role in preaching the gospel with the goal of making converts.[28] Perhaps missing, in the past, has been an emphasis on the ongoing nature of *discipling* followers of Jesus. In recent years David Bosch[29] has reminded us that it is the transforming mission of God (*missio Dei*) that provides the narrative for God's action in the world, supremely demonstrated through the embodied life of Jesus. This impacts every aspect of human life and community.[30] Movingly, research participant David's catchphrase as he spoke of his experience of dementia was: "This is my mission!"

The illness prompts questions about how this "mission" is embodied and expressed in the faith community in ways that embrace and "disciple" those who live with this disease. How might their participation in God's mission be recognized? How might their growing spiritual life be supported and nurtured?

The Bible

Belief in the central role of the Bible and its authority is a defining hallmark of evangelicalism. There is, however, diversity in the way Scripture is understood and interpreted.[31] My own evangelical tradition has emphasized commitment to the whole Bible, with awareness of the contextual (as it was written, as it is read, and as it is lived out) and to the understanding that all Scripture ultimately relates to Jesus Christ. The devotional practice of regular, prayerful Bible reading, both corporate and personal, is perceived as a way of meeting with God, undertaken in humility and dependence on the Holy Spirit.[32] Many evangelicals have followed this practice as a key element in their relationship with God, and this has been a significant part of their faith lives. Yet dementia changes this: "too difficult now to read," Alice recognized.

---

28. Harris, "Beyond Bebbington," 204; McGrath, *Evangelicalism and the Future of Christianity*, 55–56.
29. Bosch, *Transforming Mission*, xv.
30. For example, "seeker sensitive" churches and the Willow Creek movement.
31. Briggs, "Bible Before Us," 15.
32. Hoggarth, *Seed and the Soil*, 145–47.

As with Cathy's situation described at the beginning of this chapter, the experience of Christians living with dementia draws questions about how this illness affects the activity of reading the Bible, the understanding of Scripture, and the ways in which its importance is expressed in their lives. It also invites us as fellow believers to strive with the reality of God and the truth of Scripture in "the contexts and situations" of today's world.[33] For our topic that means wrestling with the questions and challenges that dementia is bringing to a biblical understanding of faith and how to understand it. Dementia brings this issue into sharp relief. The changes which the illness brings to cognition and communication mean that the Bible is likely to be—and eventually must be—accessed in new ways and understood from fresh perspectives.

PRACTICAL THEOLOGY

My research is set within the field of practical theology, bringing together both theology and experience. Andrew Root[34] affirms that "theology . . . can *only* be practical"—theologically demonstrated in the practical act of God in Jesus. Both theory and practice have a reciprocal role in the faithful practice of God's purposes. It is practical theology's transformative task and goal, as John Swinton and Harriet Mowat envision, to participate faithfully in God's mission,[35] through "critical, theological reflection"[36] on the lived experience of our contemporary world. And this is the intent of this book.

At the heart of practical theology is the activity of theological reflection on lived experience. *The pastoral cycle* is a key element, and this provides a framework for the faith learning in this book. Beginning with human experience, it seeks "to be close to people's real experience of life."[37] Ongoing reflection and questioning involves listening to a variety of perspectives. I will often use the image of "conversation"[38] to describe this dialogical process. As different insights emerge and merge, new understandings come to light in ways that can transform our understanding and practice. This is what I have sought to do as I've reflected on what the experience of those living with dementia brings to theology and biblical understanding of Christian faith.

33. Greggs, "Introduction," 3.
34. Root, *Christopraxis*, 94–95.
35. Swinton and Mowat, *Practical Theology*, 27.
36. Swinton and Mowat, *Practical Theology*, 6.
37. Lartey, "Practical Theology as a Theological Form," 132.
38. This approach draws on Pattison, "Some Straw for the Bricks."

Richard Osmer has helpfully drawn out four core tasks which are involved in this work of reflection. These are simply: What is going on? Why is this going on? What ought to be going on?[39] Then there is the pragmatic question: How, together with others, might we respond? These questions don't provide a linear structure for the thinking in this book but do underlie and inform each aspect of its content.

Practical Theology and Evangelicalism

The nature of practical theology lends itself to learning and ministry within the evangelical faith tradition.[40] It has the capacity to honor its significant, dynamic characteristics and to facilitate reflection on the experience of faith towards enabling (and transforming) practical ministry. Five key aspects are:

- *Valuing of transcendent experience.* This is significant because the experience of faith brings profound changes to people's lives. Its valuing allows the researcher to take seriously these experiences of their faith and learn how these are enabling participants' response to their illness.

- *A Christ-centered focus.* Relationship with God depends on the work of the cross bringing justification and hope of resurrection. In Christ, the divine meets human experience—and God intervenes at moments of hopelessness. In this book we hear about this encounter with Christ at a critical time and its effect on people who are living with dementia.

- *Social and relational dependence.* Practical theology is itself a relational activity, depending on listening carefully to different voices in order to deepen understanding in a particular area of faith. This reflects a biblical model of community where accountability is provided within the body of Christ. Its ministry is also relational, aiming, in this case, to bring fresh insights into how the church might support Christians with dementia.

- *A missiological and ministerial impetus.* As participant in God's mission, practical theology brings together the lived-out encounter of divine and human action.[41] Its dynamic and transformative goals resource Christian ministry in pursuing change and growth in the light of experience (and of the Word). In researching the experience of Christians living with dementia, it not only looks for new insights,

---

39. Osmer, *Practical Theology*, 4.
40. See Root's discussion, *Christopraxis*, ix–xv, 10.
41. Root, *Christopraxis*, ix–xiii.

but also seeks to bring transformation through those new insights and understandings. This work is therefore "missiological" in its purpose.

- *A biblical perspective.*[42] The issue of the authority of Scripture is an important one for Christians of an evangelical tradition—and for the author of this book. In practical theology too, it is the Bible that "sets the agenda and boundaries for the conversation."[43] The coming of dementia brings this issue into sharp relief. The changes that the illness brings mean that the Bible is likely to be, and eventually must be, accessed in new ways and understood from fresh perspectives. In fact, changing context has always and inevitably shaped our understanding and interpretation.[44] John Swinton draws on Walter Brueggemann's words to suggest a new practical theological method which seeks redescription from the perspective of the Bible.[45] He develops this motif in ways which help our exploration of faith and dementia.

> The deeper task is to see what current understandings of dementia and the practices that emerge from them look like when they are viewed and redescribed from the perspective of the strange biblical world.[46]

ORIENTATION, DISORIENTATION, AND REORIENTATION

As I reflect on the experience of living with dementia, I will keep in mind Walter Brueggemann's model of orientation, disorientation, and reorientation.[47] He has used this in his exploration of the Psalms, as a way of thinking about the settled orientation of people of God's—knowing who and where they are; disorientation, in which this is upset by loss and suffering; then transforming reorientation that comes about as hope and joy emerge out of their God-focused and hopeful orientation. Brueggemann also suggests a wider application of this reflected in the life of Jesus,[48] and in the life of the

---

42. Root, *Christopraxis*, 99–100, n33.
43. Hauerwas, *Peaceable Kingdom*, 98.
44. Vanhoozer, *Is There a Meaning in This Text?*, 460–61.
45. Brueggemann, *Redescribing Reality*, 4–6.
46. Swinton, *Dementia*, 19–21.
47. Brueggemann, *Praying the Psalms*, 3; Brueggemann, *Spirituality of the Psalms*, viii.
48. Brueggemann, *Spirituality of the Psalms*, x; Phil 2:5–11.

church.[49] I will use this idea throughout this book as we reflect on the faith experience of the participants in my research as they were living through the experience of dementia, in the light of the hope of the gospel. Here, the three elements are dimensions of the participants' experience of faith, which inform one another continuously. I hope this model will help us in our understanding of having faith whilst living with dementia—perhaps it will bring new understanding to our own experience of faith experience too.

INTRODUCING . . .

Now, let me introduce the eight people who courageously agreed to take part in the study. All were Christians of an evangelical tradition and deeply committed to their faith. At the time of our conversations, they were attending a variety of local churches, including Anglican and Baptist or other free churches. Theirs was that "intrinsic faith," where their sense of relationship with God was part of who they were. And it was this experience of relationship with God that seemed to be sustaining them in the face of dementia.

All were living with mild to moderate symptoms of dementia, and aware of their diagnoses.[50] At this stage of their dementia, they had capacity for use of language and a sense of linear time, although in some cases, these were beginning to be obviously diminished by their illness.[51] So, here was a window of opportunity for hearing their voices and perspectives, and for gaining understanding of their lived experience of faith, both in the present and in their anticipation of the future. There has been an increasing recognition of the importance of these earlier stages of the disease[52]—perhaps this is especially true for the spiritual lives of persons of faith.

Each of the participants in my study was living in their own home, either independently or with a loved one. They include Alice, Bill, David, Jess, Jill, Matthew, Rosemary, Ron, and their families. Their names, and those of their family members and other individuals used in this book, are not their real names in order to protect their anonymity.

Alice, a retired GP. She had been a missionary doctor in Africa in her earlier adult life. When we met, she was living independently in her own home, which was part of a supported-living community. Her husband had passed away a few years previously. Her upbringing had been in the

---

49. Brueggemann, *Spirituality of the Psalms*, xi.

50. Goldsmith, *In a Strange Land . . .*, 60–65; Shamy, *Guide to the Spiritual Dimension of Care*, 50–53.

51. Alzheimer's Society, "Progression of Alzheimer's Disease."

52. Kevern, "I Pray that I Will Not Fall," 293.

evangelical tradition. At the time of the interview, she was part of an evangelical, "ecumenical" (Alice's description) church. She had been diagnosed with dementia ("mainly Alzheimer's") about five years before the first interview. She said of her dementia: "It's a privilege to understand dementia from the inside."

Bill, a former policeman. As a child, he had attended a local Anglican church. At the time of the interview, he belonged to an evangelical, charismatic community church (formerly Baptist) of which his wife, Carol, was the pastor. He had received a diagnosis of early onset dementia (Alzheimer's) about eighteen months before the research interview. In spite of his illness, he spoke of God as the "best boss," and of dementia: "This side of heaven that is going to be part of my journey."

David, a retired senior teacher. He had been brought up in the Methodist denomination. For many years he and his wife, Gail, had been part of an evangelical Anglican church. He had received a diagnosis of dementia (combined vascular and Alzheimer's) about one year before the research interview. Looking to the future he said: "Even if the dementia gets worse there'll still be Jesus . . . That's the important thing . . . just becomes . . . he loves me . . . yeah . . ."

Jess was living with Andrew, her husband. She had traveled extensively with Andrew whilst he was in the army (Andrew was a chef), and they had both come to faith during that time. After returning to live in the UK, they had been involved in community work, which they were passionate about. At the time of our conversation, they were part of an evangelical Anglican church. Neither of them had had a Christian upbringing. Jess was diagnosed with Alzheimer's about two years before the research interview. She understood that she had a diagnosis of dementia ("when I was *labelled* 'memory loss'") but preferred that in our conversation we didn't refer to this as "dementia" but spoke in terms of memory loss. Other researchers have pointed out "the limitations of a society that still stigmatizes dementia,"[53] making those facing the challenges of the disease sometimes unwilling to name it. In Jess's case she wanted to tell her story in spite of her dislike of medical terms. Supported by Andrew, she said: "I have *now* . . . Today is the day of salvation."

Jill was living independently in her own home in a supported-living community. Her husband had passed away several years before the research interview. She was brought up in a "nominal" Christian home and became a committed Christian in her early twenties. She had been a teacher, and, in recent years, had been part of a local evangelical Anglican church. She had

---

53. Bartlett and Martin, "Ethical Issues in Dementia Care Research," 59.

been diagnosed with dementia about two years before our conversation. Her dementia was mainly Alzheimer's with some vascular. Asked about the experience of faith, she said: "I'm lucky knowing the presence of God . . . near me . . . within this . . ."

Matthew had been brought up in the Anglican church. Broadly, of an evangelical tradition, he and his wife, Wendy, were part of a lively, community-focused, local Anglican church. He had Alzheimer's disease that was diagnosed about six years before the research interview. He was more physically frail than some of the other participants, and throughout our conversations, concentration to think and speak clearly took time and effort. Asked whether he felt dementia was making a difference to his faith, he replied: "Yes, it makes me feel stronger."

Ron was living with Clare, his wife, at the time of the interview (he sadly passed during the writing up of this research). He had been brought up in Wales and had attended a Baptist church there as a young person, although his parents were not regular churchgoers. He had been converted whilst working in Rhodesia (Zimbabwe) as a young man. At the time of the interview, he and Clare belonged to a Baptist church. He had been diagnosed with vascular dementia about three years before this. Like Matthew, Ron was further on in his journey with dementia than others in the study, and it was difficult sometimes for him to find the precise word or expression for which he was hunting. Nevertheless, a gentle Welsh accent still shaped his expression: "I know myself that being a Christian I shall be going . . . to heaven."

Rosemary, a former teacher, was living independently in her own home, part of the same community as Alice. Her upbringing had been in the Plymouth Brethren, which she had left as a young adult. She didn't go to church regularly during the middle years of adulthood. However, following a serious illness about ten years before our research conversation, her sense of relationship with God had grown. She had been diagnosed with vascular dementia during the ten years preceding our conversation—and offered to take part in this research as a result of hearing about it through a friend. Rosemary said her goal in speaking to me was that she wanted to "just bring glory to him [God]."

Throughout this book I quote their words and refer to insights which these bring. Commitment to faith was the starting point for their responses to dementia, and it is this which had motivated them in wanting to be part of this research project: as Rosemary put it, "to bring glory to him." For such human beings, how can faith be understood in relation to their dementia?

ANTICIPATING THE CONVERSATION . . .

In this book I bring reflective accounts of the participants' faith experience and practice interweaving with exploration of theological and biblical themes arising from their words and experience. This conversation includes the voices of those who were living with dementia; and those of other writing and theology. It takes place "in the light of the Word," which sets "the boundaries and agenda."[54] I'm aware of my own inevitable "situated-ness"—my own context, life, and faith experience—and the book is written understanding that others may bring different perspectives to the issues discussed. In the final chapter I consider the implications this work might bring for other believers, pastoral ministry, theology, and the church. I believe that in listening to the voices of these Christians who live with dementia—and to the "disruptive and complex" voices[55] of Scripture—we can expect exciting, new discoveries.

In this first chapter I have introduced some of the questions raised by the experience of faith in dementia. We have looked at some of the terms used in the book, such as "dementia," and "evangelical," and at the nature of practical theology. We've also been introduced to the people living with dementia who took part in the research that underlies this book. The following chapters are structured in this way:

Chapter 2. Seeking Understanding. In this chapter, I consider some wider context for the book's focus, exploring a range of writing in the area of spirituality, religion, and faith in dementia. I draw on writing from psychology, philosophy, theology, research—and personal accounts of those who live with dementia. The chapter provides background for our thinking as we set out to discover deeper understanding of this experience of faith in dementia.

Chapter 3. Who I Am. This chapter explores theological and biblical perspectives on the issue of identity that provide foundations for and confidence in faith—even in dementia. Here is the settled orientation of faith that the coming of dementia begins to disturb. For the Christian believer knowing that you are created by God in his image, knowing that you are in Christ, knowing that you are a member of the church (the body of Christ) are fundamental to understanding of the experience of faith of Christians who live with dementia. These assumptions were embedded in the words of those who spoke with me—and questions raised—even if these were not described explicitly.

---

54. Hauerwas, *Peaceable Kingdom*, 98.
55. Greggs, "Introduction," 4.

Chapter 4. Knowing God: The Experience of Faith. Using the words of the research participants, this chapter explores individuals' sense of relationship with God, and of knowing Jesus personally. Surprisingly, they expressed their feelings of a growing, strengthening faith, and of joy, peace, and hope.

Chapter 5. Being Not Doing: The Experience of Practice. For the Christian believers in the research project, practice was an expression of their faith and *relationship* with God. However, the coming of dementia was inevitably affecting this. Using their words again, this chapter explores the nature and experience of particular practices that are significant for many Christians of an evangelical tradition, including Bible reading, prayer, and belonging to a local church.

Chapter 6. Walking through Shadow. In spite of the positive attitudes of the Christians I met, their words and expression of these disclosed shadows. In spite of their firm faith, dementia threatens disorientation. This chapter raises the issues of living with darkness as a Christian believer who has dementia, and begins to explore the nature of adversity in the life of faith. It especially considers Christ's own suffering and his identification with those who live with this illness. Challenges include: the experience of being an outsider; the inner unseen struggles of maintaining one's trust in God; and the practical challenges of participation in local church life.

Chapter 7. Memory Funding Faith. Listening to the person of faith living with dementia nudges our perspectives on memory's true nature and role. This chapter explores how memory is expressed through the *whole* person in a variety of ways, and how this embodied memory is resourcing faith in the person with dementia. Memory is also key in understanding the Bible and the story of God's people. It is therefore central to the exploration of faith experience in dementia. Ultimately, that experience is dependent on the God who does not forget.

Chapter 8. Growing Faith.[56] Can Christians with dementia grow in faith? This chapter reflects biblically and theologically on *how* maturing faith may be happening in this dementia journey from disorientation towards new, hopeful orientation in Christ. The participants' words are marked by discovery of purpose, trust in God, and Spirit-enabled endurance.

Chapter 9. Present-Future Hope. The faith of these Christians who share their experiences from the perspective of living in dementia may puzzle us. How is it that they can be so positive in the discomforting context of dementia? In conversation with Scripture, I seek to understand the transforming impact of hope in these believers' lives as they journey onwards towards a

---

56. Material in this chapter draws on my article "Growing Faith in Dementia."

new orientation in Christ. Their words and our encounters reveal not just a *distant* hope ("it'll be all right in the end"), but hope-shaped living in the present.

Chapter 10. Walking Together. In the concluding chapter, I reflect on insights which have emerged from the voices of these Christians, and from biblical reflection on their words. I consider possible implications and ways forward for ministry, pastoral care, and the nurture of faith—and raise the question of how the church might grow in its receiving of the gifts which Christians living with dementia bring.

As you begin to read this book, you'll find the participants' words threaded through its pages. These were recorded as we talked together and later transcribed. Sometimes there are gaps reflecting hesitations, misused words, or a struggle to speak—I have left these to give a sense of how they were speaking and of our conversations. At the end of each chapter there is a Bible passage and some questions for further reflection that can be used individually or by a group reading this book together.

Now . . . let's begin this task of seeking further understanding . . .

"Whenever we enter into another person's experiences of suffering, we need to tread very carefully for we tread upon sacred ground."[57]

For Further Reflection . . .

- Reflect on Paul's words in Romans 8:37–39: Nothing "will be able to separate us from the love of God in Christ Jesus our Lord." What might these words mean for the person living with dementia?
- What is your own experience of dementia—family, friends, yourself?
- What questions do *you* think this illness raises for faith?

---

57. Goldsmith, "Tracing Rainbows through the Rain," 122.

2

Seeking Understanding

"... from experience not ... some theory."

Living with the frustrations of dementia, Rosemary knew without doubt that God was with her. She was no longer able to cope with discussion of the "theory" of faith, yet her "experience" of God was evidently real and sustaining her. Alice referred to something similar: "I used to think I was quite clever!" But now . . . their experience—and my encounters with other Christians living with dementia—provoked questions that challenged my assumptions and theory. The participants in my research were also seeking understanding. Early on in my research, I had received a hesitant but determined phone call from Rosemary, who had heard of my study and wanted to take part. Dementia had come into her life, but it had not taken away a lifetime of experience and the embedded knowledge that had shaped who she was—and she wanted to share her insider perspective to serve God and help others. How could we together seek understanding?

Practical theology *begins* with experience. It is here, Andrew Root[1] has argued, that we witness encounter with Christ—and it is this experience that informs the theoretical and leads to new perspectives towards transforming

---

1. Root, *Christopraxis*.

practice. Hence, my desire to hear the voices of those who were living with dementia—and that will be the main focus of this book. But first, there is also a wealth of scholarly and practical wisdom that helps us as "outsiders" begin to understand the experience of faith in dementia. In this book I will draw on both experience *and* "theory"; the one prompting the other onward in the pastoral cycle of care. Together, insider and outsider perspectives facilitate pastoral understanding, and together contribute towards growth within the community of Christ.

Seeking understanding has included listening to firsthand experiences of dementia, but also, in the light of this, to the writing and research of others. In this chapter I consider some of this wider discussion as background and context to help in our understanding and to prompt further questions.

EXPERIENCE PROMPTING THEOLOGICAL REFLECTION

My own approach to this task was prompted by the specific needs and experience of evangelical Christians living with dementia: how could we help these believers continue to meet with God through Bible reading and prayer? Out of my evangelical tradition, further questions then began to emerge: Is "saving faith" certain if you can no longer remember God (someone really did ask me that question!)? If so, how might we make the case for this biblically and theologically? Then, how might the church nurture such faith? Dementia has been called "the theological disease" because it asks us questions about human identity and faith.[2] Such reflection has the potential to bring new insights to understanding our own faith too. Confronted by similar challenges, a small number of theologians and scholars have reflected on similar questions. I have drawn on their work throughout this book and this is helpful as we begin our own journey of understanding faith in dementia.

Theological Writing

David Keck's *Forgetting Whose We Are* was one of the earlier explorations of theological insights arising from the experience of dementia. It is sure in its encouragement to carers that their loved ones' faith is secure, but less so about their ongoing lived experience of faith in later stages of the illness. His

---

2. Keck, *Forgetting Whose We Are*, 14–15.

phrase "deconstruction incarnate"[3] has triggered some disturbing questions for Christians about identity and personal faith, especially as relevant in *later* dementia.

More recently, John Swinton's *Dementia: Living in the Memories of God*,[4] has made a major contribution to the thinking about the theology of dementia. His insistence on the continuing personhood of people living with dementia and the security of their salvation draws our attention to these significant questions for disciples of Jesus. His compassionate practical theological approach emphasizes the significance of relationships and participation in the body of Christ, the sacredness of people who live with dementia, the importance of recognizing being "in the moment," the value of "being with" others, and the importance of love. Swinton's approach reinforces the conviction that theology must connect to lived experience,[5] and that the Bible provides fresh perspectives from which to understand our present situation.[6]

There is, of course, other writing that explores theological questions and helps with our understanding of the experience of faith in dementia. Walter Brueggemann's Bible-focused theology is particularly helpful in the exploration of the suffering of God's people, and also in his understanding of this as a journey from a settled orientation of faith, through disorientation to a new orientation.[7] I will draw on these in more depth in later chapters. First, some glimpses from the current context.

GLIMPSES FROM THE CURRENT CONTEXT

In recent decades there has been a growing awareness of dementia in the Western world. Popular books such as *Iris*[8] and its subsequent film version, and the biography *Still Alice*[9] and the film that followed, are amongst several books and films that have contributed to the increasing public profile and understanding of dementia, and the experience of those who live with this condition. Sally Magnusson's[10] moving account of her mother's journey with dementia also gave glimpses of the losses, and the self that endures.

3. Keck, *Forgetting Whose We Are*, 32.
4. Swinton, *Dementia*.
5. Swinton and Mowat, *Practical Theology*, 5–6.
6. Swinton, *Dementia*, 17–21. See also Brueggemann, *Redescribing Reality*, 1–11.
7. Brueggemann, *Praying the Psalms*, 3; Brueggemann, *Spirituality of the Psalms*, viii.
8. Bayley, *Iris*.
9. Genova, *Still Alice*.
10. Magnusson, *Where Memories Go*.

Nicci Gerrard's *What Dementia Teaches Us about Love* reflects powerfully on the experience of her father's dementia, "facing truths too deep for tears."[11] Increasingly, the voices of people who live with dementia are also being heard, for example, *People with Dementia Speak Out*,[12] and the film *The Father* (2021). Jennifer Bute, who lives with dementia herself, has done much practical work to help those who live with dementia, and has written of her own experience in *Dementia from the Inside*.[13]

As awareness of dementia has grown, spirituality and religion have been recognized as significant factors in the well-being of those living with dementia. It is increasingly recognized as an important aspect of care in policy and strategy documents: "The person's spiritual needs . . . should be addressed and respected as much as the medical aspects of care."[14] For pastors and chaplains the spiritual dimension is an obvious and essential component of holistic care. However, in spite of growing awareness, in public arenas, it is often still "all-knowing medical science" that seems to have preeminence.[15] There is more to be done.

TOWARDS HOLISTIC EMPHASES . . .

The question of how people with dementia are sometimes perceived and treated by medical and social care facilities prompted the person-centered thinking of Tom Kitwood.[16] In *Dementia Reconsidered: The Person Comes First,* he argued that when the medical-scientific perspective dominates, the person can come to be treated merely as a biological object needing "physical care . . . but little else."[17] He warned of the danger of allowing diagnosis to define the person and consequently influencing the way we treat certain people. Kitwood's work on dementia and personhood[18] has done much to focus the attention of caring professionals on the *whole* person rather than just the disease, including the spiritual, relational, and social dimensions of personhood.[19] Complementing this thinking, Steven Sabat has highlighted

---

11. Gerrard, *What Dementia Teaches Us.*
12. Whitman, ed., *People with Dementia.*
13. Bute with Morse, *Dementia from the Inside.*
14. Alzheimer's Society, "End of Life Care."
15. Saunders, *Dementia,* 7.
16. Kitwood, *Dementia Reconsidered,* 1, 37–38.
17. Saunders, *Dementia,* 7.
18. See also Sabat, *Experience of Alzheimer's Disease.*
19. Swinton, *Dementia,* 71.

the harm caused to individuals through "malignant social positioning"[20] that (even unintentionally) stigmatizes those living with dementia.

Swinton also challenges a dependence on medical definitions to describe the person, especially those who live with dementia:

> Medical definitions are helpful for medical purposes, but they may be considerably less helpful for working through the contribution of theology and pastoral care to the process of defining and responding to dementia.[21]

The brain, as Rosemary and Alice's comments at the beginning of this chapter suggest, is not the *only* path to understanding.[22] Neuroscience is important, of course, but, as Swinton asserts, theology is a *necessary* lens when seeking understanding of the *whole* of being human. Such holistic thinking is essential as we try to understand the nature of being a person of faith who lives with dementia. We are "more than body, brain and breath."[23] The spiritual dimension of human life is a significant part of what it means to be human, and requires nurture, especially perhaps amidst the challenges of living with dementia.

Whilst theologians, chaplains, and other practitioners working with people who live with dementia generally agree about the importance of this holistic view, this may not be the case for all expressions of Christian faith.[24] For those for whom theological structure or doctrinal "soundness" are principal concerns, there is consequent danger of excluding and dehumanizing those with cognitive loss. The lens of theology is necessary in order to stimulate questions that lead to effective, *whole person* caring of those who are living with this illness.

SPIRITUALITY, RELIGION, AND FAITH

There has been a growing awareness of the spiritual needs of persons with dementia in recent years. Yet, whilst there are broad commonalities, there are different understandings of the terms "spirituality," "religion," and "faith." This is significant for the particular nature of faith that this book is exploring. Such different perceptions provide context for understanding the

---

20. Sabat, "Mind, Meaning, and Personhood in Dementia."
21. Swinton, *Dementia*, 47.
22. Swinton, *Becoming Friends of Time*, 13.
23. Shamy, *Guide to the Spiritual Dimension of Care*, 58–63.
24. Goldsmith, "Through a Glass Darkly," 124.

faith of Christians who live with dementia, and begin to point to why these are important for their well-being and the nature of care that is offered.

Spirituality

Spirituality is undoubtedly a difficult term to define—"an intangible multidimensional concept," dependent on subjective experience.[25] It is about the immaterial aspects of life,

> closely associated with a sense of meaning and purpose. It is particular to each person and yet, by virtue of its essential nature to all human beings, is shared with others. Some would say that spirituality is intuitive or even innate and, therefore, not easily susceptible to rational explication.[26]

It often includes ideas of transcendence.[27] It is both immanent (for example, caught in a smile exchanged), and transcendent, a "going beyond."[28] It involves, in some way, a sense of being connected to a divine or transcendent sense of purpose,[29] requiring an openness to mystery. In whatever ways it is understood, increasingly the idea of spirituality is widely recognized as "an integral, even fundamental, element of what it is to be a human being."[30]

Religion and Faith

Spirituality is often expressed through religion, and the terms are sometimes used interchangeably,[31] but spirituality does not necessarily include religion. In general, religion involves structures and provides shared practices, rituals, understandings, and language for "the working out of human spirituality."[32] Faith is a further category within human spirituality. Again, whilst often situated within religion, it has distinct characteristics. John Hull has helpfully

---

25. See Beuscher and Grando, "Using Spirituality to Cope," 584–85; Higgins, "Spiritual and Religious Needs of People with Dementia," 24.

26. Allen and Coleman, "Spiritual Perspectives," 205.

27. Sapp, "Spiritual Care of People with Dementia," 200; MacKinlay and Trevitt, *Finding Meaning*, 85.

28. Hughes, "Situated Embodied View," 200–201.

29. Stuckey and Gwyther, "Dementia, Religion, and Spirituality."

30. Kevern, "Spirituality of People with Late-Stage Dementia," 765–66.

31. MacKinlay and Trevitt, *Finding Meaning*, 17.

32. Goldsmith, *In a Strange Land . . .* , 145; MacKinlay and Trevitt, *Finding Meaning*, 20.

depicted spirituality, religion, and faith as three concentric circles, with faith at the center.[33] Spirituality does not necessarily include religion, which places human life under, and in relation to, the infinite. Faith is a further category within the religious, which Hull describes as a "trustful response to the object of religious worship."[34] This model suggests that, whilst spirituality is common to human experience, it does not necessarily include religion, and being of a particular religion does not necessarily include faith. Malcolm Goldsmith describes something similar, narrowing his discussion from the broad term of "spirituality," through "religion," and then to "faith."[35] Whilst people will have different ways of expressing a commitment to their religion, in the Christian context, he considers this faith commitment is expressed in being "a follower of Jesus," bringing the understanding of being in personal relationship with God. This is reflected in my encounters with Christians living with dementia, for whom the experience of relationship with God was preeminent in their faith ("not some theory," as Rosemary said).

Swinton helpfully brings other distinctions with his use of the terms "intrinsic" and "extrinsic" religion.[36] Whilst extrinsic religion is "detachable from [the] essential sense of self," essentially self-serving and utilitarian, intrinsic religiousness is a meaning endowing framework that extends beyond religious activities into every aspect of life, determining "who and what they understand themselves to be."[37]

These ideas of faith—suggesting trustful relationship, obedient following of God in Christ, meanings and values which are deeply engrained in the sense of identity—are present in the experience of evangelical faith explored in this book. So, what about *spirituality* in dementia?

SPIRITUALITY IN DEMENTIA

Finding Meaning

Whether expressed through religion or through faith, spirituality provides a sense of meaning. Elizabeth MacKinlay[38] writes about it in this way:

> [Spirituality is] the need for ultimate meaning in each person, whether this is fulfilled through relationship with God or some

33. Hull, "Spiritual Development," 171–73.
34. Hull, "Spiritual Development," 171.
35. Goldsmith, *In a Strange Land . . .* , 147.
36. Swinton, *Spirituality and Mental Health Care*, 30–32.
37. Swinton, *Spirituality and Mental Health Care*, 31.
38. MacKinlay and Trevitt, *Finding Meaning*, 23.

sense of another, or whether some other sense of meaning becomes the guiding force within the individual's life.[39]

If spirituality—with its dependence on meaning—is part of what it is to be human, then that quality is inherent in those who are living with dementia. MacKinlay places the *finding* of *meaning* at the center of her model of the spiritual tasks of aging in dementia. This, she notes, can be interactive with relationship with God. The sense of meaning may bring a transcendence of loss and disabilities, and the finding of hope. It is therefore a most significant element in our care for those living with dementia. For the person living with dementia, spirituality might, at least, be considered as a tool for coping with this experience.

Is Spirituality Relevant?

Some have questioned whether spirituality is even a relevant issue for those living with dementia. Yet, if this is part of what it is to be human, "our models of dementia . . . must be broad enough to encompass spirituality, not as an add-on, but as a fundamental feature."[40] And if spirituality is part of who we are, then we can support those with dementia in maintaining their sense of personhood by paying attention to their spiritual needs, even into advanced stages of dementia.

On the other hand, if we consider that personhood *is* under threat as a result of dementia, then so also is the spirituality of those living with dementia, including those of Christian faith. Perhaps, as Peter Kevern has suggested, we need to "reframe" our understandings:

> If we hold to the assumption that people with dementia retain a spirituality into the late stage of the condition, in what ways will our understanding both of spirituality and of dementia need to be revised?[41]

---

39. MacKinlay, *Spiritual Dimension of Ageing*, 42.
40. Hughes, "Situated Embodied View," 205.
41. Kevern, "Spirituality of People with Late-Stage Dementia," 771.

Developing Spiritual Resources

We need, then, to develop a person's spiritual and religious resources as they come to terms with the early stages of dementia in preparation for the future.[42] John Swinton brings this theological perspective:

> Spirituality may take a different form than it had before, but it does not disappear along with their vanishing neurons. Our inherent holiness is not affected by the neurological decline, even if our previous modes of articulating it change or become unavailable. The challenge is for those around persons with dementia to explore how best this holiness can be sustained in the midst of profound changes.[43]

Studies of those who live with dementia have found that the spiritual and religious dimensions of their lives help in the present, enabling coping with the impact of the disease, in finding meaning, and in developing spiritual resources for the future.[44] Support for the spiritual lives of people with dementia is important for their well-being. This prompts a further question for our pastoral caring: does spiritual growth *continue* in those who live with dementia? I explore this further in chapter 8.

The issue of spirituality and the questions it implies for personhood arise instinctively from the experience of Christians who find themselves living with dementia and are fundamental for our thinking about faith in dementia.

QUESTIONING DEMENTIA

For the Christian, still able to contemplate their personal experience of living with dementia, profound and (for some) disturbing questions about self-identity and the nature of faith may arise. This then brings other questions about memory and time. First, consider the question of personhood.

Perspectives on personhood

Writing about her own journey with dementia, Daphne Wallace remarks on her sense of grief and bereavement as she adjusted to the changes that her

---

42. Kevern, "I Pray that I Will Not Fall," 293; Katsuno "Personal Spirituality," 332.
43. Swinton, *Dementia*, 174.
44. Goldsmith, *In a Strange Land . . .* , 144.

illness was bringing.[45] It raised these basic questions: "Who am I? What is at the heart of who I am? . . . Is my personhood fixed or is it continuously evolving?" Christine Bryden explored similar questions of herself as she spoke of the fears of dementia:

> Our main fear is the "loss of self" associated with dementia. We face an identity crisis. We all believed the toxic lie of dementia that the mind is absent and the body is an empty shell. Our sense of self is shattered with this new label of dementia. Who am I if I can no longer be a valued member of society? What if I don't know my family, if I don't know who I am and who I was, if I don't even know God?[46]

She concludes: "Suddenly we have become a non-person."[47]

Being a Person

From the beginning of knowing that you have dementia, these troubling questions about your human identity are present. Philosophy, psychology, church tradition, and theology offer a range of different responses.

There are the rationalist criteria of René Descartes—I think therefore I am (*cogito ergo sum*)—and John Locke's definition of the person as "a thinking, intelligent being, that has reason and reflection."[48] But these do not bring solutions to the questions about personhood for those who are living with dementia and know they are beginning to lose cognitive capacity. The controversial views of ethicist Peter Singer[49] compound such perspectives, arguing that the status of personhood rests on the possession of rational capacities alone. Consequent—or at least implied—lack of compassion and empathy allow what Stephen Post has described as "hypercognitive snobbery" in which: "the category of 'need' is arrogantly displaced as the dominant source of moral obligation by the category of 'personhood.'"[50]

Tom Kitwood[51] has brought a contrasting perspective with his argument for person-centered care: the primary characteristics of personhood here are not about autonomy and rationality, but about being in relationship

---

45. Wallace, "Maintaining a Sense of Personhood," 27.
46. Bryden, *Dancing with Dementia*, 156.
47. Bryden, *Dancing with Dementia*, 156.
48. Locke, *Essay concerning Human Understanding*.
49. Kuhse and Singer, *Should the Baby Live?*, 132; Singer, *Practical Ethics*, 86.
50. Post, *Moral Challenge of Alzheimer Disease*, 79.
51. Kitwood, *Dementia Reconsidered*, 8, 9.

with others. For Christians, such a view of human identity may seem reassuringly closer to a biblical view. However, his argument implicitly *depends* on Martin Buber's relational "I-Thou" philosophy,[52] which is deeply tied to the necessity of the reality and presence of God.[53] Buber envisages a three-way relationship between God, I, and others. God is the ultimate Thou. With this missing God-element, Kitwood's answers to the question of personhood are flawed.[54]

There are other difficulties with relational criteria for personhood. If relationality is key, this doesn't answer the question for those who are isolated, or for those in the later stages of dementia where there may be no obvious clues of response in relationship. The philosophy of Maurice Merleau-Ponty draws our attention to another factor: recognition of the person in their *embodied* self is still possible: "bodily habits, gestures, and actions support and convey humanness and individuality."[55] Reflecting on this, Steven Sabat reminds us that, as this disease progresses, empathy with the inner life of individuals with dementia is important: the "self" continues but may increasingly depend for its expression on the cooperation of caring others.[56] Consequently, faith communities have an important cooperative role in enabling the maintenance and expression of the personhood of individuals.[57]

Robert Spaemann brings a further perspective. Being someone is not dependent on certain capacities but is inherent for all human beings.[58] The nature of being human *is* social and therefore relational. But this is not the starting point for his definition of what it is to be human. He asserts that every human being is above and before anything else "someone" and shares human rights and worth with all humankind, irrespective of capacities, because of our shared genealogical heritage. This idea applies to all, whether or not they own a particular faith. In recognizing this, the term "person" takes us to the heart of Christian theology,[59] which we'll reflect on further in chapter 3.

Such ideas of personhood are deeply associated with our self-identity and the meaning of memory. The relationship between these is particularly significant as we think about the impact of dementia on the experience of

---

52. Buber, *I and Thou*.
53. For further discussion of this, see Swinton, *Dementia*, 149–50.
54. Williams, "Knowing God in Dementia," 1–16.
55. Kontos and Naglie, "Expressions of Personhood," 801.
56. Sabat, *The Experience of Alzheimer's Disease*, 274–308.
57. Sabat, *The Experience of Alzheimer's Disease*, 137–42.
58. Spaemann, *Persons*, 236–48.
59. Spaemann, *Persons*, 17.

faith (and *vice versa*). In the following we take a look at some current thinking about this issue.

Perspectives on Memory and Identity

Increasingly, writing about dementia draws us to the "fragile clues"[60] of a person's identity which persist deep into their journey with this disease. These reveal unexpected perspectives about our memory, uncovering its embeddedness in who we consider ourselves to be.

Autobiographical Memory

With its recall of events in chronological order, autobiographical memory has been a benchmark in Western literature's thinking about identity. Augustine wrote about memory as containing our world and identity: "There . . . I meet myself."[61] As "the temporal glue between past and present," it is "the source of all the connections between past and present experience that allow us to have self-identity and autobiography."[62] Daniel Schacter sums up the standard view: "Our sense of ourselves depends crucially on the subjective experience of remembering our pasts."[63] Without autobiographical remembering and its time-ordered recall, ultimately, sense of self and identity is lost.[64]

Dementia then challenges the assumption of the identity of self being dependent on the chronological grasp of autobiography. With a diagnosis of dementia "past, present, and future begin to disconnect—and we begin to lose the stories of our lives."[65] However, another factor, which Jens Brockmeier has emphasized, is the importance of *meaning*. This provides another perspective for thinking about the issue of faith in dementia.[66]

These different strands of identity and memory interweave, raising questions about the nature of time itself—and for the Christian, perhaps, the mysteries of time within eternity. A holistic understanding of the person and their identity uncovers other kinds of remembering. As Eileen Shamy suggests, the whole person: "the body-soul self . . . seems to have other ways

---

60. Post, *Moral Challenge of Alzheimer Disease*, 25.
61. Augustine, *Confessions*, X.viii, 186.
62. Post, "*Respectare*," 223.
63. Schacter, *Searching for Memory*, 34.
64. Brockmeier, "Questions of Meaning," 69.
65. Post, "*Respectare*," 225.
66. Brockmeier, "Questions of Meaning," 83.

of 'knowing.'"[67] Such understandings bring hope to our perceptions of the identity of the person with dementia and deepen our awareness of how that self is expressed.

Embodied Memory

Whilst dementia eventually brings severely incapacitating cognitive loss and forgetfulness, there is increasing recognition that memory of ourselves is embedded in *every* aspect of who we feel ourselves to be. Maurice Merleau-Ponty's notion of the embodied self[68] offers insight for our understanding of the experience of faith in dementia. In the spiritual caring of those with dementia, faith response is visible not only through brain-dependent capacity, but is expressed through bodily movement, emotional expression, and gestures.[69] For example, in a Christian worship service in a care home we may glimpse the body's memory as we sing familiar hymns, as hands are raised in praise, as we join in with prayer and liturgy, or express the wish to receive communion through acquiescent gesture.[70] This embodied memory, in spite of our failing neurons, can sustain and prompt moments of clarity for people living with dementia—even into advanced stages—including in the experience and practices of faith. Such moments of memory might provide opportunities for connection with God in dementia.[71]

For those living with dementia, as cognitive capacities diminish, identity found and expressed in the body and the relational becomes increasingly significant for the expression of self. As cognitive capacities diminish, triggers to the body's memory become increasingly significant for the expression of self (and faith), and for the understanding of those who care.

THE EXPERIENCE OF FAITH IN DEMENTIA

So, we focus in on the experience itself of faith in dementia. As the person of faith diagnosed with dementia—and perhaps, especially, their loved ones—begins to wrestle with these questions, other thoughts about the security of

---

67. Shamy, *A Guide to the Spiritual Dimension of Care*, 104–5.

68. Merleau-Ponty, *Phenomenology of Perception*.

69. Swinton, *Dementia*, 237, 251.

70. Shamy, *A Guide to the Spiritual Dimension of Care*, 93–119. See also Williams, "Knowing God in Dementia," 9.

71. Read more about implicit and body memory in: Schacter, *Searching for Memory*, 161; Summa and Fuchs, "Self-experience in Dementia," 396–400; and Swinton, "What the Body Remembers."

their faith, relationship with God, and with others begin to surface. How might their perspectives—and *our* understanding—help them now in their walk with God?

The courageous autobiographical accounts of Christine Bryden and Robert Davis have brought significant contributions to this journey of understanding. Both committed Christians (Davis was a Baptist pastor), they speak passionately about their own early experiences of dementia and growing sense of new purpose as they discover new paths for serving God. Jennifer Bute has more recently written of her own long journey with dementia which, like Bryden, she describes as "a gift."[72] Movingly, she writes: "I have come to see that dementia is a glorious opportunity to demonstrate God's love for the whole body of Christ."[73] These stories are significant for us as individual Christians, and for the church, as we come to terms with living with dementia within the horizons of faith.

SEEKING UNDERSTANDING . . .

In this chapter, the writing and research explored provides wider context for the conversation of this book. The different perspectives bring into focus the questions which dementia asks us about identity and memory, and, therefore, about the nature of faith itself. Such questions are of great significance for how we regard the person with dementia, and, in particular, those whose core identity is found in their Christian faith. Deeper understanding contributes to our "being-with" those Christians who are facing the particular challenges of this disease—as well as to the understanding of our own faith in Christ.[74]

Not Just Some Theory. . .

Now, in the following chapters, we look for a deeper understanding of committed faith as we listen to and reflect on the experience of Christians who are living with dementia. In my research I used the methodological approach of hermeneutic phenomenology, which enables the exploration of this lived experience, seeking deeper understanding of this, and aiming to

---

72. Bute, "My Glorious Opportunity."

73. Bute, "My Glorious Opportunity," 23.

74. For further discussion of the idea of "being-with," see Williams, *What Happens to Faith*, 68–69.

bring new insights.[75] The voices of the Christians I spoke with bring insider perspectives of their experience of faith in dementia. These are contributing to the "theory"—and to transforming practice. (Rosemary, I think, would be pleased!)

The words of Jess, Ron, Jill, David, Alice, Rosemary, Bill, and Matthew recorded in this book are a gift. They challenge and provide important opportunity to listen, learn from, and reflect on this experience, offering potential for the bettering of spiritual care in the present, and for the funding of faith as a resource in later-stage dementia. As Christine Bryden reminds us:

> After diagnosis, there is usually a journey of several years, in which we are battling the decline. And in this journey many of us can still speak . . . There is no time to lose to hear our voice as we struggle to communicate.[76]

For Further Reflection . . .

- Reflect on these words from Deuteronomy 6:5: "Love the Lord your God with all your heart and with all your soul and with all your strength." What do you think these words might mean for the person living with dementia?
- Is the person with dementia "no longer there"? Why might you think that?
- If spirituality *is* important for all human beings, how do we recognize this in the lives of those who are living with dementia?
- How might memory be important for the faith lives of Christians who are living with dementia?

---

75. For further discussion of the research approach used, see Williams, *What Happens to Faith*, 60–87.

76. Bryden, *Dancing with Dementia*, 48.

3

Who I Am

"I am loved by God."

The coming of dementia begins to interrogate the meaning of what it is to be human. Who am I? For the believer, even in its earlier stages, the illness starts to question theological understanding of what it means to be created in the image of God, and consequently, our identity as being in relationship with God in Christ. Yet, for Alice, David, Rosemary, Bill, Jess, Michael, Jill, and Ron—in spite of initial shock of diagnoses, even anger—"I was very cross with him [the GP]!" (David)—they know *who* they are:

> "I am loved by God . . . Nothing . . . can ever separate me from him" (see Rom 8:38–39) (Alice).
> "It's a relationship" (Alice).
> "I know Jesus" (David).

Even as they were beginning to struggle with loss of words, concentration, and short-term memory, they were certain of God and their sense of identity in knowing that they were loved by him.

> "God is always with me . . . but now, even when my brain falls apart . . . it doesn't matter" (Alice).

How could they be so sure?

This chapter reflects on theological and biblical perspectives that begin to suggest answers to this question of identity—even "when my brain falls apart." Interweaving with the participants' words, there is certainty of identity. I will explore the significance of being created by God in his image, of being in Christ, and of belonging in his body—the community of faith gathered by the Holy Spirit. Caught up in this story is the participants' eschatological hope (considered further in chapter 9). This is the orientation of their faith.[1] These perspectives have profound importance for ways in which they perceive themselves, and also for the ways in which the body of Christ responds to them as fellow Christians. First, we hear some initial responses to this question from David, Bill, Jess, and Alice, then we will delve deeper into some of the theological underpinnings of their faith and identity.

"I AM ME"

When I began to talk with David and Bill about this question of identity, it was just a year or two since their diagnoses. At this stage, they both felt that dementia was *not* affecting their sense of who they were: "not a problem," said David; no difference, said Bill, "apart from these memory lapses."

In spite of the definite ways in which they spoke, I couldn't help wondering if the strength of their assertions disclosed an unwelcome recognition of the changes that dementia was bringing. As they told me their stories of diagnosis, their comments resonated with Christine Bryden's story, who writes of her diagnosis as bringing the "horror of prognosis" that is "a turning point in our lives."[2] However, both David and Bill minimized their awareness of difficulties.

> DAVID: It's one part of the brain, it's just one part . . . now if that one part . . . they don't work—but the rest of the brain does.
> BILL: I think what has surprised me is that I still feel I'm the same person before it was diagnosed. Now I've got the medication I think it's bringing it down to a stable . . .

In these early stages of the disease, David and Bill were both seeing dementia as a *medical* condition—which they knew was bringing changes to their lives—but feeling that these were not significant for their identity.

---

1. See chapter 1, 10–11, 14; Brueggemann, *Spirituality of the Psalms*, 9; Williams, *What Happens to Faith?*, 173–75.
2. Bryden, *Dancing with Dementia*, 155.

Perhaps seeing dementia in this way was enabling them to keep their biological diagnoses separate from the person they felt themselves to be, and also to retain control over their lives. At the beginning of their journeys with this illness, I wondered if, as Tom Kitwood has questioned, their medical diagnoses were already beginning to define who they felt themselves to be.[3] Nevertheless, Bill's surprise that he felt like "the same person" suggested his awareness of stereotypical images of people who live with dementia. Their protests that there was "not a problem" suggested their understandable desire to assert their sense of continuing identity as they were encountering the changes that dementia was undoubtedly bringing.

Jess was a little further on in her journey. But she had also been thinking about this question. She was uncomfortable with the word "dementia," which for her brought negative connotations and unhappy memories:

> JESS: I do agree that I have "memory loss" . . . but it doesn't affect me . . . when I knew . . . that I had memory loss . . . when I was *labelled* memory loss.

Her ironic emphasis on the word "labelled" suggested her strong objection to having her identity summarized with a medical label. Instead, she asserted that her essential identity as a person with dementia was found in relationships:

> JESS: Just because you can't remember things it doesn't make you not human. You're still a human, you're still a parent, wife . . . husband . . .
> JESS: I'm just me.

Unlike David and Bill, Alice had also lived with dementia for several years, and her words bring us to the experience of faith. Her identity was found primarily in her sense of relationship with God. She was: "a child of God, that is fact." She was "loved by God, no matter what." Instinctively, she expressed her belief in God's love for her as being prior to her own capacities in this way:

> ALICE: Our worth and value never changes . . . when God so loved the world, he gave his Son . . . our worth and value doesn't depend on how good we are or what we do or what our health is like or the state of our bodies . . . he just loves us for who we are . . . so we are complete in him.

---

3. Kitwood, *Dementia Reconsidered*, 9. See also Kevern, "Alzheimer's and the Dementia of God," 241.

For her, this was the central and most important aspect of her identity. As a former GP, she understood the nature of her illness and its consequences from a medical perspective. Yet, in spite of this, she believed and felt that she was "complete in him" (God). She recognized the physical impairments brought by dementia to her life, but this didn't diminish her sense of identity. Her emphasis on wholeness resonates with the insistence on seeing the *whole person*, rather than the illness.[4] Her words reflected this wholeness which had been brought about through her faith in Christ.

Throughout our conversations, these believers' strong sense of identity suggested awareness of the questions that dementia was bringing to others' perceptions of "who I am." In response—in a variety of ways—all of the research participants affirmed their sense of enduring identity as people loved by others and by God. Typical of Christians of an evangelical tradition, this was found in a transcendent sense of being in relationship with God ("It's a relationship"; "Nothing . . . can ever separate me from him"). It was this sense of *knowing* who they are in Christ that was framing their experience of dementia. How can we understand this?

QUESTIONS FOR THEOLOGY

Their certainty found in the experience of faith brings questions to the traditional theological ideas of what it means to be human,[5] created in God's image, and—as cognitive capacity fades—to our salvation and sureness of identity in Christ. Bryden's question, asked out of her own early experience of dementia, echoes the faith-filled certainty of these disciples of Jesus ("at what stage can you deny me my self-hood and my spirituality?"[6]). It also prompts new questions which dementia brings to theology of the evangelical tradition. What does it mean for the Christian to be formed in the image of God and in Christ when memory and other capacities are beginning to fail? Jess's daughter, reflecting on this, said:

> I have found it challenging. Because I think . . . it's made me re-address and think through some of my preconceptions . . . about who we are and what it is to be made in the image of God, and what the Christian community is all really about.

---

4. For example: Kitwood, *Dementia Reconsidered*, 7; Shamy, *A Guide to the Spiritual Dimension of Care*; Swinton, *Dementia*, 41–48.

5. See the earlier discussion in chapter 2 about identity and personhood, 25–29.

6. Bryden and MacKinlay, "Dementia: A Spiritual Journey," 71.

The answers to such questions have significance not only for theology, but for Christians living with dementia and their loved ones. For them, their prognoses and the first signs of stigmatizing behaviors from others begin to raise the question: Who are you?

CREATED IN THE IMAGE OF GOD

Traditionally, for the Christian believer, being created in the image of God provides the starting place for biblical and theological understanding of what it means to be human[7]—including those who live with dementia. Whilst the phrase "image of God" (*imago Dei*) appears in Scripture only a few times,[8] it provides a foundation for theological understanding of the Christian faith, setting a purposeful trajectory through Scripture: we are creatures of God, loved by him, and made with a purpose, "to glorify God, and to enjoy him forever."[9] This idea of who we are is presumed in Christian faith, and assumed and embedded in the words of the research participants. Their God was sovereign and the Creator. Alice expressed her purpose as being "to please him"; Bill (the former policeman) thought of God as "the Boss"; Rosemary spoke deliberately of worshipping "Creator God."

Theological understanding of the *imago Dei* relentlessly leads us forward to the image of God found in Christ (Col 1:15) and then to the discovery of the Christian's identity—whatever our capacities—as being "in him." With such an identity, the Bible points us inevitably to the hope of resurrection and the state of being-with-God forever (1 Cor 15).[10] It is this foundational understanding of the preeminence of God and his purposes that permeated the words of the participants and was giving them hope: "I know where I'm going," Ron said.

Rational or Relational?

Understandings in our contemporary Western context of what it means to be "me," have been shaped by perspectives from philosophy and psychology, often depending on *rational* or *relational* criteria. Yet, eventually, both might threaten the identity of those living with dementia. This tension is reflected

---

7. Anderson, *On Being Human*, 70.
8. Brueggemann, *An Unsettling God*, 59.
9. Westminster Assembly, "Westminster Shorter Catechism."
10. Grenz, "The Social God and the Relational Self," 83.

in Christian tradition and is important for understanding the nature of faith experience in dementia.

From Aquinas through to modern theologians such as Carl Henry and Gordon Clark,[11] the criteria for the reflected image of God have included reason as being preeminent: it is "in the rational creature alone we find a likeness of image."[12] Most Protestant thinking has been more closely associated with Augustine's focus on the human orientation towards God and the relational.[13] Yet, ultimately, Augustine also argues that to be made in God's image depends on rationality: he is "a rational soul, which raises him above the beasts in the field."[14] Modern evangelical theology has lived with an uncomfortable tension between its style of rational, linear, propositional thinking[15]—developed in response to Enlightenment thinking—and the relational aspect of faith response found in Augustine, Protestant Reformers such as Luther, and modern scholars such as Buber and Barth. Whilst Christians have emphasized the relational as an essential part of being created in the *imago Dei*, still, eventually, some have suggested an ultimate dependence on rational capacity, which leads us back to the rational criteria of Aquinas.

Evangelical theology brings emphasis on personal relationship with Christ,[16] dependent on God's gift of salvation that is freely given (Eph 2:8). Confidence in this sense of relationship with God was clear in the research participants' accounts. However, some sections of evangelicalism have also portrayed ongoing salvation status as dependent on verbal and cognitive assent to the central tenets of Christian faith.[17] Such understanding eventually seems to risk excluding those suffering with advancing dementia from relationship with God. Dementia reveals inconsistency in this. Perhaps, unwittingly, some evangelicals have implied limits on the grace of God for *some* human beings.

---

11. See Anderson's discussion of the perspective of a conservative evangelical orientation (*On Being Human*, 225).

12. Aquinas, *Summa Theologica* Ia, q.9, a.6.

13. Anderson, *On Being Human*, 74–75.

14. Augustine, *On Genesis*, 186; see also Reinders, *Receiving the Gift of Friendship*, 228–29.

15. For example, Reasonable Faith, https://www.reasonablefaith.org.

16. Zahl, "Reformation Pessimism," 82.

17. For example, drawing on Bible verses such as Romans 10:9–10 (NIVUK): "If you declare with your mouth, 'Jesus is Lord,' and believe in your heart that God raised him from the dead, you will be saved. For it is with your heart that you believe and are justified, and it is with your mouth that you profess your faith and are saved."

Such tensions are deeply embedded in the evangelical tradition. David's words hinted at this. I had asked him in what ways he felt that declining cognitive understanding affects faith. Certain of his own relationship with Jesus ("I know Jesus"), he pondered this issue.

> DAVID: The trouble is . . . when people have got dementia and it's much further on . . . they wouldn't be able to know, because if they didn't already know . . . they wouldn't be able to understand it . . . but that faith I would hope will continue with me . . .

David was sure of his own faith as he imagined his future with dementia. Yet he struggled with the question of the possibility of having faith without "knowing."

A difficulty with traditional understandings of what it means to be a human, created in the image of God, with its reason/relational dimensions, is that these do not provide easy solutions for the Christian with dementia, who knows that cognitive capacity is diminishing. For those living in the early to moderate stages of dementia, still able to envisage the future, they may understandably feel that our "hypercognitive society"[18] threatens not only their identity but also the security of their faith.

Such conclusions may feel as if they distance us untruthfully from those we know and love who live with the increasing consequences of cognitive impairment. Alice was sure of her enduring relationship with God. For her, and the other participants in the research, the certainty of being in a two-way relationship with God had preeminence: "It's a relationship to someone that I love and who loves me" (Alice). As I listened to their voices, and to the voice of Scripture, two further questions arose. From a biblical perspective, what then is the *nature* of being human (including the Christian living with developing dementia) created by God? And, what is the *nature* of God the Creator?

Being Human

"Then the LORD *God formed a man from the dust of the ground and breathed into his nostrils the breath of life, and the man became a living being" (Gen 2:7).*

The biblical story of creation begins with the will and intention of the Creator: "In the beginning God" (Gen 1:1, NIVUK). In Christian thought, unlike the perspectives of secular Western society, the human creature is *not*

---

18. Post, *Moral Challenge of Alzheimer Disease*, 5.

an autonomous being who can find fulfillment in self alone.[19] The biblical creation account makes clear: "We are not the authors of our own stories."[20] Rather, God is sovereign: he is the one who creates and gives "the breath of life," so that the human becomes "a living being," sustained by and dependent on God the Creator. The participants' words reflected this sense of the God who is in charge of their lives ("If God has asked me to have dementia . . . ," Jill).

Body-and-Soul

The creation story gives a holistic sense of what it is to be human—*together* the "dust" and "breath" form the "living being."[21] The Hebrew word *nephesh*, often translated as "soul," indicates that this is God's "breath of life." The Old Testament understanding of human creatures seems to be as "ensouled body and embodied soul."[22] However, influenced by Greek thinking, Christian tradition has over the centuries separated the physical and spiritual. In some cases, such "dualism" has persisted into twenty-first-century thinking. I noticed that David's words implied his uncertainty about this as he imagined his own future of living with advancing dementia: "Maybe the dementia gets worse, but that part of me will belong to Jesus."

In the New Testament, Paul's thinking sometimes appears to be ambivalent about this. For example: "Set your minds on things above, not on earthly things . . . Put to death, therefore, whatever belongs to your earthly nature" (Col 3: 2–5, NIVUK).[23] However, as Paula Gooder helpfully highlights, the New Testament Greek word often translated as "soul" (*psuche*) is not precise but is used in a variety of ways by Paul. In keeping with his Hebrew heritage, it

> incorporates the body, pushing us to recognize that for Paul both the words "body" and "soul" are neutral and describe who we are as people—bodies animated by a vital life force.[24]

In the case of persons living with dementia, even a subtle ignoring of the wholeness of what it means to be created in the image of God can result in

---

19. For example, Giddens, *Modernity and Self Identity*, 70–108.
20. Swinton, *Dementia*, 164.
21. "*Terra animate*," as Augustine describes the human being. See Augustine, *City of God* 20.20.
22. For further discussion of this, see Anderson, *On Being Human*, 38, 210.
23. Gooder, *Body*, 22–23.
24. Gooder, *Body*, 41.

damaging stigmatization, which those involved in the research were already beginning to experience (see chapter 6). In contrast, a unified body-and-soul understanding of what it means to be human brings reassurance, both for the person living with dementia and their loved ones.

Contrary to a fragmented understanding of personhood where cognitive capacity is definitive, a "created in the image of God" (*imago Dei*) understanding of "who I am" is of the *whole* person—body, mind, and soul—the integrated self, expressed through the unity of body and soul.[25] In these understandings of who we are as human beings there is hope—and significance for those who *know* that their cognitive capacities are diminishing: "I am much more than a diseased brain."[26] In biblical terms, the living, breathing human being, whatever their incapacities, is made in the image of God, holy and worthy of honor: "We are complete in him" (Alice).

Made for Relationship

An important part of our understanding of ourselves as created by God is that we are made for relationship. In the beginning, God said: "Let us make mankind in *our* image, in *our* likeness" (Gen 1:26, NIVUK, my emphasis). God's words suggest the inherent relationality of what it means to be human. Ray Anderson, in his exploration of the creation accounts, develops this: the "*imago* is not totally present in the form of individual humanity but more completely as *co*-humanity,"[27] reminding us that, "in the image of God . . . male and female he created them" (Gen 1:27, NIVUK).

Human beings are made for relationship, not only with God, but with one another. Before the creation of Eve, God said, "it is not good that the man should be alone" (Gen 2:18). Who we are is embedded in our human relationships. As Jess said: "Just because you can't remember things . . . You're still a human, you're still a parent, wife . . ." Anderson recalls Buber's "I-Thou," three-way interactive relationship[28] between God and people, suggesting that "it is in relationship with other persons as well as with God that the divine image is expressed."[29] From the beginning, in the garden of Eden, God himself actively sought and initiated relationship—it is an inherent characteristic of human being (see Gen 2:18, 20b–24; 3:8–9).

---

25. Swinton, *Dementia*, 166–67.
26. Bryden, *Dancing with Dementia*, 152.
27. Anderson, *On Being Human*, 73.
28. Buber, *I and Thou*; see chapter 2, 27.
29. Anderson, *Spiritual Caregiving*, 33.

The relational nature of the *imago Dei* is caught up through Scripture in the command to love God who "so loved the world" (John 3:16), followed with its consequent "love your neighbour as yourself" (Luke 10:27).[30] It is reflected in the community of God's people through the Old Testament story, and then in the New Testament in the community of believers who are *together* the body of Christ (1 Cor 12:12–31; 1 Cor 3:16, NLT). From a biblical perspective, relationality is not a criterion for personhood that can be in doubt but arises out of being made in the image of God.[31] Whilst this being-in-relationship with God is inherent in being human, relationship with others brings increasing challenge for those who live with dementia. As Rosemary said of others in the local church she had tried to attend: "They don't understand."

What Kind of God in Dementia?[32]

In asking this question, Peter Kevern recognizes that living in this freshly acknowledged *context* of dementia has potential to bring new perspectives to our understanding of God. Developing dementia does not change God. He is relational and loving in spite of this destructive illness. This is the God of whom the participants in the research spoke: I am "loved by God, no matter what" (Alice).

The Relationality of God

Theologians from Augustine to Moltmann to Zizioulas and others of the Christian tradition have understood God to be fundamentally relational in his trinitarian nature. God-as-Trinity—this difficult concept—has been understood in a variety of ways. Perhaps, in the end, a definitive definition is unimportant; rather, as Karen Kilby suggests, the three-in-oneness of God provides a kind of grammar for understanding Scripture and gives a vocabulary for Christian faith.[33] It also provides a sort of underlying grammar for understanding the *experience* of faith. Bill expressed his understanding in this way: "there are three bosses, I suppose: Boss 1: Father; Boss 2: Jesus; Boss 3: Spirit . . . and they're all working together on our behalf."

---

30. Williams, "Knowing God in Dementia," 6.
31. Swinton, *Dementia*, 159.
32. Kevern, "What Sort of a God?," 174.
33. Kilby, "Perichoresis and Projection," 443–44.

Augustine's emphasis on the oneness of God has perhaps contributed to the individualism of Protestantism and that of evangelicalism.[34] Together with his stress on the capacity of reason,[35] the person with developing dementia is left increasingly isolated. Instead, Jürgen Moltmann[36] has famously insisted on the relational nature of God the Trinity. In this there is hope for understanding of the kind of God to be found in dementia:

> God who is a Trinity of persons . . . is a perichoretic community of love constituted by the relationships of the three persons of the Trinity: God the Father, God the Son, and God the Holy Spirit; each person is inextricably interlinked in an eternal community of loving relationship.[37]

This understanding of God-as-Trinity provides new possibilities for thinking about the person with dementia, who is both part of the human family *and* in relationship with God.[38]

Being as Communion

Zizioulas's description of God the Trinity as "being as communion" brings a further perspective, helpful for us as we think about a Christian believer who lives with dementia.[39] He makes the point that relationship with God and others isn't primarily about the human ability to respond to God and others.[40] Rather, this God who exists as communion creates and draws his creatures into loving communion both with himself and with each other.[41] It is within the context of *this* relationship that human dignity and sacredness, no matter what an individual's attributes, are found:

> Human dignity, the unconditional requirement that we attend with reverence to one another, rests firmly on that conviction that the other is already related to something that isn't me.[42]

---

34. Kilby, "Perichoresis and Projection," 433–35.
35. Augustine, *On Genesis*, 186.
36. Moltmann, *The Trinity and the Kingdom*, 174–76; Kilby, "Perichoresis and Projection," 440.
37. Swinton, *Dementia*, 158.
38. Swinton, *Dementia*, 158–59.
39. Zizioulas, *Being as Communion*.
40. Zizioulas, *Being as Communion*, 17–18.
41. Zizioulas, *Communion and Otherness*, 43.
42. Williams, "The Person and the Individual."

Our humanness, as Rosalie Hudson draws out, is bound up in God the Trinity.[43] All are invited "in the person of Jesus Christ, by the personal power of the Holy Spirit . . . into the Son's personal communion with the Father." Jesus' prayer for his disciples expressed this: "that they may be one, as we are one" (John 17: 22). This inherent relationality of God and human beings is hopeful for those who live with declining cognitive capacity. Rosemary spoke of the mystery of her relationship with God in this way:

> ROSEMARY: God, Jesus his Son, and the Holy Spirit who indwells[44] . . . all . . . to me are a mystery . . . the Spirit of God is always in me. Now I am always conscious of that, even if it's really bad . . .

At the heart of this relational Trinity is the creative and redeeming impetus of God's love-in-relationship ("God . . . loves me," Alice).[45]

God Is Love

Amidst these complex doctrinal issues, there is the profound, practical, and theological quality of love, demonstrated in God's gift of Jesus (John 3:16). Reflecting out of my evangelical tradition, biblically, God's intentional love brought humankind into existence; God's sacrificial love expressed through his Son enables human beings to find relationship with him; the Holy Spirit sustains that loving relationship with God in Christ. Bill expressed it this way, his words becoming a prayer to Jesus:

> BILL: God the Father, God the Son, God the Holy Spirit—and they are here for me . . . just me. Yes, I have sinned . . . but all that is in the past and I just want to be a follower of you.

The research participants' certainty of their identity and their experience of God's love as Christians ("he loves me . . . that's it . . . yeah," David*)*, is underwritten by the New Testament understanding of being "in Christ," the true image of God (Col 1:15). Here is a key to the identity of the Christian who is living with dementia. So, in the light of participants' experience and Scripture, what does it mean for the Christian living with developing dementia to *be* "in Christ"?

---

43. Hudson, "God's Faithfulness and Dementia," 53.

44. For example, 1 Corinthians 6:19: "Do you not know that your bodies are temples of the Holy Spirit, who is in you?" (NIVUK).

45. See 1 John 4:16.

BEING IN CHRIST

The biblical story of our identity and our relationship with God centers on Christ.[46] As we move forward from the creation-centered understanding of being human, and from the tragedy of the fall in Genesis 1–3, we discover that the Scriptures (as Jesus himself affirmed) sustain this Christ-centered theme, showing how *in* Christ the true image of God is found (see Luke 24:44).

Christ's coming is the catalyst for new creation: "In the beginning was the Word, and the Word was with God, and the Word was God . . . The Word became flesh and made his dwelling among us," (John 1:1, 14, NIVUK). Paul's letters develop this theme. Jesus *is* the divine image,[47] the second Adam, who makes peace between creature and Creator (1 Cor 15:20–22; Rom 5:12–17). In spite of failing bodies, our identity "in Christ" finds its goal in the new creation, going from the past, and beyond the present into hopeful future (see Heb 1:1–4). So, out of his frailty, as we talked, Matthew was able to voice with confidence Paul's words as his own: "We shall all be changed . . ."[48]

The New Testament's imagery of being found "in Christ" (1 Cor 15:22) begins to disclose its significance for the person living in the earlier stages of dementia, bringing confidence in the security of knowing who they are and of their salvation. The ideas of *identity* and *salvation* are fused in the participants' "intrinsic faith" in Christ, and this begins to respond to questions about the loss of personhood and faith for those living with dementia.[49]

Imagining their future, the participants were confident in the security of their faith in Christ. As Swinton puts it:

> Through Christ we are included in Christ. When we come to realize that all that needs to be done has been done in Christ, we come to realize that all that we are and all that we can be is who we are *in Christ*.[50]

Where faith is core to identity, this biblical understanding and assurance of being "in Christ" is key for the person of faith in the light of their developing dementia.[51] It enables peace in the present (as well as confident hope for the

---

46. Grenz, "The Social God and the Relational Self," 80.

47. Grenz, "The Social God and the Relational Self," 80.

48. "Listen, I will tell you a mystery! We will not all die, but we will all be changed" (1 Cor 15:51).

49. Keck, *Forgetting Whose We Are*, 14, 15. See Swinton's discussion of this in *Dementia*, 9.

50. Swinton, *Becoming Friends of Time*, 187.

51. For example, MacKinlay and Trevitt, *Finding Meaning*, 22.

future). David's response to my queries about his reactions to his dementia was robust: "There is no fear through Jesus."

New Identity in Christ . . .

The stories told by the research participants reveal aspects of their individual human identities (for example: a policeman, a mother, a teacher). But the essence of who they felt themselves to be was caught up in this understanding of being in Christ: "I am born again" (Ron); "loved by God" and "a child of God" (Alice); "the core is knowing Jesus" (David). Having Christian faith was not merely a useful resource for them, it was *who they were*. Their transformative experience of knowing Christ had precedence over their experience of dementia. Their illness had happened to them as people who were finding their identity in Christ. As Karl Barth has said:

> To be a Christian is *per definitionem* to be in Christ. The place of the community as such, the theatre of their history, the ground on which they stand, the air that they breathe, and therefore the standard of what they do and do not do, is indicated by this expression. Being in Christ is the *a priori* of all the instruction that Paul gives his churches, all the comfort and exhortation he addresses to them.[52]

In the Gospel accounts we see that the lives of the disciples were transformed by their meeting with the risen Jesus on Easter Day. For them, the resurrection signaled the beginning of new creation. The day of Pentecost saw the coming of God the Spirit into the world, and their lives were changed. In a variety of ways, the participants in my research spoke of the significance of their life-changing encounters with God, which had established their life's orientation of faith.[53] This transformation hadn't arisen from information acquired so that it could be lived out but was the result of a God-initiated inner transformation. Like the early disciples, they were *given*, as Ray Anderson comments, "assurance of their own shared destiny with him as an indwelling spirit of hope."[54] Their new identity in Christ was sealed with God's gift of the indwelling Spirit (Eph 1:13,14): "The Holy Spirit is filling you (as he is)" (Rosemary). Their assurance of identity and destiny was not diminished by the advent of dementia.

---

52. Barth, *Church Dogmatics*, IV.2, 277.
53. See chapter 7, 107–111.
54. Anderson, *Spiritual Caregiving*, 152.

Being "Saved"

In spite of evangelicalism's emphasis on grace,[55] sometimes evangelicals seem to bring an additional requirement of dependence on cognitive response to Christ, accompanied by a declaration of propositional truths. Interpretations of Scripture, shaped by "Enlightenment understandings of knowledge,"[56] may seem to demand cognitive work: the ongoing understanding of the significance of the cross; ability to recall and recognize personal sin, repent, and receive God's forgiveness (see Rom 10: 9–10).[57] Yet such "knowing," situated in cognitive activity, is becoming increasingly difficult for the Christian with dementia, even before the effects of the more advanced illness. If it is subtly assumed as an essential element of being "in Christ" then the person living with early to moderate stage dementia may be understandably concerned about the *future* security of their faith in Christ. However, as John Swinton reminds us, whilst doctrine is important for the community of faith, it is not factual knowledge which saves us.[58] As cognitive abilities began to diminish ("I thought . . . I was quite clever!," Alice) the participants' words demonstrated that their experience of faith was increasingly dependent on God. Alice laughs: ". . . but now I realize everything that happens is of God."

In the Gospels we see Jesus recognizing embodied, or "tacit," faith expressed through individuals' enacted dependence on him.[59] For example, his response to the woman who touched Jesus' garment and was healed of her bleeding: "your faith has made you well" (Mark 5:25–34). The New Testament Greek word *sozo* (made well), used here, sometimes has the meaning of "saved," encompassing Christ's gift of wholeness, which embraces the person in every aspect of their self. Again, Christ's promise of paradise to the repentant, dying thief (Luke 23:40–43) suggests that a dependent trust and turning to Jesus were all that was required. For the first disciples, as Swinton has suggested, "propositional knowledge was something that emerged from the experience of trusting in Jesus rather than the other way around."[60] For those whose ability to think clearly is fading, this understanding brings reassurance. One participant (Rosemary) speaking of her intrinsic certainty of God's enduring presence with and in her said:

---

55. Greggs, "Beyond the binary," 154–55.
56. Greggs, "Beyond the binary," 164.
57. Williams, "Knowing God in Dementia," 6.
58. Swinton, *Becoming Friends of Time*, 106.
59. See Kontos and Naglie's discussion in "Tacit Knowledge."
60. Swinton, *Becoming Friends of Time*, 104.

ROSEMARY: He will be with me . . . right to the end! Even if my . . . because my feelings are still as strong, if not stronger, as my mind becomes less intellectualized and able to . . . I shall be more filled with the feeling of the love of God . . . it's here [indicates inner self] . . . I can speak from experience not from some theory.

God's grace trumps cognitive capacity (Eph 2:8).

You're Safe in Him

Those at the beginning of their journey with dementia—or those who observe and care—may anxiously ask themselves whether faith is safe in the face of all that dementia may bring: "What will happen to my faith?"[61] Paul's writing makes it clear that it is through the incarnation of Christ and his redemptive work that it has been made possible for Christians to understand themselves as being "in Christ" (Rom 6:11). There can be no separation from God "in Christ" (Rom 8:38–39). John Swinton writes:

> I am who I am in Christ alone . . . "We were therefore buried with him through baptism into death in order that, just as Christ was raised from the dead through the glory of the Father, we too may live a new life" (Rom 6:4).[62]
>
> There was therefore *never* a time when who we were was determined by the particular neurological configuration of our brains. We may have thought there was, but we were quite wrong. Who we are is who we are in Christ, and, crucially, *that is hidden*.[63]

Fortunately, for those living with dementia—and for all of us—the Christian's story is not a solitary one. I am not on my own.

BELONGING IN THE BODY OF CHRIST

Being Part of God's Story

Alice, Rosemary, Bill, and the others as they were living with dementia, were intensely aware of their *individual* relationship with Christ, yet, as

---

61. Shamy, *A Guide to the Spiritual Dimension of Care*, 21.
62. Swinton, *Becoming Friends of Time*, 188–89. See also Colossians 3:1–4.
63. Swinton, *Becoming Friends of Time*, 189.

they talked about God's will for their lives, there was an awareness of being caught up in the purposeful narrative of God's people stretching from creation to the eschaton. Their words revealed their understanding that they were part of God's story.[64]

The biblical narrative has given the Christian believer a community story that is inherently caught up in the time-transcendent purposes of God himself.[65] Stanley Hauerwas speaks of this community of believers as "formed by the story witnessed to by scripture."[66] Allusions to Bible texts are threaded through the participants' words recorded in this book. It is in this—the transcending, ongoing story narrated through Scripture—in which the participants situated themselves, shaping their autobiographical accounts and discovering meaning for their present experiences in its light. Hauerwas reminds us that "the story and its people" need a community for its "remembering, telling and hearing."[67] Without community, the story cannot be remembered, recalled, lived out in the present, or bring hope for the future.[68] The lived experience of Rosemary, Alice, Bill, Ron, Jess, Matthew, David, and Jill questions the church's understanding about such an account of collective memory. Speaking of her frustrating attempts of trying to be part of a local church, Rosemary concluded: "I can't at the moment join a congregation." How might the church of today be one that enables those who live with dementia to participate in such remembering?[69]

Being Part of the Body

And here, in the present moment of this day, *all* believers belong (are not just included) in the body of Christ. Following the resurrection of Christ, his ascension and Pentecost, this understanding of the church is developed throughout the New Testament: "So we, who are many, are one body in Christ, and individually we are members one of another" (Rom 12:5; see also 1 Cor 11:23–26). The Scriptures are clear: whoever we are as individuals, as followers of Jesus, all are "in the one Spirit we were all baptized into one body" (1 Cor 12:12–13). There is a weightiness in the meaning of this for our identity. Stanley Grenz points out that "the image of God . . . is found

---

64. See Psalm 78:1–4.
65. Keck, *Forgetting Whose We Are*, 45.
66. Hauerwas, *A Community of Character*, 15.
67. Hauerwas, *The Peaceable Kingdom*, 98.
68. Hauerwas, *A Community of Character*, 15.
69. Dianne Crowther's work begins to respond to this: Crowther, *Sustaining Persons*.

in the relationality of persons in community;"[70] it is an incorporation by the Spirit "into the dynamic of divine life."[71]

Often, if English is our first language (and we are of an evangelical tradition), we may think that Paul's "you" in his epistles refers to *me*, to an individual; but more often than not it is the plural pronoun and refers to *us*.[72] Careful reflection on this reveals the hope that corporate knowing of God brings for the individual person with diminishing cognitive capacity, for example: nothing "will be able to separate *us* [my italics] from the love of God that is in Christ Jesus our Lord" (Romans 8:39). Knowing who I am is found not only in our individual relationship with God in Christ; it is found in the community of faith. All parts of the body are of equal value; without one part, the whole is damaged and incomplete (1 Cor 12:21–26). The Spirit's distribution of diverse gifts to the "members" of Christ's body does not respect status or capacity (1 Cor 12: 4–7):

> Now there are varieties of gifts, but the same Spirit; and there are varieties of services, but the same Lord; and there are varieties of activities, but it is the same God who activates all of them in everyone. To each is given the manifestation of the Spirit for the common good.

If we understand ourselves as being part of the body of Christ, then our identity and faith (even if we live with dementia) is assured within the body of Christ and, as such, we are included in this expression of the image of God.

The lived experience of dementia asks difficult questions of Scripture, and of those of us who are part of today's church. If those living with this disease are equally recipients of God's grace and calling, *how* do we treat them with "special honour" (1 Cor 12:23, NIVUK)? How are we receiving their gifts? What does it mean in embodied practice that these Christians *belong* to the body of Christ?

There is also one other powerfully, transformative element of the Christian's identity. As Paul reminds us, we are not *only* the body of Christ, we are also the children of God and, as such, "joint heirs with Christ" (Rom 8:17). Being part of this Jesus-narrative together inevitably leads to hope. This hopeful orientation is also who we are in Christ, whatever our situation. This hopeful faith is explored further in chapter 9.

---

70. Grenz, "The Social God and the Relational Self," 89.

71. Grenz, "The Social God and the Relational Self," 91.

72. For more discussion of this see Eastman, "Double Participation and the Responsible Self."

WHO I AM . . .

This chapter has reflected on this question of knowing who we are as Christians who live with dementia. In the light of the Bible and Christian theology, the research participants' sense of "Who I am" was found in the certainty that they are creatures of a sovereign God; their identity is in Christ, the image of God; and the orientation of their lives was in the shared, hopeful narrative of God's story, within the community of faith, the body of Christ. Their confidence of being in relationship with God and their identity as Christians seemed to be resourcing them for their lives amidst the disorientation being brought by their illness. In the next chapter, we will hear more about their experience of knowing God in this strange context of dementia.

For Further Reflection . . .

- Reflect on these verses from Scripture: Genesis 1:26a; Colossians 3:1–4; 1 Corinthians 12:12–26.
- How is faith important for your sense of identity?
- What questions do the ideas in this chapter raise concerning those you know and love who are living with dementia?

4

Knowing God:
The Experience of Faith

"I'm closer to God . . . nearer my God to thee."[1]

As a young man, Matthew had been an interpreter, living and working in London. With relish, he tells me stories of his city life then—of lunchtime walks across the park, of meeting the girl he loves (who listens from another room now, with tears in her eyes). He tells me a story of faith which has grown across the years, from a lively church in the southeast of England, to involvement with conferences for *Every Day with Jesus*,[2] and to his commitment in their quiet, local village church in rural England. And now, with pictures of children and grandchildren all about, and rollator nearby, he sits by the window, watching the birds and his much-loved garden. His words come slowly. He has dementia—and faith is "stronger."

You might think that Christians who develop this disease would feel God was distant. But for Matthew, Rosemary, Alice, David, Ron, Jill, Bill, and Jess the opposite was true. Their words resonate with the conclusion of

---

1. Rosemary's words here refer to the hymn "Nearer, my God, to thee" (Sarah Adams, 1792–1872).

2. *Every Day with Jesus* (published by CWR) is a Bible reading and devotional guide.

Jon Stuckey: faith itself does not seem to be under threat because of dementia.[3] This is not to minimize the evident struggles of living with this illness, which may include doubt, darkness, and a sense of the absence of God.[4] Yet, in spite of the difficulties they were already experiencing, my conversations with these Christians revealed that vibrant faith (not religion) was increasingly providing an anchor in their lives, even in the midst of the confusion of dementia. It was their encounter with Jesus[5]—either as a conversion experience (for example, Bill), or a gentle growing awareness of relationship with God (for example, Alice)—that had given them their preeminent sense of who they were, and this had set the direction of their lives in relationship with him. And now, it was this everyday, ongoing experience of knowing God that—in spite of dementia—was still at the core of their lives: "it's here [indicates inner self] . . . I can speak from experience not from some theory" (Rosemary). And they all wanted to tell me about this . . . and to pass it on to you.

In this chapter, their words describe this experience of knowing God in dementia. Sometimes there are breaks in their quotations representing pauses or a searching for words. My commentary on what they express reflects my own responses and questions to what they said as I listened. Here, we get to the heart of the matter—this is their experience.[6] For each one of these Christians, a sense of transcending relationship with God was preeminent, in spite of their dementia. Their words revealed a strengthening sense of this, a firm conviction of knowing Jesus, and—at this time when cognitive capacity was becoming less dependable—the significance of experiencing God through feelings. As we hear their stories, let's also listen for what these might ask about our own experience and understanding of what it means to be a follower of Jesus.

STRENGTHENING FAITH

"It Makes Me Feel Stronger"

Matthew was further on in his journey with dementia than some of the others involved in the research. Since he was physically frail, concentration and

---

3. Jon Stuckey, speaking about his research in the area of faith and dementia, personal email communication. Quoted with permission.

4. Davis, *My Journey into Alzheimer's Disease*, 53–54.

5. Root, *Christopraxis*, 3–17.

6. The research sought deeper understanding of the lived experience of faith in dementia, using the approach of hermeneutic phenomenology. For further discussion of the methodology, see Williams, *What Happens to Faith?*, 60–87.

talking took time and effort. Nevertheless, his body language was welcoming towards me—he *wanted* to participate in this research. When we began to talk about his faith, I asked him whether he felt dementia was making a difference. His response was definite:

> MATTHEW: Yes, it makes me feel stronger.
> 'TRICIA: It hasn't made you doubt?
> MATTHEW: No! [speaking emphatically and strongly, sounding moved]

In contrast to what I might have expected, Matthew asserted that his faith was growing *as a consequence of* the dementia. I wondered in what sense he understood the word "stronger"? He clearly didn't feel that his evident physical frailty was weakening his faith. His "No" was firmly expressed in a voice that began to break with emotion. Doubting God was not part of his response to the experience of dementia. This breaking in his voice seemed to suggest his confidence in God, in spite of his illness.

"Faith is Growing"

David also felt that faith was growing. He seemed puzzled by the fact that whilst memory was becoming more difficult, his faith felt stronger.

> DAVID: For years . . . I relied on memory . . . but now it's much harder . . . But it's the faith bit that is really interesting I think, because faith is growing more for the moment.

He seemed surprised by this. I asked him how his dementia had made him feel about his relationship with God.

> DAVID: I think there's much more of a closeness.
> 'TRICIA : More of a closeness . . .
> DAVID: Yes, because it becomes more important. I think it becomes more important . . .

David stressed this growing sense of relationship with God and its increasing significance for him. Could it be that this sense of experience of God was greater in adversity? I also noticed his awareness of human temporality ("for the moment"), which, as some have suggested, brings a sense of urgency to the search for meaning as human beings move towards the end of life.[7]

---

7. See for example, Heidegger, *Being and Time*, 11.1, 296–304. For further discussion of this see Williams, *What Happens to Faith?*, 78–79. MacKinlay and Trevitt also discuss the growing importance of finding life-meaning in "increasing age and frailty," MacKinlay and Trevitt, *Finding Meaning*, 23.

"Closer to God"

Alice was also aware of and surprised by this paradox.

> ALICE: The less I have, the more amazed I am at what he [God] does with it. Whereas . . . when I was working, I thought some of it was me [Alice laughs]. I thought God had given me many gifts and I was quite clever! [Alice laughs] But now I realize everything that happens is of God. So in a sense, I'm closer to God because there's less of me [chuckles].

I was struck by her implication that being aware of her own abilities in her pre-dementia experience had created distance between her and God. The lessening of her cognitive capacities had brought a greater awareness of her dependence on him. Her words suggested that, as the physical symptoms of her illness were increasing, her spiritual life was becoming more intense.

As I listened to Matthew, David, and Alice, their apparent growth in faith might seem counterintuitive. It wasn't only that faith was a resource for coping in the present moment.[8] These Christians talked of their relationship with God *continuing* to grow.

Rosemary responded to my question like this: "Closer to God . . . 'Nearer my God to thee' . . ." When I prompted her to say more about her understanding of "God," she introduced another element, choosing to emphasize the mystery she felt there was in this.

> ROSEMARY: God, Jesus his Son, and the Holy Spirit who indwells[9] . . . all . . . to me are a mystery . . . I don't think we're meant . . . yet . . . to have any understanding of that really, only by reading Jesus' account when he was speaking to his Father on the cross,[10] and before it and with his ministry and everything . . . Then when, of course, he gave the Holy Spirit . . . So, the answer to that is, "Yes!"

Her acknowledgment of the "mystery" of the triune God resonated with her positive acceptance of dementia. Her words hinted that she felt that she didn't need to understand *why* dementia (or other life events) had come into her life. She simply accepted this as "mystery," and was willing to trust God without understanding. Her use of "we" ("we're meant") suggested that she felt all human life exists in this context of divine mystery.

---

8. See for example, Beuscher and Grando, "Using Spirituality to Cope."

9. For example, 1 Corinthians 6:19: "Do you not know that your bodies are temples of the Holy Spirit, who is in you . . . ?" (NIVUK).

10. For example, Luke 23:46.

RELATIONSHIP WITH GOD

One of the distinctive characteristics faith of an evangelical tradition (see chapter 1) is the sense of personal relationship with God, enabled by the Holy Spirit.[11] As the participants in the research spoke about this—despite now living with dementia—they all expressed this in terms of being in a continuing, loving relationship with God. This seemed to be at the center of their experience of dementia.

"A Relationship to Someone . . . Who Loves Me"

I asked Alice to tell me more about what she felt was most important to her in her experience of faith.

> ALICE: Well, walking with God every day and having him at the centere of my life . . . It's not a work, it's not a doing, it's a relationship to someone that I love and who loves me.
> 'TRICIA: So, are you aware of God's presence with you?
> ALICE: Well, in some ways, yes . . . I mean I know that God is always with me, because he always has been, and I know that there's nothing that can ever separate me from him.

It was this loving relationship with God that was at the heart of her faith: "It's not a doing." Her sense that "nothing . . . can ever separate me from him" (Rom 8:38–39) was grounded in her past experiences and her memory-funded faith. Again, I noticed that she instinctively used words of Scripture to describe her experience. At that present moment, it was both her cognitive knowledge and her intuitive faith that were making her confident of continuing relationship with God: ". . . but now, even when my brain falls apart . . . it doesn't matter." In spite of her medical knowledge, Alice asserted that her faith superseded cognitive capacity. The experience of her relationship with God was transcending brain-limited knowledge. This conviction was resourcing her faith and confidence in God in the present as she faced the future with dementia.

Rosemary, like Alice, had had a Christian upbringing, but it was only in the last ten years, since a serious illness, that personal faith had grown. Yet her words often showed her lifelong knowledge of faith, which, in part, was enabling her experience and expression of faith in the present.

---

11. Zahl, "Reformation Pessimism," 82.

> ROSEMARY: I love the Lord God with all my heart and all my soul . . . the Spirit of God is always in me. Now I am always conscious of that, even if it's really bad . . .

Rosemary was passionate about her feeling of love *for* and commitment *to* God. Her knowledge of Scripture ("all my heart and soul") helped her to express the totality of this.[12] She loved God with the *whole* of her being, irrespective of failing cognitive capacity.[13] I noticed that Rosemary did not use the word "mind" here, which is included in the Gospel reference to this verse, and might be assumed to suggest cognitive function.

Her deliberate reference to the Holy Spirit may have arisen from the understanding, from her evangelical tradition, that a defining characteristic of what it means to be a Christian is the indwelling presence of the Holy Spirit within the believer.[14] In spite of her dementia, she believed that the Spirit of God would always remain in her. Her experience was of a mutual relationship which was sustained by God the Holy Spirit, even when her symptoms of dementia were "really bad."

"It's over to You Now, Mate!"

Jess's words expressed her sense of relationship with God more informally.

> JESS: I think when I knew . . . that I had memory loss . . . I said, "God, it's over to you now, mate! I'm all right!" [chuckles] . . . you know, "You keep me going and . . . ," I feel that God has kept me going.

Whilst circumstances had changed for Jess, her conversational relationship with God remained constant. Her hesitation before saying "that I had memory loss," perhaps subconsciously registered her dislike of the word "dementia." Her sense of close, informal friendship with God was giving her strength to cope with her illness. Her words also revealed her dependence on God: "You keep me going."

> 'TRICIA: Do you feel that God is with you?

---

12. Mark 12:30: "You shall love the Lord your God with all your heart, and with all your soul, and with all your mind, and with all your strength." See also Matthew 22:37; Luke 10:27; as well as Deuteronomy 6:5: "You shall love the Lord your God with all your heart, and with all your soul, and with all your might."

13. See chapter 3 for further discussion of "wholeness," 39–40.

14. See Galatians 4:6: "God has sent the Spirit of his Son into our hearts, crying, 'Abba! Father!'"; 2 Corinthians 1:22: "put his Spirit in our hearts as a deposit, guaranteeing what is to come" (NIVUK).

> JESS: Yes, I'm sure of that. And that's why the fact that I can't remember, my memory loss, doesn't matter . . .

For Jess, the sense of God being with her was more important than her memory loss. Her confidence in God's presence with her made her feel secure, so she could say, astonishingly perhaps: "my memory loss doesn't matter."

"The Best Boss"

Although each of the research participants talked about God in terms of relationship, their choice of words disclosed differing aspects of their understanding of God. Bill used the word "Boss" to indicate God, recalling his experience of working under direction in the police force.

> BILL: "Boss" is a sort of colloquial . . . 'cause we, at the police station, we call whoever is in charge, we refer to him as the "Boss" . . . God . . . best boss . . .

Bill's words seemed to be removing anxiety about his present experience of dementia. His questions arising from dementia were not about *why* God had allowed this in his life, but about *how* God, who was "in charge," wanted him to live with the illness.

Bill was also aware of God as the Trinity: "Boss 1: Father; Boss 2: Jesus; Boss 3: Spirit . . . and they're all working together on our behalf." Here, his words recall some of our earlier discussion about our own and God's identity in chapter 3.[15] Bill thought of the different persons of the Trinity as being both in relationship with one another and with himself. God as Trinity was both in control, and also working for our well-being. I noticed that in Bill's use of the first-person plural ("on our behalf"), he instinctively identified himself as part of community.

"Creator God . . ."

Matthew and Rosemary both spoke of how creation played a part in their sense of relationship with God. Matthew, who had limited mobility, spent much of his time looking out of the window at his garden. I asked him if he could tell me if his dementia was making him feel differently about God. After a long pause, he answered.

---

15. See chapter 3, 41–43.

> MATTHEW: Yes, I think it has . . . because I can look out and I see the birds of the air . . .
> 'TRICIA: And what does that make you think?
> MATTHEW: Well, in the book of Genesis, God created the sea, things that . . . birds that sweep over the sea . . . seagulls . . .

Matthew's words "the birds of the air" bring to mind Jesus' words in Matthew 6:26, which speak of not being worried and trusting instead in God's care.[16] Matthew was also thinking about God's role in creation and seemed to relish this with his poetic expression "sweep over." His words seemed to suggest the evidence he was seeing in creation of God's power and care.

Rosemary also spoke of creation as being significant in her relationship with God, as she was enjoying walks in the surrounding countryside.

> ROSEMARY: I relate when I'm out in the country and I'm so aware of the beauty around me that I'm literally worshipping God the Father who's created this beautiful earth and it brings out the feeling of the Creator God in worship. I think that's very important.

Seeing the beauty of the countryside prompted Rosemary's gratitude for the gift of creation and inspired her worship of "the Creator God."

KNOWING JESUS

More than the sense of knowing God, participants also spoke of their sense of personal relationship with Jesus—and the "living reality" of his presence in their lives.[17]

"I Know Jesus"

Even though Matthew was beginning to struggle with recall and concentration, he retained this strong sense of relationship with Jesus.

> 'TRICIA: Do you feel you have a relationship with Jesus?
> MATTHEW: Yes, I do [very definitely].
> 'TRICIA: And do you feel, as you go through this, he is close to you?
> MATTHEW: Yes.

---

16. Matthew 6:26: "Look at the birds of the air; they do neither sow nor reap nor gather into barns, and yet your heavenly Father feeds them. Are you not of more value than they?"

17. Zahl, "Reformation Pessimism," 82.

KNOWING GOD: THE EXPERIENCE OF FAITH   59

For Matthew, as for other participants, the sense of Jesus accompanying him through the dementia was significant, and I was struck by his deliberate "yes" to my questions. Later, I discovered that his wife, Wendy, had overheard his assertions of faith from a nearby room and was deeply moved, explaining that she had not heard Matthew speak in this way before.

David also spoke of his secure sense of relationship with Jesus as he anticipated the future:

> DAVID: I know Jesus, and that's the most important thing. I know Jesus very clearly and . . . as I go on, maybe the dementia gets worse, but that part of me will belong to Jesus. I feel very strongly. When you've got that sort of faith, it's there.

David's words, "I know Jesus," demonstrated that, for him, his faith was about relationship with God's Son, Jesus. His words suggest a transcendence, and belief in a reality beyond human physical existence. He was confident in his relationship with Jesus as he imagined the future with dementia. His words and firm manner of speaking them conveyed confidence. His trust in Jesus in the face of the unknown was sure in its expression. Thinking of other Christians who were further on in their journey with dementia, David talked about faith *holding* them: ". . . but maybe it's sometimes that very thing that holds onto them . . ." Rather than his holding onto faith, his words implied that he believed it was Jesus who would hold onto him.

"Jesus Is There"

When we met for our first conversation, David had recently been unwell with a virus. The impact of this added to his reflection about his dementia.

> DAVID: And in this difficult time . . . you know that Jesus is there. In the last few weeks, it's been pretty dire and I know that he's there, that faith is there. It's not going to go away, just doesn't go away [dementia]. Once you've got it, you never lose it, and that's it.

David recognized the presence of dementia in his life and was accepting it, although this was not easy. But this did not threaten the sustaining sense of the presence of Jesus.

> DAVID: Dementia may be going one way, but there's Jesus there . . . even if the dementia gets worse there'll still be Jesus. That's the important thing. We can still bring Jesus and dementia together [chuckles] . . . Yes . . . [long pause] I think it's the core of

> everything now. The more I understand, the deeper it gets . . .
> But the core is understanding Jesus, and knowing Jesus . . . It's
> knowing Jesus personally.

In the adversity of dementia, David expressed his sense that in some way Jesus was present with him. It was as though he felt that the "knowing Jesus" was enabling him to make sense of his dementia and to live with it.

For Jill, there was a further dimension. Her answer was preceded by a long pause.

> JILL: . . . I know Jesus . . . I've known Jesus for a long time [chuckles] . . . and I long to know him more in my illness.

Here was positive anticipation of knowing and understanding *more* as a result of her developing dementia.

"God and Man"

For Bill, the incarnation of God in Christ was significant.

> BILL: The person that I find it more easy to relate to is Jesus because he came to earth as a human being, so in a sense there is an identity between me as a human being and Jesus as a human being . . .

Christ's humanity was strengthening his sense of relationship with Jesus because he felt that Jesus understands human experience.

Jess also chose to emphasize the humanity of Christ.

> JESS: . . . I think God sent his Son into the world . . . he chose Mary and Joseph to look after his Son . . . so he wanted his Son to be man . . . he's God and man . . . the only person that's been God and man . . .

She stressed her awareness that Jesus, as a human being, shared in common human experience.

> JESS: He . . . came into the world to teach us about God and he paid the sacrifice of being a human being so that we could find God.

Jess's word "sacrifice" may first bring to mind the death of Christ on the cross. However, here Jess was applying it to the life of Christ. The sacrifice was in becoming human, so that in sharing human experience (including human suffering) he was able "to teach us about God." Her words remind me that Jesus carried our weaknesses and sorrows, as well as our sin (Isa 53:4).

EXPERIENCING GOD THROUGH FEELINGS

Whilst evangelicalism has sometimes seemed to emphasize the necessity of an underlying (at least) cognitive understanding of faith, conversations with these believers, living in the context of dementia, revealed that feelings and emotions seemed to be playing an increasing and significant role in their experience and understanding of relationship with God.

"Feelings Remain when Facts are Forgotten"

Alice spoke about the significance of her feelings for the life of faith in dementia.

> ALICE: It's a matter of knowing you're loved. And because feelings remain when facts are forgotten, it's possible for anybody with dementia, no matter what the stage of their dementia, to know that they're loved and because God is God and it's not what I say but the Holy Spirit is alive and real God . . .

Feelings were enabling a *different kind of knowing*. For Alice, this relationship with God depends on "knowing" that one is loved by God, and, on the activity of God the Holy Spirit. Speaking from her own situation as a Christian with dementia, she believed that "feelings remain" and, in spite of facts being forgotten, these feelings were a true indicator of relationship with God.

Alice also talked of the ways in which the expression of her emotions had changed in dementia. Smiling now, she told me about a mishap with lemon curd-making, resulting in smashed jars and a sticky mess—ending for her with an emotional "meltdown."

> ALICE: Some things I have very little emotion about that I would have in the past. But other things, I have more emotion about . . . Things that didn't upset me before, upset me now . . . So, yes, my emotions have changed. . . . With dementia . . . the layers come off, so we become more vulnerable . . . As a Christian, God accepts me as I am with all my mixed-up emotions, with all emotional unzipping . . .

Emotions were much closer to the surface in Alice's life because of dementia; her illness was bringing a greater sense of vulnerability. There was an acceptance of this as part of the experience of dementia. Her belief that God accepted her with "all my mixed-up emotions" was enabling her to be resilient in living with dementia.

"Exquisite Joy"

Sometimes the accounts of the research participants revealed that their feelings were not to do with expression of emotions related to events, but were transcendent experiences of *received* love, peace, and joy. The words of John Swinton resonate with this, "Jesus is our joy." In the midst of suffering: "Joy is the settled assurance that God is with us and for us in all circumstances and at all times."[18]

Rosemary's words bubbled over as she told me about her feelings of great joy that she was experiencing as a Christian living with dementia. Her rapidly spoken words were preceded by a long pause and intake of breath.

> ROSEMARY: It's partly celebratory because I have something that is so wonderful that fills me very often with exquisite joy, and still allows me though to know the dark night of the soul . . . how it makes me feel? Oh . . . infinitely better than if I had been an intellectual type of person worried and concerned in every way about what was going to happen to me after death, what will I do and how will it be going through that dark tunnel of not knowing anything . . . I think I have . . . sometimes a joyful time because I've got the dementia and I can accept it through God being with me. He will be with me . . . right to the end! Even if my . . . because my feelings are still as strong, if not stronger, as my mind becomes less intellectualized and able to . . . I shall be more filled with the feeling of the love of God.

Rosemary communicated passionately that her Christian faith was giving her great joy. Even though she sometimes experienced "the dark night of the soul," this did not overcome the sustaining sense of joy she felt that relationship with God was bringing her. Like Alice, she felt that she was becoming more aware of God because of the intensifying of her feelings in dementia: "better than if I had been an intellectual type of person." She also attributed the lessening of anxiety about the future as being partly due to her increasing strength of feelings. The emotional experience of her faith was bringing increasing confidence in "the love of God" that would be with her "right to

---

18. Swinton, *Finding Jesus*, 82–83.

the end!" There was even a sense of gratitude that she had dementia because it seemed as if it was bringing a greater sense of relationship with God.

Ron also described his feeling of joy in knowing God in his dementia:

> RON: The joy of being born again is always there. You can't separate one or the other . . . and therefore, I'll never lose that joy, but I have lost my memory.

When he came to faith as a young man (at a Billy Graham evangelistic meeting in Rhodesia [Zimbabwe]) he felt that he had received a special kind of joy, which was still with him now, in spite of his dementia. This sense of coming into relationship with God was synonymous with his experience of joy. His confidence in its permanence was striking: "I have lost my memory," but he felt certain that he would "never" lose the joyful sense of God's presence in his life. Ron's words suggested a questioning of the meaning of memory. There was another kind of memory which was at work in addition to the remembering of information. "Memory" was lost, he said, but not the joy—the presence—of his faith.

"Overwhelmed with Love and Peace"

This sense of relationship with God was also expressed in terms of love and peace. I asked Alice *how* she knew that she was loved by God.

> ALICE: There have been occasions when one has felt overwhelmed with love and peace when one has been praying with God or talking to others about him, or praying with them. But most of the time, it's just knowing that the longer I've lived—through all the rough times—he's never let me down . . . never . . . never . . .

This sense was reinforced through her conviction that God had always been with her in difficult times throughout her life. Her belief in God's intervention in her life was bringing sustenance in and transformation of difficult moments now.

Jill also talked about the experience of knowing peace in and about her situation:

> JILL: I think I have a kind of peace . . . which doesn't come from me. I think it comes from God.

As Alice's words had suggested, Jill likewise felt that this peace did not originate in herself, but was dependent on God's intervention. Her words remind me of the encounter with God that Andrew Root has described in

Christopraxis[19]—God meets us (perhaps unexpectedly) in the midst of difficult experience and brings transformation.

Listening to the words of Jill, Rosemary, Alice, and the others, we begin to realize the potential of understanding that—for people living in the early to moderate stages of dementia—their spiritual lives and sense of relationship with God are experienced and expressed through feelings and emotions, even though cognitive resources are lessening.

KNOWING GOD IN DEMENTIA . . .

The surprising words of these disciples of Jesus tell of an increased sense of the closeness of God and a stronger relationship with him arising from their illness. In their experience, as Alice and Rosemary emphasized, knowing God was not dependent on their cleverness or a cognitive "knowing." Increasingly, awareness of him was experienced and expressed through intensity of feelings.[20] Counterintuitively, it seemed that as brain capacity was declining, there was a growing confidence in their faith. Knowing Jesus was at the core of their lives—and central in their relationship with God ("the core is knowing Jesus," David). And in spite of the acknowledged struggles of living with dementia ("the dark night of the soul," Rosemary), their awareness of God's love for them and peace received from him were paramount. Their overarching sense of relationship with God was not diminished by the advent of dementia. Their words were expressions of living and active faith, a participating in God's mission, through which they desired to "bring glory to him" (Rosemary).

In this chapter, the words of these Christians have revealed further glimpses of the dynamic "intrinsic faith" that was sustaining them. But their relationship with God was not only about this *inner* experience of faith. It was also about practical, outward expressions of that faith—Bible reading, prayer, participation in the worship and activities of local communities of faith. These practices were becoming more difficult, but were also bringing sustenance. In the next chapter I explore their particular experience of faith *practice* as they live with the disorientating changes and challenges brought by their dementia.

---

19. Root, *Christopraxis*, 3–8.

20. The words of others, both those living with dementia and researchers, confirm the growing significance of feelings for the person living with dementia. See for example, McFadden et al., "Actions, Feelings, and Values," 76–78.

For Further Reflection . . .

- Pause to reflect on Jesus' words to the disciples in John 14:15–21. How do you experience his presence with you?
- In what ways have you been aware of the sense of relationship with God in those you know who are living with dementia?
- What might we learn from their words and lives about our own faith?

5

Being Not Doing: The Experience of Practice

"It's a relationship . . . not 'a doing'"

What does Christian faith mean in practice for the believer who lives with dementia? I asked Alice. She is a person with passionate beliefs and a gift of powerful expression. I had been thinking about the *difficulties* dementia might be bringing to traditional practices of faith, like regular Bible reading, prayer, and involvement in church activities. Alice's sharp, quick response shifted the perspective: "It's a relationship . . . it's *not* a doing, it's a relationship to someone that I love and who loves me."

Alice's words recall those differences explored earlier: between religion and faith;[1] between extrinsic faith—where religion is adhered to through religious practices—and intrinsic faith that permeates every aspect of who we are.[2] Her words speak of that familiar characteristic of evangelical faith: the overarching sense of personal, transcendent relationship with Jesus Christ.[3] Her strong sense of the preeminence of that loving relationship re-

---

1. Chapter 2, 21–23.
2. Chapter 1, 5.
3. Chapter 1, 5–6.

calls the "Who I am" question, and Martin Buber's concept of the three-way "I-Thou"[4] relationality that undergirds the Christian's sense of who we are. *I am* in relationship with God, which is expressed in my personal devotional practices; *I am* also in relationship with God and others as we participate in the body of Christ through its corporeal practices. Both bring difficulties (and sadness) for the Christian living with dementia. Both aspects bring challenge to the wider community of faith too. I guess that for many of us, church, with its busy rounds of meetings and programs, is about "doing." How are we attending to sustaining this I-Thou relationship *in practice* both for individuals living with dementia, and in relationship with one another as the body of Christ?[5]

In this chapter, keeping in mind Alice's words about the nature of faith as relationship, we first focus on Bible reading and prayer in terms of hearing from and talking with God. Then we listen to our research participants' experience of taking part in the practices of a local faith community (reminding us of our dependence on one another). The words of Alice, Ron, Matthew, Jill, David, Bill, Rosemary, and Jess begin to disclose the experience of these faith practices for Christians living with dementia, and something of how these were contributing to their experience of continuing faith and well-being. As we read, let's allow their words to question us about our own assumptions of theology and practice.

A RELATIONSHIP NOT "A DOING"

For all the participants in the research, not just Alice, their sense of relationship with God was at the center of their faith, rather than practices. The love of God and response of loving him was the foundation of this ("someone ... I love ... who loves me," Alice). Christian practices had always included activities like Bible reading and prayer, but these were not essential to certainty of relationship with God.

> ALICE: It's very important to me but I don't think my relationship with God will stop if I didn't do it. But it's very important ... it kind of starts and ends my day. It reminds me that that's how my life is centered, that God is the center of my life ... but ... it's not legalistic. If I forget, I'm not going to get worked up about it.

---

4. Buber, *I and Thou*. See chapter 2, 27; chapter 3, 40.
5. Bryden, "A Spiritual Journey Into the I-Thou Relationship."

Bible reading was helpful, but not a "legalistic" practice that oppressed her. Nevertheless, these core practices of Bible reading and prayer, characteristic of evangelical Christian faith, were important for all the participants in different ways. Providing familiar rhythm for each day, these were happening as a result of, or within the context of relationship, and were often described by the participants in terms of talking with, or listening to, God. For those like Jill, Rosemary, and Alice who were living independently, Bible engagement was primarily a solitary activity. For others who were married it was shared, as for Tom and Cathy whose questions began this book.

Bible Reading: Hearing from God

For the evangelical Christian, a primary way of meeting with God has traditionally been through the practice of Bible reading.[6] For example, Scripture Union's aim in its Bible materials is to help people meet with God daily as they read his Word; the practice is inherently relational. Mysteriously, the line between *knowing* the preexisting Christ who is the Word (John 1:1), and listening to God's revelation of him in Scripture becomes increasingly difficult to discern.[7] I was interested to hear how this was working out within the experience of dementia.

"I Hear God through the Bible"

At this early stage in her experience of dementia, Bible reading was an important aspect of Jill's interactive relationship with God.

> JILL: I read the Bible every day . . . and . . . I hear God through the Bible . . . I think more than any other place where I hear God . . .
> 'TRICIA: What do you mean you "hear" God through the Bible?
> JILL: An example would be . . . I have choices to make . . . I want to know God's will over something . . . I read the Bible and pray about it . . . and I get an answer . . . not always, obviously . . . but a lot of the time I get an answer.

Jill felt that God was guiding her through her Bible reading in decisions she was making. She stressed the importance of Bible reading for her faith as something through which there was a reciprocal relationship of talking and

---

6. For example, Scripture Union International Council (SUIC), "Aims, Beliefs and Working Principles."

7. Briggs, "The Bible Before Us," 16.

listening. I asked her if, in the light of her dementia, she thought it would continue to be important for her. Her response was emphatic:

> JILL: Oh yes . . . that would be devastating . . . if it was taken away for any reason.

For Alice, Scripture was important, not because it was a practice which was part of her Christian tradition, but because it was a resource in her loving relationship with God.

> 'TRICIA: Do you feel God is speaking to you through . . . [the Bible]?
> ALICE: I believe he can—but sometimes he doesn't. But I believe in obedience . . . Obedience is God's love language. And I believe that faithfully doing that is important . . . God knows how much I love him, but it's just an act of service, if you like, to let him know that I really do. And . . . on occasion, does say these wonderful things to me. If we don't give him the opportunity then, well, we're the losers.

Alice's words communicate that, above all, her faith was about loving God, but that needed to be expressed in faithful action. In this way, there was a connection between the practice of Bible reading and her sense of relationship with God. Taking time to read the Bible was providing an opportunity to hear from God. Yet, dementia was increasingly beginning to make that difficult.

"Too Difficult Now to Read"

For Alice, the practice of Bible reading had been instilled in her from early childhood: "I was in a sense . . . soaked in Scripture from a child, and I do forget." Dementia was bringing some challenges, but engaging with Scripture in other ways was still central to her faith practice: "I can't read the Bible because it's too difficult now to read, so I listen to it every day." Alice had found a solution in *listening* to it being read. CDs and online resources were making this possible, and this was much easier than reading herself. I was interested that she also spoke about understanding Scripture differently, because she was reading out of her context of dementia:

> ALICE: Everything he [Jesus] taught has something in it for whatever level you're at . . . of ability or maturity or social station . . . so I'm understanding the Scriptures like that . . . in a different kind of way, that you can, you know there's something in

Scripture . . . whatever illness you have, whatever state of your mind or brain or stage of life, and that is exciting for me, to see it in a wider context . . . So I'm very grateful for that.

Scripture was an integral part of Rosemary's life too. References to Bible texts peppered her responses during the interview. At this stage in her life, the familiarity with Bible text was giving her a language that expressed and enabled relationship with God: "I've got texts around me everywhere . . ." She had deliberately placed the words of Bible texts around her home to help her remember God, and to express her feelings towards him. The embeddedness of Bible text was enabling her to discover it as a resource in her present circumstances. For others, the support of loved ones and church groups were significant.

"We Get Fellowship"

For some of the participants in the research, reading the Bible with others was easier than reading alone. I noticed that those who were married spoke of this aspect of their faith life being shared. Like Tom and Cathy, Ron and Clare have regularly followed a routine of Bible reading and prayer together throughout their marriage: "Oh yes . . . we get fellowship together . . ." Bible reading and prayer continued to be important for Jess too.

> JESS: Well, I don't do much as a Christian now except going to church. I'm not very active physically . . . but I read the Bible every day, pray every day.

Andrew, Jess's husband, told me later that they have a regular routine of reading the Bible and pray *together* every day.

David didn't emphasize individual Bible reading, but enjoyed *hearing* the Bible read in his "home group," where it was a group activity:

> DAVID: I tend to read it much more in home group . . . I've never been somebody who will read daily passages, but with the home group . . . going through the passages and while we talk about it . . . it makes it, I find it much easier.

The group interaction was making understanding and learning easier. David also talked about the role of the group in his Bible reading as his memory loss was beginning to affect him.

> DAVID: If I was doing it right now with the people involved, I would remember it, but I probably wouldn't because it's a day-to-day thing, so that's quite difficult for me . . . I've read one

section of a Bible reading ... all I've got to do is to go back and find the Bible reading ...

As memory difficulties were increasing, the group event and then the physical Bible itself were resources that could trigger memory of what had been said. The interaction within the supportive group had helped David to continue to engage with the Bible.

Prayer: Talking with God

"My Whole Life Is Prayer"

Whilst prayer had always been part of Alice's life experience, I wanted to understand how dementia was affecting her experience of prayer.

> ALICE: Well, prayer is my whole life. I mean, all the day I pray. That's not me anymore. I can't do that ... my prayer is more, I look out of the window and I say, "Lord I'm so grateful for this wonderful view and these flowers." ... My whole life is prayer in a sense now ... rather than just a portion of the day ...

Alice described prayer as a kind of ongoing conversation with God about all aspects of her life as she lived each day. Lack of concentration and loss of short-term memory meant that she could no longer pray deliberately at specific times, but now, she felt that her "whole life is prayer."

Rosemary's experience of prayer was also as a conversation throughout the day:

> ROSEMARY: When I'm in my bed at night and talking to him during the day, having the talks with him when I'm just walking along with the dog and experiencing the glory all around me of his creation ...

This talking with God was an intimate and interactive part of her life. Here, she highlighted that creation and "experiencing" its "glory" as natural stimulants for praise and pointers towards God as Creator.

"Without It, We Are ... Naked"

Ron told me about his experience of prayer now in the context of living with dementia and its continuing importance as part of his and Clare's devotional life *together*:

> RON: Oh . . . the presence . . . as far as that is concerned is always there, because Clare and I often pray together. It's like everything else, without it, we are, to put it bluntly, naked . . . Clare and I have always prayed together, so that is . . . something which is automatic-like . . .

Ron's use of the term "the presence" in the context of our conversation seemed to imply his feeling that God was always present. The word "naked" seemed to suggest that he felt that he would be vulnerable without prayer, as if it was a kind of protective covering. This life of prayer was "automatic-like," an instinctive and natural part of his Christian life.

For Jess and Andrew, prayer is also a shared daily practice:

> JESS: . . . but we pray every day . . . we thank God for the new day. We thank God for . . .

Praying and Bible reading together was a simple, daily routine. Jess chose to focus on their shared thankfulness to God, expressing a positive response to God in spite of their current life situation.

"Allow God into Situations"

For Alice, prayer was about "allowing God into situations."

> ALICE: if we allow God into situations, he can transform them . . . not necessarily by making a situation good . . . but because of . . . the inner resources he gives us in that situation, we're able to cope with it and almost rejoice in it.

It wasn't that prayer was about making difficult situations good, but that, through these, God provides the inner resources to cope. Speaking out of her own situation, Alice concluded that prayer's transformation enables rejoicing in spite of circumstances. It was as though recognizing God's presence through prayer changed the perspective on her personal experience.

BELONGING TO A FAITH COMMUNITY

The personal, individual walk with God has often been the focus for Christians of the evangelical tradition. Some of us may assume that personal faith is principally understood with reference *only* to our individual relationship with God. We may be less comfortable with the idea of "embodied

Christianity," which mediates faith through its life *together*[8]—"church," we might feel, is a useful resource, but not who I am. Yet, as we reflected earlier, together *we are* the body of Christ, with its individual members called to comfort one another with the comfort with which we have been comforted (2 Cor 1:3-7). Dementia brings questions to our understanding of church, and how "being church" is lived out in the situations where God has placed us—whoever we are, whatever our capacities. As believers, faith is not just about our own personal experience. Living amongst the challenges of dementia, the social, relational truth of our faith may be more disturbing—but also more hopeful—than concentration on the individual's faith life.

With such thoughts in mind, I was interested to explore how the experience of belonging to a church community and relationship with other Christians was significant at this stage of the participants' lives—and to see how dementia was affecting their belonging to a local congregation.

Going to Church Services

"Getting Together and Having Fellowship"

Living independently and having dementia meant that Rosemary was finding it increasingly difficult to be part of a local church.

> ROSEMARY: . . . living in here [a supported living community] . . . we only have . . . twice a month a service, a communion service . . . I don't like missing a time of . . . "If two or three are gathered together in my name I'm there in the midst."[9] It's the collective, the getting together and having fellowship . . . and that matters I think a lot even though you're wholehearted in tune, and you're with God, and with the Lord, [the] Holy Spirit is filling you (as he is) . . .

Rosemary clearly valued meeting with other Christians, but this was difficult in the community where she was resident. Sometimes there was a service, but practical issues made it difficult for this "getting together" to happen regularly. It was clearly frustrating for her. However, she felt that "fellowship" was what was most important for her about "church." The coming together with other believers was significant in enabling a sense of meeting with God, even though she felt personally "in tune" with God.

---

8. McFadyen, "Embodied Christianity," 123.
9. See Matthew 18:20: "For where two or three are gathered in my name, I am there among them."

Rosemary had tried to go out to a local church, but had found it difficult.

> ROSEMARY: They said, "Well you're always welcome to come here." But they were very much more . . . trivial about it . . . it was routine . . . I can't at the moment join a congregation. You feel different when you are . . . here . . . and you know your brain is deteriorating.

Her words tumbled out rapidly. It had taken deliberate effort to go out to visit a local church. She was clearly disappointed with the welcome from, and interaction with, regular members of that congregation. There was a sense of frustration that she was unable to do more to be involved in churchgoing. Her sadness and sense of aloneness in this was apparent: "They don't understand."

"It's Easy . . . I Don't Remember What I Hear or What We Did!"

Those who were not on their own had a different experience of churchgoing. Jess, for example, went to church regularly with her husband, Andrew, and spoke of their involvement in church as a joint activity. Jess speaks with gentle, self-aware self-mockery:

> JESS: It's easy to go to church . . . I don't remember what I hear or what we did . . . or things like that . . .
> JESS: I don't suppose many people recognize that I can't remember things . . . people have always been very kind to me . . .

She was continuing to be part of a local church and had good relationships with others in her church. Attendance at services was "easy," perhaps because the practical aspects of this were organized by Andrew, although she didn't remember what happened or what was being said. Nevertheless, she appreciated the *kindness* of people.

"Too Loud, Too Noisy, Too Much"

Being on her own meant Rosemary had a different experience:

> ROSEMARY: The difficulty sometimes is church itself [chuckles]. . . I felt embarrassed having gone up to the communion rail (it was the evangelical St. P's where I was living before I came here) and . . . I would go up to the rail and take communion, but I lost my way coming back . . . I suddenly thought which is

> my pew? And there'd be people guiding me and beginning to think, "Oh this poor soul, she's forgotten where she's going"... I don't altogether find that people sometimes who are the church community [chuckles] are most understanding of people with dementia. It's almost as though they themselves can't quite deal with (although, of course, there's always people in that church who can give you special understanding, help and friendship) ... you feel it's beginning to be too loud, too noisy, too much, too... you want to get out of it, go quietly home and dwell on it and not have to socialize any more...

Rosemary's words highlighted her sense of a lack of people's understanding of dementia, which was making it difficult for her to be involved in church, as well as the practical problems in the service, embarrassment, and noise and loudness. Her description made clear the kind of inner confusion and turmoil she felt as a result. Whilst she appreciated the help and understanding of some, she felt that others "can't quite deal with it." Sometimes she felt that she wanted "to get out of it" and find some quiet.

Although different in personality, Alice's words echoed Rosemary's thoughts in some ways. The following is an extract from my research journal based on a paraphrase of her words from one of our conversations:

> Alice sometimes finds the informality and noise difficult. She sits against a wall which provides her with a better sense of security. Anything unusual happening is difficult, for example, if the service leader asks people to move around or get into groups.
>
> However, she has helped church members to understand what things are difficult for her and someone now sends her the service outline in advance so that she can be prepared for what will happen. Alice likes the old hymns, but her church mainly uses newer ones, although they always try to include an older one too.

Alice's account highlighted the possibilities of how someone like her might be helped to feel more comfortable in a church service. She was a naturally confident person and therefore able to help other church members understand how dementia was affecting her—and they were looking for solutions to help with her difficulties. I was aware that not all Christians with dementia would have the same confidence or facility in explaining their situation to their church community. We must listen (with imagination).

"I Do the Flowers Instead . . ."

Unlike Rosemary, Jess, with Andrew's support, felt that *going to* church was "easy." Nevertheless, there was a sadness as she spoke about how she felt dementia was affecting how others view her.

> JESS: I just support him [Andrew] now because my memory loss has interfered with my being somebody or something, doing something. I do the flowers instead . . . they don't argue with you. You don't make a mistake if you're doing the flowers . . .

Jess's words suggested how she felt other people *might* be judging her when she was not seen to have a public role in her church community. She recognized that there was loss, and that she could no longer do some things that had been part of her earlier life. Her wry "I do the flowers instead . . . they don't argue with you" suggested her own resilience and determination to continue her purposeful involvement in the community of church. But her words also hinted at sadness, possibly revealing a sense of regret and, perhaps, a lack of felt-awareness or support from others in her wider church community.

Dependence on One Another

In spite of describing challenges, participants in the research group also expressed a sense of dependence on others in their communities of faith for support in their spiritual lives—and their gratitude for this. This support was experienced both within church services, in small group meetings midweek, or in their daily relationship with their spouse.

"People Are Aware. . ."

Bill talked about the sense of support he feels that his church community is providing:

> BILL: I don't have a problem in telling people that are close and or even in the church. In fact, when we had the diagnosis confirmed, Carol, during the service, said, "I just want to let you know that Bill has now had a diagnosis of early onset Alzheimer's." . . . The number of people who then came and said we're really sorry for what you're going through! And also, to Carol, because the carer is perhaps is carrying much more than the patient themselves.

And I think that was good because then people are aware that this is what is happening...

Bill and Carol (Bill's wife) felt part of their church community and cared for in a way that allowed them to share the news of Bill's diagnosis publicly. The relationships were warm and strong enough to have enabled people to come to Bill and express their sympathy and understanding, and their desire to support *both* of them. Bill felt that telling people about his diagnosis would help them to understand what was happening in their lives. At this early stage in his dementia, he recognized that his illness had difficult implications for Carol too, and his need for her support in this. I also noticed that Bill, by implication, referred to himself as "the patient," assuming a medical definition of himself. Whilst he was possibly being lightheartedly dismissive of himself, I wondered if he was also reflecting back a perception of self that he felt others would now have of him.[10]

"Members of the Church . . . Very Kind"

Matthew, similar to others who were married, spoke about involvement in his local church as being a joint activity and commitment. He referred to his village church life frequently throughout our conversation.

> MATTHEW: Yes . . . the members of the church seemed to . . . be very kind . . . and actually when we celebrated our fiftieth wedding anniversary . . . which was last year . . . we . . . the former vicar and his wife both came . . . and a lot of church members came . . .

Matthew was aware of and appreciative of the kindness of others. There was a sense that he was well-known and loved in the church community. Its members were supportive of him in his health difficulties. His words suggested that he felt he belonged to this community of caring Christian people. Matthew's own attitude of thankfulness towards others suggested mutually responsive relationships.

Relationships that were nurturing faith—apart from attendance at church services—were important for the participants too. For Bill, "home group" was an important expression of his church life. He emphasized the relational nature of his group. They were mutually supportive, and he was already valuing that support in the early stages of his dementia.

---

10. Goffman, *Stigma*, 154; Bryden, *Dancing with Dementia*, 142.

> BILL: We pray, we pray for each other . . . I think that the people . . . that group is very supportive anyway . . . it's sort of there for you; it's there for them.
> 'TRICIA: As the journey with dementia goes along, do you think there are going to be people around you, like the home group, who will support you?
> BILL: They already are . . . [with feeling]

"The Spiritual Side Comes with Gail"

For those like David, Matthew, Ron, Bill, and Jess whose spouse was in the role of primary carer, this relationship was felt to be very significant for their spiritual well-being. Ingrid Hellström has noted the impact of this shared relationship in discussing the effects of dementia on identity: "couplehood is multidimensional, constructed and shared between the spouses."[11] This seemed to be evident in these couples' shared spiritual lives.

As in earlier examples given about church involvement, married participants named their wife or husband specifically as being key for their spiritual support. David joked, "Well, first of all I've got Gail. . . [laughs] That's the key one!" David clearly saw her as being his primary spiritual partner. He also mentioned the support of his wider family.

For Ron, Bible reading, prayer, and going to church were done as a couple unit. The relationship with Clare was crucial for his faith practice.

> 'TRICIA: Who gives you most support in your Christian life?
> RON: Well, the most . . . Clare, in particular, naturally . . . but, whenever you . . . actually have fellowship with another church, or with the Baptist church . . . well that is it . . . and you're always in that situation . . . whereby you get fellowship . . . and it's mighty good!

I noticed that whilst Ron considered Clare was most important in giving him spiritual support, the role of the wider believing community was also clearly significant for his faith sustenance and enjoyment.

This unity of spiritual support was also clear in Jess and Andrew's relationship:

> 'TRICIA: And as you go through this time in your life do you feel that God is with you . . . or Jesus . . . or the Spirit . . . is with you?

---

11. Hellström, "'I'm His Wife Not His Carer!'"

> JESS: Yes, I'm sure of that. And that's why the fact that I can't remember, my memory loss, doesn't matter. And the other thing is that . . . I've got [Andrew] looking after me. And he's . . . very good at looking after me . . .
> JESS: Andrew is . . . my protector, my director. And he is in charge and I just do as I'm told! And also he loves me a lot . . . which is very nice because I am safe with Andrew.
> 'TRICIA: Do you feel that you're safe with God?
> JESS: . . . I'm totally reliant on God . . . and his relationship with Andrew as well.

Jess had a great sense of assurance of God's presence and Andrew's care. She also had a sense of safety because of her relationship with Andrew. It was her trust of Andrew's relationship with God that seemed to enable her reliance on him.

This resource of a loving spouse's spiritual support was not available for the participants who were living independently.

"It's Hard for Me Living in Here"

Rosemary would like more spiritual support, but this was not regularly available. She was missing regular "fellowship" and, as expressed earlier, church attendance outside of the community where she lived was difficult. Yet, being together with other Christians was very important for her. The community's chaplain and a Christian friend were significant in supporting her spiritually: "In a spiritual way, [that] help has been the closest thing . . ."

Whilst Alice also did not have the immediate support of Christian family nearby, she coped with this by actively seeking to encourage others in their faith. She primarily seemed to find resilience to her life's circumstances through her own dependence on God:

> ALICE: I know that God is always with me, because he always has been, and I know that there's nothing that can ever separate me from him.

Her own sense of being loved by God and her security in that, was enabling her to focus on the needs of others.

> ALICE: . . . and there's always something that we can encourage people about and help them . . . and all the difficult times we go through are just to encourage us to do the same [laughs].

For Alice, her dementia seemed to be motivating her to be an encourager. In this way, she was finding spiritual sustenance in her interaction with others. The giving and receiving were a mutual experience.

BEING NOT DOING . . .

As I listened to the voices of these Christians talking about their experience of faith as they lived through dementia, it became clear that for them being in relationship with God had precedence over the *doing* of faith practices. Faith practices such as Bible engagement, prayer, and going to church services were not significant of themselves, but were important as means and expressions of relationship with God and other believers. Yes, failing concentration and memory were making habitual, routine Bible reading and prayer difficult, but these practices remained central in their ongoing relationship with God. And, they were finding other ways of using these resources of Bible and prayer. I was interested that none of this group chose to mention communion or "the Lord's Supper"—possibly because of their churchmanship (Alice, for example, countered my question about this by saying that her relationship with God was ongoing, all-encompassing, "not just reduced to a rite"). I will look at this "practice" further in connection with memory in chapter 7.

Attendance at church services had positive value for participants, bringing familiar triggers of awareness of God's presence. However, their words also highlight particular challenges for the local church in facilitating this in ways that can express their mutual belonging as members of the community. Dependence is part of the experience of being a Christian believer, whoever we are.[12] The responsibility of support and care is mutual, but is especially significant for the person living with dementia. For those who were married, the partnership was clearly offering significant spiritual support—but the spouse or family member needs spiritual support too. For those who were living independently, there are issues to be resolved about how such support can be enabled. As we reflect on the issues raised by these disciples of Jesus, what might we learn about how we might accompany them in their walk of faith?

In spite of the lightness and positive words, I also noticed hints of shadow and darkness that were bringing a sense of disorientation to these believers' experience of faith. In the following chapter, in light of Scripture, theology, and other writing, I reflect in more detail on the struggles and pain dementia is introducing to their journey of faith.

12. Stott, "The Age of Dependence."

For Further Reflection . . .

- Reflect on the words of Hebrews 10:19–25 in the light of these experiences of faith practice.
- What do you think are the challenges of faith practice for Christians who live with dementia?
- How could we set about "encouraging one another" practically (Heb 10:25)?

6

Walking through Shadow

"... like the sun that's gone behind the clouds"

Rosemary's urgent words began the moment I entered her home: ebullient, full of passionate confidence in God, sprinkled with Scripture and song, mildly absorbing my questions, she continued to speak—somewhat breathlessly—until her concluding "Amen." Full stops and paragraph breaks were barely noticeable, but later, as I reflected on her bright words, shadows began to appear.

> ROSEMARY: Yes, of course, there's the dark night of the soul... It's always been used to describe people who have moments like that... but they're not dominating my life. My life is dominated by the Lord... a very minor thing...

Like Rosemary, in a variety of ways, for all of the research participants, this *orientation* of faith was expressed confidently—even determinedly. Yet the coming of this illness was inevitably bringing shadows of *disorientation*.[1]

---

1. See the discussion of Brueggemann's model of orientation-disorientation-reorientation in chapter 1, 10–11. As Swinton notes in his discussion of other mental health issues, it is possible to experience all three facets of this experience in one day. See Swinton, *Finding Jesus*, 91.

As I listened to their words, remembered the unspoken communication present in our embodied encounters,[2] and sought further understanding through theological reflection, the hiddenness of some painful aspects of the lived experience of dementia began to emerge.[3] I was aware that in our conversations, those involved in the research were *wanting* to give positive accounts of their faith in dementia, despite the tragedy of their illness and experience of difficulties. Their honesty and courage were apparent in their words, as was their trust in God. It was as though the struggle of living with dementia was assumed and accepted, whilst it was the experience of faith that provided their preeminent sense of being.

However, I was conscious of a danger of colluding with their positivity in the desire to affirm the faithfulness of God. I became aware of the risk of an apparently triumphalist perspective, which did not acknowledge the *hidden* pain of living with the darkness of dementia. Yet, their nuanced allusions to struggle, frustration, and alienation prompted further questioning of this experience of faith as they walked through the shadows of this illness. What is it like as a committed Christian to experience these moments of anguish in the context of a relationship with God, even in the earlier stages of dementia? Why might it be that these Christians living with dementia seemed unconcerned to speak of their own pain? Why did they, in some senses, seem even to be "rejoicing" in their suffering?

In this chapter, we explore further the conundrum of this experience of joyful faith in the midst of darkness. As I have listened to participants' accounts of their dementia, which sometimes seemed to conceal pain, I am mindful of John Swinton's important description of practical theology as the art of perception.[4] Helpfully, for pastoral understanding and ministry, he highlights the difference between "the action of looking" and "the act of accurate perceiving." Such perceiving, in which we seek to look from God's perspective and through the lens of the cross, has the potential to transform our understanding in ways which may enable the spiritual flourishing of those most directly affected by the disorientation dementia is bringing. We need to pause, to observe, to listen, to pause again, to reflect—to be attentive to how the God who loves us might perceive this suffering.

I begin with the question of how we, as Christians, respond to adversity—which, of course, will shape our response to the issue of the suffering of those who live with dementia. In the following, I reflect on a pastoral theology

---

2. Manen, *Researching Lived Experience*, 130–31.

3. For further methodological and philosophical discussion of this see Williams, *What Happens to Faith?*, chapter 4, 69, 71–72; chapter 8, 198.

4. Swinton, "Reforming, Revisionist, Refounding," 5.

of suffering, the cultural context within which we minister, and the New Testament "norm" for this issue. I then look more closely at the nature of affliction, grief, the particular shadows of dementia—and the importance of the cross in our thinking about faith in this context. In the light of these perspectives, we reflect further on the words of Rosemary, Matthew, Bill, Jess, Ron, Alice, David, and Jill to discover what these disclose about walking through the shadows of dementia as disciples of Christ. How might we respond?

RESPONDING TO ADVERSITY

"He is my strength, my rock . . . my salvation."[5]

A Pastoral Theology of Suffering

Human adversity of any kind provokes two kinds of questions, debated through the centuries of Christendom. There is the theodical question of evil—why does a good God allow suffering? Then, there is the distinct theological pastoral question of how we understand and respond to suffering within the context of Christian faith. Whilst the first might suggest doubt and denial of a sovereign God,[6] the second arises out of belief and expresses trust, in spite of suffering. A familiar biblical model of response to suffering is found in the story of Job. In the midst of his anguish and loss, and in spite of his friends' unhelpful words about who was to blame and other unanswerable questions, he declared, "I know that my Redeemer lives" (Job 19:25). In the end, he didn't seek answers from God, but simply asserted his trust in him.

In the light of the lived experience of the participants in this research, I focus primarily on this second question, seeking understanding of their experience of faith that dementia brings within the context of trust in God in a fallen (or "broken") world:

> ALICE: And I think, well Lord, this is something that you've allowed me to have (I don't believe that God beats us up, or gives us bad things). He allows things in this broken world, and so he's allowed it.

---

5. Rosemary was referring here to verses from the Psalms, for example, Psalm 18:2.
6. See Job 1:9–11.

The Wrong Question

The confusion between the two questions (to doubt God or to trust him) has potential to bring deep frustration and further pain to people of faith who are beginning to live with dementia. Alice, for example, recounted how fellow Christians insisted that she must be "blaming" God for the advent of her dementia: "'So are you blaming God for all this?' I said, 'No I'm not.'" Jill also used the word "blame" in this connection, out of concern that others might think that her own failures had in some way brought this suffering on herself ("he [God] doesn't blame me"). In both cases, the questions being asked of their illness have echoes of the conversation between Job and his friends: either Job might reasonably deny God who had allowed such undeserved suffering (Job 2:9), or it was Job's evil actions that had brought punishment from God (e.g., Job 15:5–6). In both cases, it was the questions of *others* that had potential to bring additional suffering through the expression of their own uncertainties. As Stanley Hauerwas has reminded us, such questions may be of interest, but meanwhile, "we are torn apart by what is happening to real people, to those we know and love."[7] Practically, our inquiry here concerns how God's people respond to the experience of dementia, and the nature of and reasons for such response.

It is interesting that the word "blame" used by participants assumed fault: in one case, disbelief ("Are you blaming God for all this?"); in the other, sin ("as if it's my fault"). This inclination to focus on sin in the context of suffering is also evident in the Gospel accounts of Jesus' miraculous healings. For example, in the case of the man born blind, the disciples wanted to know whose sin had caused his condition (John 9:2). Taking Job as an example, theologian and ethicist Hans Reinders has pointed to the difficulty of such assumptions of a divinely controlled "moral geometry": those who are apparently deserving of punishment go free, whilst those who are innocent are deeply affected by adversity.[8] The falseness of this is clearly shown in Job's story where the righteous man suffers great loss. Yet, at the end of Job's conversation with God, he recognizes his own unworthiness, apart from any specific wrongdoing. In spite of his suffering, he ceases to question God about his personal condition and affirms his trust in God (Job 42:1–6).[9] In one of my conversations, Jill's words implied the question, "Why not me?!," which, perhaps, seems a more appropriate one from the perspective of faith. Again, this points to the primacy of the pastoral issue

---

7. Hauerwas, *Naming the Silences*, 1–2.
8. Reinders, *Disability, Providence, and Ethics*, 1–15.
9. Reinders, *Disability, Providence, and Ethics*, 121.

of the nature of our response to the experience of suffering. How might we walk with those who suffer?

The Relationship between Evil and Suffering

Throughout the centuries, theological discussion has linked evil and suffering (again, remember Job and his friends). The issue of dementia may raise these familiar questions. How can a good God permit this suffering in his good creation? For the purposes of this particular topic, I am seeking here a pastoral *response* to this pain, which happens *within* the context of the questions about evil[10] ("this broken world," Alice).

John Swinton points out that Augustine seemed to conclude that evil has no being in a creation which God himself declared "good":

> . . . unless in his omnipotence and goodness, as the Supreme Good, he is able to bring forth good out of evil.[11]

Swinton's discussion derives from this, that it is *the turning away* from God which is evil.[12] Other theologians echo Augustine, similarly concluding that evil arises from denial of God.[13] The theological debate is complex, and, as we strive with Scripture, we may disagree with some of the theologians' conclusions. However, here we are primarily concerned, as Hauerwas has reminded us, with people we love who are suffering. The people in this research were definitely *not* turning away from God; in their living with dementia, deliberate commitment to God was evidently the context for the suffering they were enduring.

Whilst the nature of evil, apart from human transgression, is difficult to define, it also raises the pastoral question of sin and the possibility of forgiveness for those living with dementia. Keck, with a controversial choice of words, has raised the difficulty of repentance for the "de-subjected patient."[14] In response, I remember an elderly resident in a dementia unit of a care home who, disturbed by guilt ("I've been wicked"), responded joyfully when assured of Christ's welcome and forgiveness.[15] There are ways, apart from the cognitive, in which those living with dementia might be

---

10. Swinton, *Raging with Compassion*. See especially chapter 1, 9–29.
11. Swinton, *Raging with Compassion*, 22; Augustine, *Enchiridion* 3.11.
12. Swinton, *Raging with Compassion*, 22; Augustine, *City of God*, 11:9.
13. For example, Hauerwas, "Seeing Darkness," 36–38. Hauerwas draws on Jenson's discussion of Barth. See Jenson, "Nihilism"; Barth, *Church Dogmatics*, 3.3, 519–31.
14. Keck, *Forgetting Whose We Are*, 166.
15. See Williams, "Knowing God in Dementia," 8–9.

supported in acknowledging sin and troublesome guilt, and receiving Christ's forgiveness. However, in the experience of the participants in this study, whilst sadness and struggle are discernible, these are the result of their illness, not their sin. Sin is not mentioned by them apart from their assurance of forgiveness ("I feel I have been forgiven . . . I don't think we have to carry a burden," Jess). In their experience, within the suffering of dementia, they confidently affirmed their growing sense of trust in God ("Faith is growing more," David).

Cultural Context

As well as the theological questions, it's important to acknowledge the cultural context within which we encounter the sadness and suffering brought by dementia. Before the Enlightenment, reservations about the apparent inconsistency of belief in a good God alongside the experience of suffering were not considered.[16] It was with the coming of post-Enlightenment Western culture that questions of theodicy (the goodness of God; the presence of evil and suffering) became apparent. Modern culture was one in which "reason supplanted faith as point of departure"; "human planning took the place of trust in God."[17] Post-Enlightenment culture has, in consequence, dethroned God, becoming human-centered. The difficulties that the Enlightenment brought for Christian faith of the evangelical tradition are evident in its emphasis on individualism[18] and the attempts to rationalize Christian faith. Arising from our post-Enlightenment framework, a logical question to ask in response to the suffering of illness is: "Why does a good God allow bad things to happen to good people?"[19] However, if we accept the metanarrative of Enlightenment reason and autonomous human beings, the questions of "theodicy" are, in fact, wrongly addressed to God. Why, after all, does *medicine* not cure all illness and its associated suffering?[20] If theodicy involves doubt of God, it suggests denial of God. Consequently, if we give space to this argument, human beings are left alone to face the tragedy of human suffering. Such questions, if they are allowed to stand unchallenged, bring deep discomfort to those living with dementia.

Yet, this is not the position of God's people who inhabit the biblical narrative in which God is sovereign. In Walter Brueggemann's reflections

16. See Swinton, *Raging with Compassion*, 34.
17. Bosch, *Transforming Mission*, 269–71.
18. See for example, Zahl, "Reformation Pessimism," 82.
19. Hauerwas, "Seeing Darkness," 37.
20. Bosch, *Transforming Mission*, 266.

on suffering and hope in the experience of the Israelites,[21] he asserts that amnesia leads to despair—yet, remembrance of God brings hope. It might be that whilst denial of God in the lived experience of dementia brings anguish, trust in him—as shown in the lives of the participants in this study—transforms their experience, bringing hope. As pastoral theologians are discovering, the experience of suffering for the Christian believer does not of itself result in "a crisis of faith."[22] Hauerwas redirects us to the biblical account of suffering:

> The realism of the Psalms and the book of Job depends on the presumption that God is God and we are not. When Christians think theodical justifications are needed to justify the ways of God at the bar of a justice determined by us, you can be sure that the god Christians now worship is not the God of Israel and Jesus Christ.[23]

This overarching metanarrative of Scripture is the one within which the participants locate their experience. It is within *this* cultural context that response to the question of suffering, in relation to their faith, must be sought.

The New Testament Norm

For New Testament Christians, suffering wasn't a surprising factor in their lives. Hauerwas points out that, for them, it did not require explanation:

> For the early Christians, suffering and evil . . . did not have to be "explained." Rather, what was required was the means to go on even if the evil could not be "explained."[24]

Peter's expectation of suffering is conveyed in his first letter: "In this you rejoice, even if now for a little while you have had to suffer various trials" (1 Pet 1:6); Paul also assumes the presence of suffering: "We also glory in our sufferings" (Rom 5:3, NIVUK).

Of course, the fundamental thread through the Gospels and the epistles is the Christ who chose the life of the suffering servant, who "made himself nothing," and bore our *suffering* on the cross (Phil 2:6–8, NIVUK; Isa 53:4). His call to take up our cross and follow him (Matt 16:24) suggests that

---

21. Brueggemann, "Suffering Produces Hope," 97.
22. Swinton, *Raging with Compassion*, 111.
23. Hauerwas, "Seeing Darkness," 36–37.
24. Hauerwas, *Naming the Silences*, 49.

believers should not be overwhelmed by the advent of suffering: Hauerwas writes, "Any truthful account of the Christian life cannot exclude suffering as integral to that life."[25] For Ron, Rosemary, Alice, and the others involved in my research, it was becoming an accepted part of their lives: "all right, we've got a bit of difficulties, but we're all right . . ." (Ron).

As those called to follow Jesus, their focus was on him, and their hope was found in the resurrection (I look further at this experience of hope in chapter 9). Their Christ-centered orientation was providing the perspective for understanding their suffering. In spite of the losses being brought by dementia, their faith resonated with Job's affirmation of trust in God. No matter what their physical and material circumstances, this was their faith ("I know there's nothing that can ever separate me from him," Alice).

Into this certainty comes the particular disorientation of dementia. In the lives of Christians who live with dementia, this is where theory meets lived experience in the "now" of their temporal, embodied existence.

EXPERIENCING SHADOW

Affliction

Knowing the theological and biblical theory of response to suffering is a different matter from the experience of living in shadow, or (in this case) knowing the sadness of dementia as it affects one's own life. Simone Weil thoughtfully and movingly refines the anonymous questions of suffering with her use of the word "affliction," which is experienced by a particular human being.[26] She uses the word to refer to the experience of enduring pain, not a passing physical pain, but one which engulfs the whole person:[27] "an uprooting of life," affecting every part of life: "social, psychological and physical." Aileen Barclay[28] takes this understanding and uses it to explore her own experience of living with her husband's Alzheimer's, which becomes "an inescapable part of existence."[29] At times, its darkness might even make the believer *feel* God is absent.[30] Rosemary, whose words are at the head of this chapter, questioned her experience in this way: "Is it like

---

25. Hauerwas, *Naming the Silences*, 85.
26. Weil, *Waiting on God*, 63–78.
27. Weil, *Waiting on God*, 63–64.
28. Barclay, "Psalm 88," 96–98.
29. Barclay, "Psalm 88," 96.
30. Barclay, "Psalm 88," 96; Weil, *Waiting on God*, 66; Davis, *My Journey into Alzheimer's Disease*, 53–54.

the sun that's gone behind the clouds?" Weil envisages the transforming love of God *alongside* the experience of affliction, available for all who turn their gaze toward him: "It rests with them to keep or not to keep their eyes turned towards God through all the jolting."[31] The discovery of this illness in the participants' lives was unavoidably affecting every part of their existence ("completely engulfed," Ps 88:17, NIVUK), yet the participants in my research expressed unfaltering trust in God's presence with them in their experience of dementia.

Like Paul who lived with the affliction of his "thorn . . . in the flesh" (2 Cor 12:7–10), they mentioned the realities of their suffering in passing ("It's a very minor thing," Rosemary; "all right . . . we have a bit of difficulties," Ron); yet these were a present reality in their lived experience. Perhaps, especially in the earlier stages of dementia, there was a strange reticence in naming the nature of this suffering.

The Naming of Grief

Malcolm Goldsmith, reflecting on the experience of dementia, talks about a "process of denial and collusion." Through this, he notes that friends and loved ones might be seeking to protect, but in fact, this might remove the possibility of preparation for the further development of this disease.[32] In his exploration of the psalms of disorientation, Walter Brueggemann points to a deeper possible reason for this reticence. He suggests that for some Christians there is "a mismatch between our life experience of disorientation and our faith speech of orientation."[33] He notes: "It is a curious fact that the church has . . . continued to sing songs of orientation in a world increasingly experienced as disoriented."[34] Whilst the "Yet I will rejoice in the LORD" of Habakkuk (Hab 3:17–18) is an expression of faithfulness to God in spite of tragic and terrifying events, the observer of those who suffer might conclude that such declarations arise from "wishful optimism,"[35] or perhaps even a refusal to contemplate the suffering which some endure.[36] The acknowledgment of the disease and its disorientating influences was attested to in my research by evident grieving, frustration, or sadness of participants, and the quiet tears of their loved ones as we spoke. However,

---

31. Weil, *Waiting on God*, 69.
32. Goldsmith, "Through a Glass Darkly," 129.
33. Brueggemann, *Spirituality of the Psalms*, 25.
34. Brueggemann, *Spirituality of the Psalms*, 25.
35. Brueggemann, *Spirituality of the Psalms*, 26.
36. Barclay, "Psalm 88," 89.

they did not choose to dwell on the difficulties of their dementia. Perhaps our faith culture has resisted the embrace of negativity, as if to do so "was somehow an act of unfaith."[37]

Yet, as Brueggemann points out, it is strange that a Bible reading-focused faith community should often not pay more attention to the psalms of lament. The psalmist, who is overwhelmed with his troubles ("my soul is full of troubles," Ps 88:3) declares his grief, and the exiles sit down together and weep far from home (Ps 137:1). Jesus himself legitimates this activity of lament as he quotes from Psalm 22 in the extremity of his agony on the cross: "My God, my God why have you forsaken me?" (Matt 27:46; Ps 22:1). Such lament is *not* to deny God, or his power and control. Rather, it might be perceived as "an act of bold faith."[38] The one in anguish continues to address God in searching for a solution. The laments of the psalms are conversations which take place within the arena of faith, within a community that trusts in God.

Reflecting on dementia as an experience of disempowerment, Malcolm Goldsmith asks whether it is not acceptable at times to rage in response to the losses that dementia is bringing, even though such raging may be difficult for others.[39] I remember an event at a local church about dementia. One woman, whose parent was living with dementia, had listened quietly through the evening. Finally, angry and frustrated by the gentle expressions of compassionate understanding throughout this evening, she burst out: "I am *not* all right with this! I *am* embarrassed by what [her parent] will do next in church!" Her unexpected raging was an honest naming of grief, and in keeping with the voices of the psalmist. In spite of some surprise and mild embarrassment, the community of faith was an appropriate place in which to express her anger and grief.

Lament (naming our grief) in this context may be a necessary part of the wrestling with God that leads to perceiving of the light, reorientation, and celebration of his sovereignty ("they shall . . . proclaim his righteousness to a people yet unborn, that he has done it," Psalm 22:31, ESV).[40] In a sense, the research conversations at the center of this book are themselves expressions of lament.

---

37. Brueggemann, *Spirituality of the Psalms*, 26.
38. Brueggemann, *Spirituality of the Psalms*, 27.
39. Goldsmith, "Tracing Rainbows Through the Rain," 124.
40. See also Psalm 22:27–31.

Disclosing Shadows

In the following I reflect on some glimpses of the struggle and darkness the participants were experiencing: the sense of becoming a stranger, and the unseen struggles of the inner life. The first has to do with our relationships with others; the second has to do with the sense of relationship with God. In each circumstance, these were always expressed in their felt context of "Even though . . . you are with me" (Ps 23:4). There was an unfailing recognition of Christ's presence with them in the confusion of their developing dementia.

Becoming Strangers[41]

The moment of diagnosis brings the shock of sudden shift of self-perception, and of grief, as revealed in David's words: "I was quite staggered by this . . . I was really quite shocked." Christine Bryden also recalls this sense of shock of diagnosis and the immediate change that dementia signified for the whole of her life: "The day before my diagnosis I was a busy and successful single mother . . . The day after I was a label—Person with Dementia."[42] Whilst she is reluctant to use the word "dementia," Jess's words echo this: "When I was *labelled* 'memory loss' . . . my memory loss has interfered with my being somebody or something, doing something."

EXPERIENCING STIGMA

Bryden suggests that there are "two burdens from our disease": the "struggle with the illness itself" and the "disease of society," which, perhaps unconsciously, stigmatizes and disempowers.[43] Aileen Barclay, exploring her husband's experience of dementia, uses the words of Psalm 88 to powerfully evoke the resulting sense of isolation and exclusion: "You have taken from me friend and neighbour—darkness is my closest friend" (Ps 88:18, NIVUK).[44] These shadows of exclusion, and struggle with darkness, are present in the lives of those who are living in the early to moderate stages of dementia. Even then, anguish results from the perceived reactions of others to their illness, which begin to distance them from their wider communities. Unseen by others, such struggles bring moments of darkness.

---

41. For further discussion of becoming a "stranger," see Swinton, *Dementia*, 257–78.
42. Bryden, *Dancing with Dementia*, 156.
43. Bryden, *Dancing with Dementia*, 142.
44. Barclay, "Psalm 88," 93.

This sense of stigma affecting those who feel labelled with "dementia" is in itself a disabling problem. In his broader discussion of disability, Hans Reinders has highlighted: "Many would say that they feel neither wronged nor harmed by their disability, but by how other people treat them."[45] Steven Sabat talks about this as "malignant social positioning."[46] Simone Weil, in her reflection on affliction, challenges the community of faith with this statement: "Except for those whose whole soul is inhabited by Christ, everybody despises the afflicted to some extent, although practically no one is conscious of it."[47] How might *we* sometimes be guilty of this?

In spite of the research participants' positive outlook, there was awareness of being, in some senses, *less* than they had been, "despised," and of becoming "strangers" to others.[48] For example, Jill spoke of her concern for others that her dementia might be an embarrassment *to* others.

> JILL: Yes. I think they're embarrassed about naming it . . . [laughs] . . . you see nobody has asked me questions like you ask me . . . very rarely do people acknowledge that I have dementia.
> 'TRICIA: Is it helpful to have it acknowledged?
> JILL: As long as I'm not made to look a fool [laughs] . . . or as if it's my fault.

Jill's response to her dementia was, at this stage, double-edged. She feared that it might be embarrassing for others, and that she might "be made to look a fool," even that others might think that it was her fault (echoes of Job and his friends). Yet her words also conveyed that she did not believe herself "a fool" and did not regard having this illness as her own fault. Like other participants in this research, Jill's response to the sense of unspoken judgment of others arose out of her faith, as she said: "He [God] doesn't blame me."

Jess, a little further on in her journey with dementia, questions her role in church—now, "I do the flowers instead." Jess had told me of difficult childhood memories of her grandmother's treatment in an "asylum." Perhaps her sense of stigma may have partly resulted from historical negative views of mental health disorders.[49] Erving Goffman has drawn attention to this hidden perspective, that the image of self is confronted by the image of themselves which others reflect back to them.[50]

---

45. Reinders, *Disability, Providence, and Ethics*, 7.
46. See also chapter 2, 20–21.
47. Weil, *Waiting on God*, 40.
48. Barclay, "Psalm 88," 93; Swinton, *Dementia*, 258–59.
49. Kitwood, *Dementia Reconsidered*, 42–45.
50. Goffman, *Stigma*, 154.

Here are Bryden's "two burdens." Both Jess and Jill were beginning to feel the impact of the isolating tendency of the reactions of others to their illness. Both were confident in their own sense of personal identity, yet there was underlying concern about how others might see them. Jill's fear was not so much of the disease itself, but of the possible responses of others to this which might lead to stigmatizing reactions. For disciples of Jesus, in addition to "malignant social positioning,"[51] there is an additional source of stigma.

Malignant Spiritual Positioning

Perhaps even more significant for the Christian living with dementia is an insidious "malignant spiritual positioning" that may confront sufferers in their local church community.[52] In this expression of stigmatization, others may make negative assumptions about one's spiritual life. Thoughtless words may suggest doubt of a person's faith, which, in turn, threatens separation from God. Alice, for example, spoke indignantly of fellow Christians who questioned her relationship with God because of her increasingly apparent illness:

> ALICE: So they said . . . "Aren't you angry with God?" I said, "No, I'm not!" So they didn't believe me! [laughs] . . . And they said, "Well, you've obviously forgotten because of your dementia. You can't remember that you're cross with God." I said, "I've never been cross with God!" [frustrated laughter] . . . [quietly] It doesn't help . . .

She concluded with exasperation, "They nullify my Christian walk!" Unintentional in their effect maybe, such words are felt as an insult and bring discomfort. Swinton suggests that difference in others can bring uncomfortable questions for all of us:

> Those who come proclaiming that the standard ways of relating to God might not apply to them will inevitably create a dissonance that is at best disorienting and at worst offensive.[53]

How can the experiences of such "stigma" be understood theologically? The biblical story of exile brings insight for a faith understanding of this experience.

---

51. Sabat, "Mind, Meaning, and Personhood in Dementia."

52. Barclay, "Psalm 88," 90. In her use of the phrase "malignant spiritual positioning," Barclay is quoting from a personal conversation with John Swinton.

53. Swinton, *Dementia*, 269.

Aliens and Exiles

This "becoming a stranger" finds echoes in the believer's participation in the continuing biblical story of faith. Brueggemann has drawn on the experience of the loss and chaos in Jerusalem that preceded the people's journey into exile.[54] Goldsmith also looks for understanding of the experience of living with dementia in this image of the exiled Israelites.[55] Their homeland in ruins, displaced as exiles, how could the Israelites sing the Lord's song in a foreign land?[56] The imagery persists into the New Testament: the writer to Hebrews reminds the readers of this pattern of living as strangers (Heb 11:1–39). Peter speaks of the community of faith as "aliens and exiles" (1 Pet 2:11).[57] From a biblical perspective, all believers, whatever their capacities, live as "strangers" in this world.

Ultimately, this being a stranger resonates with participation in Christ's own suffering—"the sacrifice of being a human," as Jess said. Rejected by the Jewish people, Jesus became the supreme outcast, accursed by his death on the cross.[58] The prophet Isaiah's surprising picture of the coming Christ shows him as: "despised and rejected by others; a man of suffering, and acquainted with infirmity" (Isa 53:3). Jesus identified himself as the outcast, and as being in allegiance with those who suffer: "For I was hungry and you gave me food, I was thirsty and you gave me something to drink, I was a stranger and you welcomed me (Matt 25:35)."[59] This is the Christ whose disciples are called to follow and serve.

Unseen Struggle

Despite welcome, warmth, good humor, and an evangelical faith—"I don't know where I'm going in the way that *you* know . . . but I know myself that being a Christian I shall be going . . . to heaven" (Ron)—the unseen struggles of dementia were rippling the surface of the faithful lives of my research participants. Their words disclosed moments of private darkness and struggle as they recognized, amongst other symptoms of their illness, encroaching memory loss: "I had a memory then, I haven't one now . . .

---

54. Brueggemann, "Suffering Produces Hope."
55. Goldsmith, "Dementia."
56. Goldsmith, "Dementia," 127–28.
57. See Swinton, *Dementia*, 274–76.
58. "Christ redeemed us from the curse of the law by becoming a curse for us" (Gal 3:13).
59. Swinton, *Dementia*, 276.

it's not funny" (Ron). Throughout our conversation, Ron's hesitance (and sometimes misplaced words) suggested the frustrations he was feeling.[60] Rosemary also talked about her overwhelming experiences in everyday life resulting from her failing memory, so that, when she felt unable to cope, "I just . . . crumpled underneath it." The conversations themselves disclosed the struggles of words going missing and slowness of thought during our exchanges.

Allusions to apparent forgetfulness of loved ones hinted at our society's fear that dementia steals our knowledge of one another. Alice spoke of a meeting with a loved one when she had forgotten her name. This was not an easy moment for either person, but from Alice's insider perspective, it didn't matter: they still *knew* one another. Failing neurons do not take away the essence of loving relationship.

However, for some Christians as dementia advances, there is an even more disturbing experience (which some have spoken of as intermittent): the sense that relationship with God himself goes missing.[61]

> ROSEMARY: . . . but . . . I . . . still . . . do experience sometimes . . . when it's a . . . deep down . . . feeling . . . of the worst of it all . . . when I can't . . . find myself . . . in that state where God . . . seems to have shut . . . and you read about it in Psalms[62] . . . "Oh God, where are you? Why have you . . .? I'm calling out to you and I can't at this moment connect . . ." But he knows . . . And sometimes when I'm feeling those dark nights of the soul I can cry out to God and say, "Where are you God?" Where is this feeling of joy which I so often get, which I'm just not feeling now. Is it like the sun that's gone behind the clouds?

Rosemary's sense of struggle with dementia and her frustration were clear: her words reflected a frightening sense of separation from God and her own sense of lostness. Evidently, this was *not*, as she sought to minimize, "a very minor thing." In these "dark" times she felt alone and sad. Her words echoed those of the pastor Robert Davis,[63] whose dementia initially brought a similar sense of loss:

> Now I discovered the cruellest blow of all. This personal and tender relationship that I had with the Lord was no longer there . . . There were no longer any feelings of peace and joy . . . I could

---

60. MacKinlay, "Listening to People with Dementia," 101, 104.
61. Davis, *My Journey into Alzheimer's Disease*, 47–48.
62. For example, Psalm 22:1: "My God, my God, why have you forsaken me?"
63. Davis, *My Journey into Alzheimer's Disease*, 47–48.

only cry out bitterly to the Lord, "Why, God, why? . . . Why have you made my sunlight turn into moonlight?"[64]

On several occasions during our conversations, some of the participants were close to tears as they sought to describe these inner experiences of dementia in the light of their faith. Matthew, for example, frail and visibly moved, spoke of Christ's crucifixion and resurrection:

> MATTHEW: I wouldn't be afraid to die . . . because . . . Jesus went up to Calvary . . . and on the third day . . . he rose.

In this suffering, through these struggles, God brings us to "the foot of the Cross."[65] This demonstration of divine solidarity[66] with our human experience provides a metaphor for these disciples of Jesus who live in the light of the cross, in spite of the shadows of dementia. And, as the psalmist discovered, the Good Shepherd walks with us through this valley of the shadow of death (Ps 23:4).

The Shadow of the Cross

As Paul explores, Christ, the image of God in humankind, becomes the suffering servant, who in obedience to his Father lays down his life for others (Phil 2:6–8). The Gospel accounts reveal the incarnated image of God *being with* those who suffer and are rejected. The very nature of God-in-Christ is revealed as the one who stands with the stranger.

During one of our conversations Bill intentionally showed me a wooden cross. He had hammered nails into this, as an expression of his confidence that Christ was, and would be, with him in the uncertainties of his illness. Dietrich Bonhoeffer,[67] in his exploration of the suffering of believers, puts this into perspective alongside the suffering of Christ on the cross: "In the hour of the cruellest torture they bear for his sake, they are made partakers in the perfect joy and bliss of fellowship with him." Aileen Barclay, reflecting on the darkness of the cross, highlights revelation in this serendipity: those who are afflicted share in Christ's own desolation on the cross.[68] This seems to be Bill's experience as he adjusts to the presence of dementia in his life.

---

64. Davis, *My Journey into Alzheimer's Disease*, 47.
65. Weil, *Waiting on God*, 69. For discussion of Luther's pastoral theology of the cross, see Heuser, "The Human Condition."
66. Explored further in Moltmann, *The Crucified God*.
67. Bonhoeffer, *The Cost of Discipleship*, 81.
68. Barclay, "Psalm 88," 97.

Christ on the Cross

In this "brokenness of God on Calvary," Keck suggests we can find identification and hope. The crucified Christ, suffering and despised, allows those walking in the shadow of dementia to see Christ as fellow sufferer:

> The tangles and plaques in the brain of the Alzheimer's patient can be seen in the matted hair and blood-stained garments of Christ. Both this disease and the Cross are prolonged experiences of death.[69]

Such anguish sets the scene for apocalyptic desire and resolution as we observe this suffering: "Let it be over." In response to this, Peter Kevern has insisted on the profound relevance that Christ's suffering on the cross has to the *lived* experience of the person living with dementia in the temporal, corporeal moment of "now."[70] If heaven is the *only* focus for comfort, then God is placed outside the experience of living with dementia amidst the change and physical deterioration of the present. This insight is helpful to those with mild to moderate dementia, who need assurance of Christ's presence with them *now* and as they imagine the future progress of their illness. Christ's suffering is pivotal in human understanding of the story of redemption: he is able to redeem us *because* "he is subject to all the weaknesses and contingencies inherent in being human."[71]

Christ's experience of darkness is the extremity of suffering, unknowable by humankind. His separation from God "is the Father's deliberately giving his Christ over to a deadly destiny so that our destiny would not be determined by death."[72] Theologically, this takes us to the mystery (and hope) of the self-giving love of the Trinitarian God. Even in the extremity of affliction, Christ, as part of the Trinity, is held within the loving communion of God. The believer's being "in Christ" envisages the one living with dementia caught up in the mystery of this bond of love.[73]

Comfort in Darkness

Still able to welcome me and communicate, these research participants were not—at the time of our conversations—suffering the extremities of

---

69. Keck, *Forgetting Whose We Are*, 171–72.
70. Kevern, "Sharing the Mind of Christ," 411–12.
71. Kevern, "Sharing the Mind of Christ," 417–18.
72. Hauerwas, *Cross-Shattered Christ*, 63.
73. See discussion in chapter 3, 44–45; Weil, *Waiting on God*, 70–71.

the symptoms that advanced dementia brings. Nevertheless, *these* struggles are part of the unseen, inner experience of faith that requires response in the present moment. They were also living each day with the knowledge of the future development of their illness. For a people embedded in *God's story*, there is the comfort of his words and presence: "For just as we share abundantly in the sufferings of Christ, so also our comfort abounds through Christ" (2 Cor 1:5, NIVUK).

WALKING THROUGH SHADOW . . .

Interweaving with sadness and loss, dementia brings a shifting of perception of the journey of faith. In some ways, its advent undoubtedly brings disorientation. Yet, for the participants in my research, knowing themselves as being "in Christ," the finding of purpose and hope was also possible in the light of his resurrection. A reorientation seemed to be happening as these disciples of Christ were keeping their gaze fixed on him.[74] How might we walk with them?

In the following chapters, we begin to explore further how their experience of reorientation in this new context of dementia was happening. I begin by reflecting on the issue of memory as a surprising resource for faith for those who are living with dementia.

For Further Reflection . . .

- Thinking of those you know who live with dementia, reflect for a few moments on the words of Psalm 23.
- What "shadows" of dementia are you aware of in the lives of those living with this illness?
- Is your local church—or are you—ever guilty of stigmatizing those who live with dementia? In what ways?
- How might we bring comfort to our brothers and sisters who are quietly walking through these shadows?

---

74. Weil, *Waiting on God*, 69.

7

Memory Funding Faith

"I'll never lose that joy, but I have lost my memory . . ."

Ron is sitting quietly in a comfortable chair in the living room of his home when I arrive. There are books and newspapers on a table nearby. As I am introduced by Ron's wife, Clare, he is friendly and welcoming. Ron understands that I have come to talk about having faith in dementia (although sometimes he will seem to forget the purpose of my visit). My first question sparks a lengthy and enthusiastic account of his life and his coming to faith. All is spoken in his soft Welsh accent (although he is far from that particular homeland now). There are hesitations, digressions, and repetitions, but the strength of his faith is clear: "The joy of being born again is always there . . . and therefore, I'll never lose that joy . . . but I have lost my memory . . ." Ron considers further and then says reflectively, "I haven't got a memory . . . but I have." What does he mean? What and how is he remembering? His words reveal apparent paradox in this experience of dementia. How can memory be significant for his faith now?

Dementia is sometimes characterized as the disease that is labelled with "loss of memory." "His memory has gone," people say of the dementia sufferer. It is tragic, but we must accept that this person's story (and faith?) is over. Some people might also add, "I don't visit him anymore; there's no point."[1] Facing the grief brought by dementia, this is not an uncommon reaction of loved ones affected by the illness of their father or mother. Yet, such a notion—no memory, no longer there—does *not* bring simple answers. In fact, it suggests a limited view of the nature, power, and scope of memory, and has the effect of excluding this person and the gift of their living presence: "My memory loss has interfered with my being somebody," Jess says. Habitual thinking in such ways may mean that we fail to recognize aspects of being the person who is living with this illness. For Christians, this might include ignoring, undervaluing—even just not noticing—the nature of their present, even strengthening, experience of God. So, dementia begins to question our assumptions, and consequently, the meaning of faith for Christians who live with dementia—and the importance of memory for funding that faith. If we watch closely, we observe faith and memory interweaving, bringing a reorientation of faith that is taking place amidst incipient dementia. As Walter Brueggemann has written intriguingly, memory is an essential ingredient of faith in times of loss:

> The primary ingredient, the primary resource of faith that is indispensable in a season of loss is active, determined, concrete, resilient memory.[2]

How can this be true for Christians who live with the losses that dementia brings? Surprisingly, the participants' experience unveils this paradox. Memory funds their faith despite the loss of memory.

In this chapter, I consider first some current thinking about memory's role in our identity as human beings.[3] Then I reflect on some biblical perspectives on memory that remind us of our place in God's story and affirm our faith and hope in him. We pause again to hear the words of the Christians who spoke with me about their memories in the light of their "engrained faith"—and remember, with them, the God who promises, "I will not forget you! See, I have engraved you on the palms of my hands" (Isa 49:15–16).

REMEMBERING: FRAGILE CLUES

Increasingly today, writing about dementia and memory draws attention to the *fragile clues*[4] of a person's identity that persist deep into their

---

1. Paraphrase from a radio interview with a sports celebrity talking about his father.
2. Brueggemann, "Suffering Produces Hope," 96.
3. See also chapter 2, 28–29.
4. Post, *Moral Challenge of Alzheimer Disease*, 25.

journey with this disease. For example, on a visit to a home for those with advanced dementia, I recall a smartly dressed (pearls-in-place) lady. Her upright stance, manner, and words ("This is not good enough!") reflected her former commanding role in organizations—and still had power to intimidate! I remember a playful, teasing Irish lady who would proudly greet me in Gaelic, outdoor coat on and bag in hand—then excuse herself, "must get on, lots to do!" My comment on someone's broad Scottish accent (we were in the south of England) brought the good-humored riposte: "I haven't got an accent . . . *you* have!" As I meet with all the social mix and diversity of those living in this home—the dancer, the farmer, the doctor, the Baptist pastor—I am confronted with these "fragile clues" to the identity of those with whom I speak (and I am aware that they pick up on such clues about me too). These reveal unexpected perspectives about memory and its embeddedness in whom we consider ourselves to be. As we reflect, different kinds of memory—both autobiographical and embodied[5]—are disclosed through "fragile clues" in our encounters with one other, including those who are Christians living with dementia.

This Is My Story

The story of their lives is *not* missing for the participants in this research. Whatever the *theories* of memory David, Bill, Matthew, Alice, Rosemary, Ron, Jess, and Jill—albeit somewhat fragmentedly—told me with eagerness, warmth, sadness, and humor about the experiences of their lives and travels, from childhood through youth and adulthood to the present. As we explored earlier, their sense of self in the present was caught up in this remembering of their past lives:[6] the good, the difficult, the romances, careers, callings, and faith. This is who they are. Precise time-ordering may have become less significant, but the impact of their memories told in and through our embodied encounters is powerful still. Threaded through all these are the memories and testimonies of their faith and its *meaning* in their lives.[7] They certainly had *not* lost the story of their lives.

Even so, loss of some functions of memory was a troubling concern for those feeling the immensity of the challenge of their ongoing decline:[8] "You asked me something . . . then it will fade away," Rosemary said. Neurons may be less efficient—and that is frustrating—but these persons are

---

5. See chapter 2, 28–29
6. Schacter, *Searching for Memory*, 34.
7. Brockmeier, "Questions of Meaning," 83.
8. Post, "*Respectare*," 223.

powerful in their presence. As John Swinton reminds us, memory is *not* just about cognitive recall; rather, it is embedded in every aspect of who we feel ourselves to be.[9] As we meet, we recognize clues to the other's identity: our speech, gestures, interactions with our environment,[10] style of dress, books, photos, choices of music and media. Stephen Sapp, in his writing about Alzheimer's disease, speaks of the interweaving of memory and identity which come from the: "experiences that the person has had in and through his or her body . . . thus . . . creating memories and a personal history."[11] We encounter this embodied story as we meet with another, no matter what our condition. As examples of "fragile clues" described above demonstrate, body memory of the self is seen in our habits and practices, and in bodily interaction with others.[12] Of course, for the Christians participating in this research, there is the further dimension of faith-ed memory too.

We noticed earlier how body memory is revealed especially in Christian worship—through singing of familiar hymns and other expressions of our faith.[13] If you know Christians living with dementia, even in its later stages, you will probably have seen such glimpses of faith's response expressed through bodily movement, emotional expression, and gestures.[14] John Swinton reminds us that this body memory "potentially acts as a powerful conduit for knowing Jesus even if one has forgotten who Jesus is."[15] Recognition of embodied memory becomes increasingly important for the funding of faith of those who live with this illness.

For the Christian believer there is this further dimension of memory that faith brings to our understanding—found in the enduring sense of transcendent relationship with God. Remember Alice's words: "There's nothing that can ever separate me from him . . . even when my brain falls apart." Before we hear more about the participants' own recollections of dementia's impact on memory and faith, I'll first consider the bigger story of memory, found in God's Word.

---

9. Swinton, "What the Body Remembers."
10. Matthews, "Dementia and the Identity of the Person," 173.
11. Sapp, "Living with Alzheimer's."
12. Summa and Fuchs, "Self-experience in Dementia," 399–400.
13. Shamy, *A Guide to the Spiritual Dimension of Care*, 93–119; Williams, "Knowing God in Dementia," 9.
14. Swinton, *Dementia*, 237, 251; Kontos, "Alzheimer Expressions," 3–4.
15. Swinton, "What the Body Remembers."

BIBLICAL PERSPECTIVES: HEART AND MEMORY

As people who are caught up in God's bigger story,[16] memories of divine-human interaction and God's Word were engrained in *who* the research participants felt themselves to be. Rosemary's words reflected this when she said: "I love the Lord God with all my heart and all my soul."[17] Her words recalled Scripture, suggested her intentional present experience, and resonated with biblical understandings of memory. Such understandings shape the language of faith. Biblical perspectives on the meanings of memory have potential to illuminate the experience of these believers who live with dementia.

Old Testament Perspectives

The language of the Old Testament brings understandings that help us in our thinking about faith memory in dementia. Brevard Childs has highlighted the connections between the Hebrew concepts of memory (*zkr*) and the "heart" (*leb*).[18] The word for "heart" is sometimes translated as meaning the "inner man, mind, will, heart," signifying the core of what it is to be human.[19] The word for memory (*zkr*) signifies not merely cognitive activity of the brain enabling recall, but is associated with the whole person. Like the Old Testament understanding of the *wholeness* of the person relating to their identity, so these Hebrew words for "memory" and "heart" are also associated with the whole person—body, soul, and mind.[20] The Israelites' *remembering* of God at significant points in their history brought renewed trust in him, and hope for the future in the midst of loss, resulting in changed living.[21] The remembering of God in the Scriptures always involves an intentional turning towards him of the whole person—resulting in transformation. Such heart remembering is affirmed in the teaching of Jesus. To live in harmonious relationship with the divine (and others) is summed up in this call to *remember* God in loving him with heart, soul, and mind (Matt 22:37; Deut 6:5), as Rosemary's words reminded me.

---

16. See chapter 3, 47–48.
17. See, for example, Mark 12:30.
18. Childs, *Memory and Tradition*, 17–19.
19. Strong, "3820 *Leb*."
20. See chapter 3, 39–40.
21. Brueggemann, "Suffering Produces Hope," 96–99. See also, for example, the resolution of the Israelites to rededicate themselves to God during King Josiah's reign (2 Chr 34–35).

As God's people remember him in this essential way in the face of new circumstances, there is inevitably a radical redirecting of life and purpose.[22] The words of the research participants, in the light of their dementia, suggested this deliberate reframing of their lives in the light of dementia. Bill said, "This side of heaven that [dementia] is going to be part of my journey."

New Testament Perspectives

In Paul's writing, the Greek word for heart (*kardia*) still carries this sense of the core of inner being with its will and affectivity. But here, the heart is also the place where Christ dwells through the Spirit. Paul writes to the Ephesian church:

> I pray that, according to the riches of his glory, he may grant that you may be strengthened in your inner being with power through his Spirit, and that Christ may dwell in your hearts through faith, as you are being rooted and grounded in love. (Eph 3:16–17)

Paul's designation of the heart (*kardia*) as the locus of the Spirit's work is not made to differentiate it from the rest of the person, but, as N. T. Wright suggests, it is "the place from which life and energy go out to the whole of the rest of the person, body and mind included."[23] In participants' experience it is their rootedness *in Christ* that brings transformed living to the whole person, and to their impact on others (see Eph 3:14–21). Intriguingly, we might see in this a connection between the Hebrew understanding of memory and "the New Testament emphasis on belief and conversion."[24] As with the Hebrew understanding of memory (*zkr*), conversion also entails an intentional turning of the whole person towards Christ. And God the Holy Spirit, through whom the believer is born into God's family, is a key participant in this process. As Paul reminds Timothy, the Spirit's work is crucial in the believer's inhabiting of our collective memory as God's people: "Guard the good deposit . . . with the help of the Holy Spirit who lives in us" (2 Tim 1:14, NIVUK).

---

22. For example, in Nehemiah 8–10 the biblical narrative recalls the recommitment of the Israelites to God after their return from exile.
23. Wright, "Mind, Spirit, Soul and Body."
24. Keck, *Forgetting Whose We Are*, 50.

Memory of the Word

For the participants in this research, God's Word plays a significant part in their relationship with God and growth as disciples of Jesus: "I hear God through the Bible . . . I think more than any other place where I hear God," Jill said. Their stories were scattered with references to the words of Scripture, which have informed their lives and present experience:

> ROSEMARY: I've got [Bible] texts around me everywhere . . . They will come into my head and I'll say them: "You are my strength and my joy . . . you are my rock and my salvation" . . . even in the midst of difficulty . . . yes![25]

The story, words, and meaning of Scripture permeated their accounts—this was their script.

Dennis Lennon[26] has reflected on how this synchronicity of heart and memory resonates with evangelicalism's focus on God's Word. The Bible itself is a store of vital "radical and dangerous memory" which provides "memory-sight" and transforms our lives "because it invites us to faith."[27] To keep God's word "in your heart" means in your memory, reforming and informing the mind and heart. The stored memory of Scripture, written "on the tablet of your heart," means that "we become empowered . . . by our memories" in the present, to see as God sees. Lennon's exploration echoes Brueggemann, who has likened the Scriptures to a "compost pile" that is full of "generative material."[28] Whilst the traditional practice of daily, sequential Scripture reading is becoming more difficult for the participants, the Word in their hearts is funding their ongoing remembrance of God and bringing growth.

These understandings of the interplay between heart and memory resonate with the participants' rich accounts of their encounters with God, and these were bringing persistent transformation to their experience in the present. This relationship between memory and faith was having a growing significance for participants' reorientation of their faith in the new context of living with dementia.

---

25. Rosemary was referring to verses from the Psalms, for example: Psalm 27:1; Psalm 95:1.
26. Lennon, *Eyes of the Heart*, 84.
27. Lennon, *Eyes of the Heart*, 89.
28. Brueggemann, *Texts Under Negotiation*, 61.

FAITH-ED MEMORY

Faith brings a different perspective to memory. My question to Jess, "Do you feel that God is with you?" brings a feisty response: "Yes, I'm sure of that! And that's why the fact that I can't remember—my memory loss—doesn't matter."

As I listened to Jess and the other participants in the research, I became aware of how autobiographical and embodied memory were both significant in their experience of faith. The telling of their stories required our social interaction, facial expressions, and gestures adding significantly to our mutual understanding. Tears were shed, hands grasped in comfort. Then as we began to talk about the memories of their faith, there was this other dimension of felt awareness of the mysterious, divine, loving interaction both in the memories described and in their retelling. I noticed how *past*, pre-dementia experiences of encounter with God were radically affecting and transforming their living in the *present* with dementia. Andrew Root's writing (mentioned earlier) about his own encounter with God described something similar: a childhood experience of encounter with God had transformed his life, and led eventually to his notion of *Christopraxis*,[29] in which faith involves the experience of Christ's unexpected intervention in our lives, as well as our subsequent response to him. Memory and faith interweave—as I saw in the following recollections of encounter with God.

Encounters with God

For all of the research participants, there was a difference between knowing *about* God and commitment to relationship with Jesus.[30] For some, as characteristic of many Christians of an evangelical tradition,[31] this development had been marked by a conversion experience of being "born again," or another memorable encounter with God. As Root suggests, our faith reality is not only socially constructed; it also recognizes that divine intervention is a possibility—God intervenes. For some participants, churchgoing had been a familiar part of their lives from childhood, and adult faith commitment had arisen out of that background. Their stories and coming to a personal faith—in a variety of ways—had provided and created the context for their understanding of the advent of dementia in their lives.

---

29. Root, *Christopraxis*, 3–8.

30. See discussion of intrinsic and extrinsic faith e.g., 5, 23, 66.

31. Harris, "Beyond Bebbington," 204; McGrath, *Evangelicalism and the Future of Christianity*, 55–56.

Memories of God's faithfulness through difficult times were also helpful for present confidence in God and as the future was anticipated. These remembered encounters with God had had transformational impact for the participants' lives and continued to transform their experience in the present. They were eager to tell me their personal faith stories, revealing how these memories were funding experience of faith in the present. Let's listen again.

"So Engrained"

David had been brought up in a churchgoing family. He recognized that this was significant for his later and present faith commitment and understanding.

> DAVID: But I had that background . . . It's much easier if you have a background of churchgoing as a child . . . That core . . . of having that understanding of Jesus as a child, I think, is always there after that . . .

His memories suggested the importance of faith memory for his experience of faith in the present. But in spite of his background, David remembers a key time in his life in his twenties when faith began to make more sense and he made a personal commitment to Christ:

> DAVID: When I met Gail . . . it really was . . . she challenged me, she brought me to faith . . . I knew about Jesus, but I hadn't really taken it on board . . .

His words suggested that his present faith awareness had begun with his childhood experience, but then there was this subsequent sense of encounter with Jesus brought about through his friendship with Gail. "Knowing Jesus" seemed to be the core of what it meant to have faith. He felt that this relationship would endure as his dementia progressed: ". . . so now engrained in what I believe . . . because it's so all-encompassing." It was not a cerebral belief alone, but something which was "engrained" throughout his whole person.

"It Is Something That Doesn't Leave You . . ."

Ron had grown up in the chapel culture of South Wales in the middle years of the twentieth century. He was further on in his experience of living with dementia than some of the other participants and, as a result, his words and recall were not always fluent, but his experience of knowing God was communicated powerfully. His parents' faith had been nominal:

> RON: . . . My mother and father wasn't . . . they were churchgoers . . . but never professed much on it . . . It was I . . . of the family . . . actually participated in the church . . .

I noticed that even in childhood, though his parents were not committed to faith, Ron had *chosen* to take part in local church activity. His independence was also evident in his decision as a young adult to go to Rhodesia [Zimbabwe], where he lived and worked for several years. It was here that he went to an evangelistic meeting at which Billy Graham was speaking, and he made a personal faith commitment to Christ. He described his experience as being "born again":

> RON: Well, that was where I got converted . . . "born again." And the thing is that . . . it's a lovely feeling . . . It was a personal thing . . . that I said to the Lord, "Thanks a lot," . . . because I always had someone that I could turn to . . . There's . . . there is no satisfaction in the way that you would get if you wasn't "born again" . . . and it is something that doesn't leave you . . .

It was a moving testimony. Sitting there in his armchair, Christian books to hand—Ron was near to the end of his life.[32] Decades after that experience of being "born again," his relationship with Christ was sustaining him now through dementia—and prompting him to share this experience with others.

"Living Words"

For others, like Ron, faith in early childhood was also "nominal." Bill had been taken to church regularly, although he didn't recall his family having a strong sense of personal faith.

> BILL: I was Church of England to start off with . . . I just went because I was taken. I went to Sunday school, sang in the choir.

As a teenager, a cousin had invited Bill to go with him to a Christian youth club. He recalled a time of conversion that came about through a leader of this youth group:

> BILL: They were living words as opposed to what I perceived to be dead words . . . It was through him, I think, that I made

---

32. Sadly, Ron passed away whilst this research was being written up.

> that "conversion" . . . from being a pew-sitter to somebody who actually had a faith . . . that was the point I went . . . believed in Jesus as being my Savior . . .

The "dead words" of his past experience were replaced with "living words" which led to personal faith and a sense of relationship with Jesus and dependence on him ("my Savior").

Like David's experience, Bill's coming to personal faith was triggered through relationship with others. For him also it was a transformational moment of meeting with Christ. Now, in these later years, it is his relationship with Christ that is the context for his living with dementia.

"My Near-Death Experience"

Rosemary's coming to personal and active faith had not been straightforward. She recalled a Christian upbringing in the Plymouth Brethren—and a teenage trip to a Billy Graham meeting, at which she had "gone forward":

> . . . It was so joyful . . . this wonderful and handsome American . . . And he would draw you forward . . . to the front and . . . It was very emotional and I do have . . . feelings about that.

However, in adulthood, life had brought various challenges, and for a time, she had moved away from active commitment to faith. Then, ten years before our conversation, serious illness had brought fresh encounter with God:

> ROSEMARY: I was sixty-eight when I had my near-death experience—exactly ten years ago . . . I'm . . . coming up to seventy-eight. It's ten years ago and all that time it's been a time of learning from God and being shown . . . every day something happens . . .

A separate conversation with Rosemary's family confirmed her account of this changed relationship with God, brought about through the experience of her illness. Her daughter told me that when she came round from her coma she was "completely different . . . talking about God a lot more, like she does today . . . about Jesus . . . how he does things for her and her relationship with . . ." Now, living in her dementia, Rosemary expressed a sense of faith that was vibrant and energetic, sustaining her evident sense of joy and peace.

"Always, Always"

Alice's experience of God had begun in another way. For her it was an ongoing encounter. Her family had been deeply committed in their faith; her parents had always been involved in various kinds of Christian ministry. She had always had a sense of relationship with God.

> ALICE: Always, always. Even when I was little . . . I can still remember that God was the center of our home. And talking with God about everything. He wasn't a member of the family in the sense he was equal with us . . . he was . . . always in charge . . . in love . . . and . . . yes, always.

Her faith hadn't been founded in churchgoing, but in its sense of relationship with God who was in control, "in love." Her sense of the reality of God's presence in her family's life was embedded in her daily existence. This deeply held belief in a loving, but authoritative, God was evident in how she was responding to her dementia in the present.

Tough Times Remembered

Some of the participants talked in detail about their memories of difficult times in their lives and of God's intervention in these. These memories seem to have prepared them in different ways for funding their faith in God as they were enduring the challenges that dementia was bringing.

"I Had a Vision"

For Jess, unlike other participants, churchgoing was *not* part of her early experience. Habitual faith practice had not been instrumental in shaping her adult faith. She described instead a difficult early life:

> JESS: I had . . . a difficult childhood . . . [says quietly] I don't want to remember it actually [chuckles] . . .

In the light of this—Jess recounted her experience of a transformative encounter with God as a teenager:

> JESS: No, I'm not a Christian because I go to church. I'm a Christian because when I was about fifteen I had a vision. And it changed me completely . . . The trigger that makes me know this is that I stopped swearing. I never swore after that.

Her early awareness of God had come from outside of herself and her situation. She felt that God had intervened to help her at a difficult time. The encounter was remembered as a significant turning point in her life that changed her behavior; now, it reminds her of God's faithfulness to her when she was growing up. Later in life, Jess and her husband were both drawn further into faith through their experiences as they travelled with the army.

"I'm . . . Grateful for All These Dreadful Experiences"

In contrast to Jess's experience, Alice's family had had a profound commitment to faith, yet the experience of adversity was also formative throughout her childhood. Her mother had died when she was a child.

> ALICE: When my mother died, my father . . . it was very sudden . . . struggled a bit to start with and he gave up being a Baptist minister . . . Initially we [Alice and her sisters] were distributed round the family—grandparents and aunts and uncles.

In spite of the disruption brought to her family life by the death of her mother, memories of Sunday school and church remained unquestioned, positive aspects of normal life.

Gratitude and faith marked her responses to the difficult memories of her childhood and youth. With reference to a particular, unhappy incident, she said this:

> ALICE: Because if I hadn't had that I wouldn't have understood people who have these dreadful experiences . . . And, in a sense, I've always said my shattered remains were nailed to the cross . . . and . . . I'm very grateful for all these dreadful experiences.

Alice chose to resolve the "dreadful experiences" in her life and their destructive results positively, to help her to understand the suffering of others, and by perceiving them as caught up in the suffering of Christ on the cross. Coping with adversity in this way and her choice to be thankful seemed to have equipped Alice for later events in her life, and now at this stage of her life, in her experience of living with dementia.

Other Ways of Remembering

As I listened and reflected on this funding of memory that happens in a variety of ways within embodied, relational contexts, its power is disclosed in the lives of these Christians. And, with our faith-ed perspective, I notice this further dimension of God's intervening life and grace.

"Music . . . Brings . . . That Peaceful Sense of Joy"

Today the connections that music and singing bring are widely recognized as significant for those living with dementia.[33] For Christians, the power of Christian songs and hymns with the words they bring to memory can be transformative. Rosemary recounts how she often sings whilst walking:

> ROSEMARY: Music, songs, anything that . . . it just brings you into that peaceful sense of joy and happiness . . . I just love singing those choruses and hymns . . . I don't care even if somebody is walking past me, I'll still sing, "Praise my soul the King of heaven" . . . and know all the words . . . you've learnt them, and they come back to you.[34]
> 'TRICIA: Do you think that's about memory, or is it about your experience of God as well?
> ROSEMARY: I think it's what your memory has deeply taken in from the early days . . . As you're going through the dementia you come more and more, come back into . . . and it means more to you all those early influences are so . . .

Rosemary recognized that it was memory that had laid down the familiarity of the music and words of the hymns, but once they were brought to her *present* awareness, she felt that they "mean[t] more" to her now, bringing peace and joy in the present moment.

Naomi Feil's work has demonstrated powerfully how words and music of remembered familiar songs can bring faith response even in those living in the advanced stages of dementia.[35] Pondering an example of her work, John Swinton comments that this shared experience of singing songs of praise acts as a "holy conduit for the movement of the Spirit as it draws the memory of Jesus gently through Gladys' heart."[36] Yes! Jesus loves me . . .

---

33. For example: https://musicfordementia.org.uk/.
34. "Praise My Soul the King of Heaven," Henry Francis Lyte, 1834.
35. See https://www.youtube.com/watch?v=CrZXz10FcVM.
36. Swinton, *Becoming Friends of Time*, 149.

"It's Given Me a Memory . . . Church"

Even though all the participants in the research knew that memory and concentration were beginning to cause them difficulties, they spoke of the importance of being with other believers. Matthew, Bill, and David all talked appreciatively about the value of being with their church community. As Rosemary said: "It's the collective, the getting together and having fellowship . . . that matters." And Jess spoke of the importance of going to church services even if she couldn't remember details later. Ron's words similarly picked up on the importance of being with other believers. He puzzled over the nature of his memory and his faith: "That is dementia . . . a memory is there and it's not there," but his continued involvement in church was helping him to access this faith memory:

> RON: It's given me a memory which I haven't got, but by going to church, it has . . . it's there . . .

The memory prompt of going to church translates into Ron's *present* experience: "it's there . . ."

However, as some of the participants' accounts showed, church and faith practices were becoming more difficult for those living independently.[37] Perhaps the possibility of memory funding faith is less easily available for those who live alone.

Remembering Jesus Together

As *practice* of faith becomes more challenging for all of those who live with dementia, the significance of the Jesus-remembering community becomes especially significant. The Lord's Supper initiated by Jesus himself—". . . do this in remembrance of me" (1 Cor 11:2–26)—provides us with powerful memory cues of Jesus' death and resurrection, and of our being part of the body of Christ. I was interested that participants in my research chose not to talk very much about this.[38] But as some have found, this shared, physical remembering brings for many a profound experience of connection with God. Perhaps that is especially true for those in later dementia who choose to receive communion—I remember the wonder of a whispered "Amen" from those who were mostly silent.

Such communal remembering of Jesus, whatever our tradition, is at the heart of biblical faith and our life together in Christ. The Lord's Supper

---

37. See chapter 5, 73–76, 80.
38. See Alice's comments, chapter 5, 80.

recalls God's story and embodies his life and presence with us. The invitation from Jesus himself calls each individual—whatever their capacities or status—to take their place in the remembering body of Christ.[39] Physical presence together and sharing of bread and wine evoke the senses and time-travelling memories, which connect us to the presence of Jesus now. This shared meal is hopeful for Christians who live with dementia, bringing not only assurance of mutual dependence and support, but connection with Christ in this present moment of collective remembering.[40]

Memory and Faith Interweave

The experiences of interweaving memory and faith—both individually and with others—are not surprising if we remember that we are integrated, "body-and-soul" creatures, created by God, with our part to play in his heart-and-memory story.[41] Having ordered autobiographical memory of ourselves isn't what makes us human. We are emotional, relational, embodied—and then there is this further spiritual dimension, the intervention of God himself in our being. We see a significant working example of this when Jesus re-calls Peter, prompting him to remember their earlier meeting on the shore of Lake Galilee (John 21; Mark 1:16–18).

During my conversations with Rosemary, Ron, and the others about memory and faith, I became aware that my prompts to *remember* God were having *present* impact. For example, Rosemary's irrepressible expression of her faith in God as she was speaking to me concluded with a firm "Amen"; Bill's description of his experience became a prayer addressed to Jesus ("I just want to be a follower of you"); Jill paused mid-sentence to remind herself that God would keep her in his peace in future trauma ("He keeps his word . . . [then quietly to self:] he keeps his promise"). Sometimes, as David Keck has suggested, to remember God seems to be synonymous with belief.[42] It is as though the experience and its memory are "interwoven in all aspects of our relationship with God."[43] Reminiscent of these Christians' account of their faith memories, he suggests that to remember God results in behavior which "resembles an experience of faith . . . Remembering the

---

39. Saunders, *Dementia*, 19.

40. For further discussion about sharing of communion or the Lord's Supper with people who live with dementia, see Mast, *Second Forgetting*, 139–41.

41. See chapter 3, 47–48, 50.

42. Keck, *Forgetting Whose We Are*, 48–49.

43. Keck, *Forgetting Whose We Are*, 52.

divine" is not "a neutral, dispassionate epistemological process," but combines "both cognitive and affective elements."[44]

The remembering of each of the research participants was not so much about recalled events on a linear timeline, but about a state of being which was encompassing, and making sense of their faith experience in the present moment. Memory and faith interwove, undermining the specificity of autobiographical time. Other research has revealed a similar interweaving:

> Their spiritual life was not separate from life. In this way, the experience of spirituality seemed to be woven into the fabric of their life, part of them, and therefore dependable and sure.[45]

Such interweaving of memory and faith seemed to be funding participants' personal experience of relationship with God, both in the present and in their imaginative anticipation and preparation for future living with their illness. The transforming impact of hope will be explored further in chapter 9.

MEMORY FUNDING FAITH . . .

In this chapter we have reflected on how faith is immanent in both our remembered autobiographical stories, and in our embodied living. As people of God's book, there is a further spiritual dimension as memories of the heart interweave with faith, and God himself intervenes to fund our faith, keeping our eyes fixed on Jesus (even as we live with dementia). As Rosemary said, "God's . . . not forgotten me."

For Further Reflection . . .

- What might the significance of the words of Isaiah 49:15–16 be for those you know who live with dementia?
- What do you know of their stories of faith and life?
- What "fragile clues" do you see to their faith, in spite of their illness?
- How might you build on these in ways that may help to "fund" their faith for this journey?

---

44. Keck, *Forgetting Whose We Are*, 48–49.
45. Dalby et al., "Lived Experience," 82.

8

Growing Faith

"I know Jesus . . . I long to know him more in my illness."

Reflectively—almost to herself—Jill says quietly, deliberately, and with resolution: "I know Jesus . . . I long to know him more in my illness." Pause for a moment to consider this woman who is beginning to understand the challenges of dementia for her life and faith. She is not only speaking about her past and present experience of faith. Courageously, she asserts a longing (and expectation) that her relationship with Christ will *grow* in the future as she lives with this illness. How could this be? Whilst the typical narrative of the progression of dementia is one of "decline and loss," Scripture and lived experience of faith suggest a different story.[1] As pastoral ministry reveals, this illness, astonishingly, brings opportunity for spiritual growth.[2]

In the face of dementia, Peter's injunction to early believers—to keep on growing "in the grace and knowledge of our Lord and Saviour Jesus Christ" (2 Pet 3:18)—presents a double-edged challenge to the church. There is the question of ongoing faith growth for those who are experiencing dementia;

---

1. Brockmeier, "Questions of Meaning," 86.
2. See Kevern, "Dementia and Spirituality"; Williams, "Growing Faith in Dementia;" Crowther, *Sustaining Persons*, 182–84.

and then, for other members of the church too. What about our own growth in faith in the face of dementia? The pattern of orientation and disorientation seems to lead inevitably to a reorientation of faith.[3] Such reorientation does not "mean going back to the ways things were before."[4]

As I talked with Jill and the others, I became aware of their spiritual growing, even as the shadows of dementia were extending across their lives. How could it be that this transforming faith was *growing*—even in dementia? And, how might the church walk with them towards a mutual growth? In this chapter, I reflect on this experience of growing faith, and explore it further particularly in the light of Paul's words to the suffering church at Rome (Rom 5:1–5).[5]

FAITH THAT GROWS . . .

At the beginning of my research, I had wondered whether Christians with dementia might feel more distant from their faith. However, for the participants in my research this was emphatically not the case. Their faith did not seem under threat because of dementia.[6] This is not to minimize the struggles of life with dementia that, for some, may *include* doubt and questioning. But for Matthew, Jill, David, Rosemary, Alice, Jess, Ron, and Bill their faith increasingly seemed to be providing an anchor in their lives.[7] In fact, they spoke about how the cognitive loss brought by their dementia was bringing a greater intensity to their sense of secure relationship with God: "Faith is growing . . ."

As I thought about their relationship with God, and talked with them further, it became clear that in the midst of their experience of dementia, faith was becoming, as Matthew said, "stronger." David, Alice, and Rosemary each talked about there being a greater sense of closeness to God, in spite of—or perhaps because of—a lessening of their own capacities. Their apparent growth in faith may seem counterintuitive. It wasn't that faith was a resource for coping in the present moment; the participants talked rather

---

3. Brueggemann, *Praying the Psalms*, 3; Brueggemann, *Spirituality of the Psalms*, viii.; see chapter 1, 10–11.

4. See Swinton's discussion of this in relation to other mental health challenges in *Finding Jesus*, 108.

5. Material in this chapter draws on my article, "Growing Faith in Dementia."

6. See discussion of doubt in Williams, *What Happens to Faith?*, 53–54.

7. Drawing on personal email exchange with Jon Stuckey, speaking about his own research in the area of faith and dementia. Used with permission.

of *relationship* with God which was continuing to grow: "Nearer my God to thee...," Rosemary said.[8]

At first, we may be surprised by their words. The challenges of dementia are of a particularly disorientating nature and these were evident in some of our exchanges—increasing short-term forgetfulness, diminishing capacity for concentration, and some confusion in spoken communication. But relationship with God does not end with a diagnosis. Although "spiritual growth" may need to be perceived differently, still it seemed possible for these disciples of Jesus who are living with dementia.

A BIBLICAL MODEL FOR GROWING FAITH

In the Old Testament, the emergence of hope out of suffering is clear in Israel's remembering of their faithful God.[9] In the New Testament, suffering and difficulties are assumed as a normal part of the life of faith in the communion of Christ (1 Pet 4:12–13). The following words of Paul, written to the suffering Christians in Rome, might seem to suggest a model for spiritual growth—from the disorientation of suffering to reorientation of joyful hope in Christ:[10]

> ... through our Lord Jesus Christ ... we boast ["rejoice," ESV] in our hope of sharing the glory of God. And not only that, but we also boast ["rejoice"] in our sufferings, knowing that suffering produces endurance, and endurance produces character, and character produces hope, and hope does not disappoint us, because God's love has been poured into our hearts through the Holy Spirit that has been given to us. (Rom 5:1–5)

Resonating with this Scripture, as I reflected on the participants' words, I perceived a *growing* experience of relationship with God in the midst of their suffering, sustained by faith's onward path of hope in Christ. In their words—in the light of Paul's encouragement to the early Roman Christians—decisive signposts for this journey of growing faith emerge. These do not signify a linear progression, but are characteristics that interweave through Paul's words and in the participants' faith. Key markers for this journey seemed to be: perception of God's purpose, a relational trust in God, endurance of suffering—and then faith's trajectory of hope that encompasses this lived experience (more about this in chapter 9).

8. Words of hymn. Lyrics, Sarah Adams, 1841.
9. Brueggemann, "Suffering Produces Hope."
10. Brueggemann, *Spirituality of the Psalms*, viii, 7–15.

Perception of God's Purpose

Meaning or Purpose?

In some models of spiritual growth, the finding of meaning is highlighted as a key goal, enabling transcendence of loss and disabilities, leading to hope.[11] Elizabeth MacKinlay and Corinne Trevitt's reflection on the experience of dementia reflects such models.[12] Whilst they were writing about a broader area of spirituality than the specific focus of this book, their work suggests that the experiencing of dementia may be "the starting point for spiritual growth," bringing a deeper sense of relationship with God.[13] In some respects, such a model might seem to mirror what is happening for the participants in this research. However, in the case of these Christians living with dementia, the accounts of their experience suggested that the finding of meaning—or the failure to do so—was not at stake. Their faith in Jesus had priority. This places them—just as Paul's listeners—firmly in the context of God's story within the body of Christ, not their own. There is a theological question here about the understanding of God's purpose; but the pastoral question concerns acceptance of this, enabling transcendence of despair and the envisioning of hope. How might we help those who are beginning this journey and walk with them?

Made for a Purpose

It might seem strange that those involved in this study had a strong sense that dementia had purpose in their lives, and that its arrival in their lives had meaning that they wanted to understand.[14] As committed Christians, their seeking of *purpose*, even whilst living through the disorientation of dementia, made sense in the light of their belief in being created by a sovereign God. For example, as Jill said: "If God has asked me to have dementia . . . then I know he will be there." She understood her purpose as being set within the purposes of God.

---

11. Erikson's model of psychosocial stages of aging, for example, show the possibility that transcendence leads to hope (Erikson, *Life Cycle Completed*). See also Frankl, *Man's Search for Meaning*; Fowler, *Stages of Faith*.

12. MacKinlay and Trevitt, *Finding Meaning*, 86.

13. MacKinlay and Trevitt, *Finding Meaning*, 86. See also chapter 2, 23–24.

14. The seeking of ultimate meaning is generally regarded as fundamental to human growth. See for example Frankl, *Man's Search for Meaning*; MacKinlay and Trevitt, *Finding Meaning*, 15, 20–24.

Returning to the biblical story, in the creation accounts we see Adam in a working relationship with God (Gen 1–2), within the boundaries God had provided (Gen 2:15, NIVUK). In the New Testament, the disciples were sent out by Jesus to partner with God in his mission to the world (see Matthew 28: 19, 20; Acts 1:8). For Jill and the others, their unwelcome illness is part of the bigger story and plan of God's will and purposes. They seemed to have no doubt about this in their experience of developing dementia. David said: "Faith says to me, I can make a difference to other people." Alice's words reflected the broader orientation of her faith life: "My purpose is to please him, not anybody else." Such understanding and certainty may be ongoing signs of growth for these disciples, and perhaps also for that of the wider faith community as it witnesses and acknowledges God's sovereign purposes.

Choosing to Accept

Alice's words point us to the assumption underlying Paul's words to the suffering Roman Christians: the loving purpose of God's sovereign plan (Rom 5:1–2). Whatever changes dementia was bringing to their lives, the participants' sense of acceptance of their illness was a clear marker of their growth, caught up in this sense of being involved in God's hopeful purposes for their lives: "I will accept it," Jill said decisively. Here and now, living with dementia, there is challenge for those who are followers of Jesus. In Gethsemane, Jesus faced the climactic moment of acceptance of his Father's will. In the context of dementia, as Peter Kevern has reflected, Jesus' acceptance reiterated his commitment to the enacting of his Father's purposes, which involved the way to the cross.[15] In his Gethsemane prayer Christ was not searching for meaning, but was identifying with and accepting God's purpose for his life (Matt 26:39).

Writing of their own experiences of dementia, both Christine Bryden and Robert Davis describe how choosing to accept God's purpose was transformational.[16] Davis speaks of new understanding of the words, "Thy will be done," which had enabled him to find peace in his life as he trusted in Christ. Similarly, it was these research participants' identification with and "in Christ" that enabled their own crucial step of acceptance.

Paul's encouragement to the suffering church—"All things work together . . . according to his purpose" (Rom 8:28)—is no triumphalist

---

15. Kevern, "Sharing the Mind of Christ," 419.

16. Bryden, *Dancing with Dementia*,169–70; Davis, *My Journey into Alzheimer's Disease*, 56–58.

assertion, but a costly and courageous statement of trust: "I choose . . . instead of raging wildly at the things I have lost. I must thank God . . ."[17] The transcendence of suffering, following from acceptance of God's will and purpose, was reflected in the participants' accounts of their experience. Alice's words became a prayer addressed to God in the midst of our conversation:

> ALICE: Lord, this is your gift for here . . . Therefore I will accept it as this gift and with your help I will do what I can in order to reflect your glory in it.

This journey of acceptance may be a painful one both for those who live with dementia and their loved ones and fellow believers. Yet, lived out commitment to God, in spite of the evident difficulties this illness was bringing, asks questions of our own faithful *acceptance* of God's purposes. As we serve Christ in our brothers and sisters, how might we more effectively *accompany* those who are beginning this journey?

Reframing Purpose

The advent of dementia in the life of a Christian unavoidably shifts perception of one's own place in God's purposes. God's story and God's faithful covenantal love have set the grand narrative for the believer. The immediate contextual question that underlies the participants' responses is not, therefore, "Why would a loving God allow this to happen to me?"[18] Rather, it is, "What is God's purpose for my life in this new context?" This implicit sense of the participants' experience of dementia is within God's loving hold on their lives, and is evident in their words (Rosemary: "What will be, will be . . . when it comes, in your time, Lord, and your will"). It is not "that God is indifferent to the suffering that dementia brings." Rather, it has purpose both for the person living with dementia and others—albeit "a mystery," it is "firmly rooted in God's creative and redemptive actions in and for the world."[19] This energizing new sense of purpose was reflected in my encounters with participants and their words. For example, whatever happened in this stage of her life, Rosemary asserted that she just wanted "to bring glory to him." Recognizing the reality of her dementia, Alice said:

---

17. Davis, *My Journey into Alzheimer's Disease*, 57.
18. See chapter 6, 84–87.
19. Swinton, *Dementia*, 184.

> ALICE: My purpose is to please him, not anybody else. And to please him is to, like the boy with the loaves and fishes, just giving him the little that I have.[20]

Into this arena of acceptance of God's purpose, the transformative phenomenon of trust in God's faithfulness is disclosed.

Trust in God

Trusting in God's Love

Returning to Paul's words to the Roman Christians, I notice that this ability to transcend suffering is embraced in the assurance of the Trinitarian love of God, through Christ, and the gift of the Holy Spirit (Rom 5:1–2, 5).[21] The participants' words reveal not a reliance on propositional truth, but on being held within this loving relationship with God: "It's not some theory," Rosemary asserts. Her faith is about "the God who I trust and believe in"; "God is with me," says David; ". . . a relationship, not a 'doing,'" Alice reiterates. As the symptoms of dementia advance, John Swinton suggests that this word "trust" has potential as providing a way of understanding the faith of those who are living with cognitive incapacity.

Dependence involved in *trusting God* becomes the primary ingredient of faith, which is a simple reliance on God's relationship with us.[22] So, Rosemary said:

> ROSEMARY: I can accept it [dementia] through God being with . . . as my mind becomes less intellectualized and able to . . . I shall be more filled with the feeling of the love of God.

The participants' experience affirmed that it was their illness which was resulting in this increasing trustful dependence on him. Alice made this point: "I am closer to God because there's less of me." As Christians of an evangelical tradition, despite proclaimed dependence on God's grace, we may sometimes appear to default to an underlying dependence on the ability to articulate doctrinal propositions. Yet such a dependence becomes increasingly difficult for those who live with dementia. To be a disciple of Jesus—whether or not we live with dementia—means a relinquishing of any trust in our own abilities or status.[23] John Dunlop writes:

20. See John 6:8–9.
21. See chapter 3, 43; chapter 4, 57.
22. Swinton, *Becoming Friends of Time*, 102–3.
23. Hauerwas, *Peaceable Kingdom*, 86.

> Trust is not just a cognitive activity . . . We trust when we stop wrestling with our questions and rest in God. Jesus invited people to come to him as little children.[24]

None of us are able or need to understand everything. In their illness, each of the participants, knowing that their cognitive capacity was changing, expressed an increasing sense of their faith as being this trustful dependence on God.

How might such trust/faith challenge our own understanding? Perhaps sometimes our unintentional emphases on cognitive understanding excludes those who Christ welcomes. In seeking to learn from those who live with dementia, their voices may ask us to redress the balance between emphases on propositional truth as opposed to this experience of relational trust. As the shadows of dementia intrude on these believers' lives, how might we support them in receiving the lightening grace of Jesus?[25]

Trust in God's Faithful Memory

This pattern of suffering that impels believers to find themselves closer to God is a familiar biblical one. Trust in God's faithful memory is underwritten by its foundation in the biblical story of covenantal relationship between God and his people. In situations of extremity, the Israelites found themselves recalled to God. In the exile of Babylon, as they remembered God, their tears mixed with songs. Walter Brueggemann points to their *trust* in the covenant faithfulness and steadfast love of God with his people:[26]

> Know therefore that the Lord your God is God, the faithful God who maintains covenant loyalty with those who love him and keep his commandments, to a thousand generations. (Deut 7:9)

It might seem, as we witness the anguish and sadness brought by dementia, that in the face of human pain and struggle, God's sovereignty is in tension with his fidelity to his people.[27] However, in this fallen, broken world, as Brueggemann has suggested, God's sovereignty insists on a committed engaging of his covenant partners (his people) in a long-term perspective on *his* purposes ("He allows things in this broken world," Alice). Yet there is also the certainty that "God is with me" (Rosemary). As

---

24. Dunlop, *Finding Grace*, 162.
25. Williams, "Growing Faith in Dementia."
26. Brueggemann, "Suffering Produces Hope."
27. Brueggemann, *Unsettling God*, 63.

I witness the faith of the Christians involved in this research—"Stronger!" says Matthew, through tears—I understand that something miraculous and transformative is happening in the midst of their trouble. Such trust brings assurance that "God is doing something new that is congruent with God's past actions."[28]

As explored in the previous chapter, memories of God's past faithfulness in participants' own individual lives were building their faith in the present, bringing assurance for an unseen future: "He's never deserted me. He keeps his word . . . his promises" (Jill); "He loves me" (Alice). The writer to the Hebrews sums up the continuing promise of God to his people: "I will never leave you or forsake you" (Heb 13:5). These perceptions of purpose and trust in God were enabling endurance, in the light of hope in Christ (Rom 5:2–3).

Endurance under Pressure

"Endurance" in Paul's understanding (sometimes translated "perseverance"[29]) is a key word that informs our understanding of the suffering and the believer's response to it (Rom 5:3–4). The New Testament Greek word for this (*hypomone*) has the sense of endurance whilst living under pressure.[30] Of course, diagnosis of dementia acknowledges a chronic illness that is not a passing interlude: "Dementia is not just an end stage, it is a journey . . . There are many steps along the way."[31] It requires endurance, and needs the support of others in Christ's body, the community that Paul addresses in these verses as "we." The local church must also *endure* for the length of this journey. Or, will the absence of those who suffer bring forgetfulness?

As we listen to Ron, Alice, and the others, we discover a further element in their experience of growing faith: it is characterized by joy and hope.

---

28. Brueggemann, "Suffering Produces Hope," 98.

29. For example, see Romans 5:3–4 (compare NRSVA and NIVUK translations).

30. Stott, *Message of Romans*, 141–42. The same New Testament Greek word is used for "endurance" in 2 Corinthians 1:6, NIVUK. See also Scripture4All, "Romans 5" and "2 Corinthians"; Cranfield, *Romans*, 103–6; Dunn, *Romans 1–8*, 264–65; Fitzmyer, *Romans*, 395–98.

31. Bryden, *Dancing with Dementia*, 40, 48.

Rejoicing in Suffering

Alongside the accounts of the shadows of dementia,[32] these stories of experience were marked by "rejoicing" (Rom 5:2, ESV) and thankfulness:

> RON: I'll never lose that joy, but I have lost my memory.
> ROSEMARY: I'm so grateful for what God's offered me and given me that I can relax and just say, "What will be, will be . . . in your time Lord and your will."

At first glance one might think this is a mystery (or even miraculous).[33] Yet others researching these questions have also found that joy and thankfulness seem to be part of the Christian's response to the suffering of dementia.[34] It is as though *acceptance* of being within God's plan enables a sense of security.[35] John Stott's comments on Romans 8:17 bring further illumination:

> The recognition that there is a divine rationale behind suffering [brings reassurance]. . . . We are co-heirs with Christ, if indeed we share in his sufferings in order that we may also share in his glory.[36]

The participants' joy and thankfulness echoes Brueggemann's account of reorientation in the psalms where praise results from acknowledging and accepting the will of a sovereign God, and from the affirmation of trust in his faithfulness to them.[37] This movement of interweaving acceptance, thankfulness, and even joy is reflected in the words of Alice:

> ALICE: Thank you Lord, this is your gift for here . . . therefore . . . I will do what I can in order to reflect your glory in it.

Above all, this mystery of joy in suffering takes us once more to the Christian's implicit sense of the presence of Christ in their lives, and to his suffering on the cross. This paradox of joy within suffering should not surprise us. As John Swinton recognizes, the presence of Jesus *is* joy—and suffering is an integral part of that joy: "Joy is the key point of resistance *within* the struggle."[38] Echoing Paul's words in Romans, James writes this:

---

32. See chapter 6.
33. Brueggemann, "Suffering Produces Hope," 98.
34. Goldsmith, "Tracing Rainbows through the Rain," 132.
35. Katsuno, "Personal Spirituality," 325.
36. Stott, *Message of Romans*, 141.
37. Brueggemann, *Spirituality of the Psalms*, 46–74.
38. Swinton, *Finding Jesus*, 80–82.

> Consider it pure joy, my brothers and sisters, whenever you face trials of many kinds, because you know that the testing of your faith produces perseverance [endurance]. Let perseverance [endurance] finish its work so that you may be mature and complete. (Jas 1:2–4)

And, as Alice's words suggest, her joy in her suffering is a gift—an aspect of the growing fruit of the Spirit (Gal 5:22–33). This joy is also inherently hopeful—it is eschatological, looking beyond time:[39] As Paul writes, "We rejoice in hope of the glory of God" (Romans 5:2, ESV).

But before this hope is fully realized, Paul's model suggests a further function of the endurance of sufferings in our lives here on earth. This joy—in spite of suffering—is *part* of a maturing towards the hope of faith which does not disappoint (see Rom 5:3–5): "endurance produces character, and character produces hope." These disciples of Jesus were growing in their faith.

Growing More . . .

To speak of those who are living with dementia as growing spiritually[40] might seem difficult to envisage—even inappropriate. Yet, being conformed to the likeness of Christ is for *all* who are called by him (Rom 8:29); and this did not seem unimaginable for the participants in this study. David said that his faith was "growing . . . much more of a closeness"; Rosemary seemed to feel that her life was increasingly being aligned with God's purposes, "if God had not willed me . . ."; and Jill simply stated that she longed to know Jesus more *in* her illness.

Even as cognitive awareness was diminishing, the participants' experience echoed Paul's words about the work of the Spirit in the believer's life—"in your inner being"—strengthening the awareness of Christ and his love (Eph 3:16–17). The word "character" following "endurance" suggests (as in James 1:3–4) a *maturing* towards this hope of faith: "endurance produces character, and character produces hope" (Rom 5:4). Scripture points to the evidence of love, joy, and peace arising from the presence of the Holy Spirit within the believer; the research participants' words and embodied expression resonate with this (Gal 5:22–23). Scripture suggests that it is in these fragile, human "jars of clay" that the life of Jesus is revealed (2 Cor 4:7–12).

---

39. Swinton, *Finding Jesus*, 82.
40. See, for example, Romans 8:29.

In their research, Elizabeth MacKinlay and Corinne Trevitt framed *finding meaning* as being one of the spiritual tasks of aging.[41] In the light of this, they proposed that this path of spiritual growth can lead to self-transcendence that, even in the tragedy of dementia, brings growth and enables hopefulness.[42] The evidence of the lives of the participants in my research bring their own particular affirmation of this. Pastoral theologian John Dunlop takes this further, suggesting that early dementia may provide a renewed opportunity to trust and rest in God.[43] He points to the ways in which the fruit of the Spirit are being developed in the lives of those who live with this illness, and the transformation of its struggles in ways which honor God. Such aspects of growth, together with their sense of purpose in serving God through their dementia, were characteristic of those involved in this research.

Their testimonies to growing faith pose questions to the community of Christ. How will the church continue to support and facilitate their spiritual growth? How will the church receive their Spirit-given gifts, so that together, as the body of Christ, we might be "rooted and built up in him and established in the faith, just as you were taught, abounding in thanksgiving" (Col 2:7)? In the here and now of living with dementia, what is it that is enabling these followers of Jesus to endure and live positively as they walk through this illness? Remember, we are not on our own.

Enabling Endurance

THE REMEMBERING COMMUNITY OF FAITH

Importantly, *endurance* of suffering in New Testament writing is within the context of the supporting, Jesus-remembering community,[44] the Spirit-indwelt body of Christ.[45] In a world that emphasizes individual and personal autonomy, dementia reminds us that as disciples of Jesus "we were all baptized into one body" (1 Cor 12:12–13). For the person with diminishing cognitive capacity, this assurance of corporate knowing enables the endurance of growing disciples.[46] Stanley Hauerwas, speaking of those who live with adversity, reminds us that those who suffered in the New Testament

---

41. MacKinlay and Trevitt, *Finding Meaning*, 23.
42. MacKinlay and Trevitt, *Finding Meaning*, 166.
43. Dunlop, *Finding Grace*, 162.
44. Hauerwas, *Peaceable Kingdom*, 98.
45. See chapter 3, 48–49.
46. Eastman, "Double Participation."

"had a community of care that has made it possible for them."[47] John Swinton challenges us:

> Response to the . . . existence of suffering was not to question God's goodness, love, and power, but rather to develop faithful forms of community within which the impact of . . . suffering could be absorbed, resisted, and transformed as they waited for God's return.[48]

The weight of suffering is to be mutually carried: together, we rejoice; together, we suffer (1 Cor 12:26a; 2 Cor. 1:3–7).[49]

Although the participants in the research knew that memory and concentration were beginning to cause them difficulties, they spoke of the importance of being with other believers. Kindness and welcome were remembered, even if the words of sermons were forgotten.[50] The experience of living with dementia highlights the importance of the corporate nature of the community of faith. Where believers have prized "individual privatized commitment over corporate participation,"[51] those living with dementia challenge the church itself to find new orientation, in its awareness of being as community, the body of Christ. Christine Bryden's words remind us:

> As I travel towards the dissolution of my self . . . my relationship with God needs increasing support from you, my other in the body of Christ . . . I need you to minister to me, to sing with me, pray with me, to be my memory for me.[52]

However, as attendance at church services and conversation with others becomes more difficult, the local church itself may, unintentionally, become deeply forgetful of its members who live with dementia.[53] Difficulties in this area were reflected in conversations with some research participants, particularly I noticed for those who were living independently. Their voices and experience are reminders that in this time of early to moderate dementia there is a special moment of opportunity for the church.[54] Christians living with dementia are able, in some measure, to express their present needs, to prepare for, and to anticipate what might be helpful in their ongoing

---

47. Hauerwas, *Naming the Silences*, 53.
48. Swinton, *Raging with Compassion*, 35.
49. See Crowther, *Sustaining Persons*, 167.
50. See chapter 5, 74, 77; chapter 7, 114.
51. Kent, "Embodied Evangelicalism," 108.
52. Bryden and MacKinlay, "Dementia: A Spiritual Journey," 74.
53. Mast, *Second Forgetting*, 105.
54. For example, Bute, "My Glorious Opportunity," 23.

experience of trust in God. Dianne Crowther, in her exploration of spiritual care for those with dementia, speaks of the necessity of the local church's solidarity with those who live with this illness.[55]

The challenges raised by the shadows of dementia can find response in and through the community of faith.[56] Within the body of Christ, with its mutual reverence and sharing of one another's burdens, there is the potential to enable perseverance in faith "until he comes" (1 Cor 11:26). But, of course, this human community of faith may sometimes fail. God, in his mysterious mercy, has provided another way for enabling the endurance of suffering too.

THE PRESENCE OF THE HOLY SPIRIT

As dementia progresses, knowing *about* God may become more difficult, but the Spirit within the believer seems to be ever reminding them of God's attentive presence ("Oh . . . the presence . . . is always there," Ron).

In Paul's understanding of suffering, its endurance (sustained by hope) is enabled by God's love and mediated through the indwelling Spirit: "God's love has been poured into our hearts through the Holy Spirit" (Rom 5:5–6). Reflecting on this, John Stott draws out two reasons for the believer's awareness of God's love: the presence of the Holy Spirit, and the knowledge that God has demonstrated his love in giving his Son.[57] Stott emphasizes that this sense of God's presence is *dependent* on God's loving intervention:

> It is God's love for us, not ours for him, which is in mind . . .
> What the Holy Spirit does is to make us deeply and refreshingly aware that God loves us.

This is especially important as we think about those living with developing dementia: this is about the love of God *for* the believer, not dependent on *my* (or *their*) ability to love him. The sense of God's love and the resulting peace was expressed on several occasions in participants' words ("overwhelmed with love," Alice; "I have a kind of peace . . . I think it comes from God," Jill).

This confident dependence on God, expressed by the participants, emerges from the experience of their deeply engrained, "all-encompassing" faith.[58] Theologically, we understand that it is the Holy Spirit who is at work enabling this transcendent sense of relationship with God:

55. Crowther, *Sustaining Persons*, 167.
56. Hauerwas, *Naming the Silences*, 53.
57. Stott, *Message of Romans*, 143.
58. See chapter 7, 108.

> But you have received a spirit of adoption. When we cry, "Abba! Father!" it is that very Spirit bearing witness with our spirit that we are children of God, and if children, then heirs, heirs of God and joint heirs with Christ. (Rom 8:15–17)

In John's Gospel, Jesus assured his disciples of the Spirit's presence as the ultimate reminder of God and his words.

> The Advocate, the Holy Spirit ... will teach you everything, and remind you of all that I have said to you. Peace I leave with you; my peace I give to you. (John 14:26–27)[59]

When words go missing, the Spirit helps us in our weakness: "We do not know how to pray as we ought, but that very Spirit intercedes with sighs too deep for words" (Rom 8:26–27).[60] In this intimate work, there is comfort for those who are beginning to lose the language of words because of their dementia. For those who observe and care, there is a reminder here of the mysterious, unseen work of God's Spirit in those whose ability to remember is diminishing. Ron's words—"I haven't got a memory, but I have...."—recall this puzzle of cognitive decline alongside his "remembering" of God. As dementia progresses, knowing *about* God may become more difficult, but the Spirit within the believer reminds them of God's attentive presence and his knowing of them.

As we come alongside those living with dementia, we might find ourselves being channels for God's "comfort"; surprisingly, we might find that we also are recipients, humbled by the presence of Jesus in those who are living with dementia, bringing *us* his transforming hope:

> The hope of the glory of God ... does not disappoint us ... because God has poured out his love into our hearts by the Holy Spirit. (Rom 5:2 ,5, NIVUK)

HOPE THAT GROWS

The last of these key markers signaling faith growth in this journey through dementia is faith's hope: "I know where I'm going," says Ron. This hope—faith's horizon—threads through the circle of Paul's pastoral cycle of growth (Rom 5:1—5), and through the lives of Alice, Rosemary, Ron, Jill, Matthew, David, Bill, and Jess: "we boast in the hope of the glory of God ... and hope does not put us to shame" (Rom 5:2, 5, NIVUK). In fact, this future

---

59. See also Luke 12:12.
60. Mast, *Second Forgetting*, 67.

hope encompasses and permeates every other aspect of growth and life in the research participants' experience—and is strangely present in their lives now. We will explore this further in the following chapter as we reflect on their present-future hope in Christ.

GROWING FAITH . . .

At the beginning of this chapter, I asked how growth of faith could be possible in dementia. Our perspective on what this looks like in dementia may need to change. But as we have listened to the voices of these disciples of Jesus in the light of the Word, we have surely seen faith that is growing. We have become aware of their perception of God's purpose, and their decisive acceptance of that, even with thankfulness and rejoicing. We perceive their trust in God and in his faithfulness. We witness their endurance in the face of suffering and struggle, supported by communities of believers, enabled by the presence of the Holy Spirit. We have heard Jill's desire to know Jesus *more* in her illness. In the light of hope in Christ, a reorientation of faith was happening in this experience of dementia, bringing transforming spiritual growth.

For Further Reflection . . .

- Reflect on Paul's words in Romans 5:1–5. Imagine what these might mean for a Christian who lives with dementia.
- Remember those you know who are living with dementia. In what ways do you see faith growing in them?
- How might you and your church walk with one another on this journey?

9

Present-Future Hope

"... We shall all be changed."

"There is no fear through Jesus!" David's response firmly rebutted my question about whether his dementia has made him fearful. Theologically, he is right, of course—"perfect love drives out fear" (1 John 4:18). Being *in* Christ, there is no fear: we are forgiven; caught up in his eternal love, we are safe. There may be ups and downs as dementia develops, but, in spite of struggles and darkness, David knows that his hope in Christ is secure (Heb 11:1). Hope was evidently sustaining Ron too. In spite of the effort needed for concentration, he asserted: "I know where I'm going . . . we are content." And Matthew almost shouted his "No." Gripping my hand, his voice breaking with emotion, he spoke of Christ's resurrection, and his hope that "we shall all be changed."[1] In the light of this hope of glory (Rom 5:2, 5), I witness faith that is growing in present experience. In the midst of these encounters with those living with dementia, I found myself *surprised* by this hope.[2]

---

1. Matthew is referring to 1 Corinthians 15:51.
2. Wright, *Surprised by Hope*.

This chapter reflects on the mystery of this experience in dementia: how it is generally understood as enabling resilience and the transcendence of suffering; and the particular part hope plays in the believer's story. Like other issues explored in earlier chapters (identity, suffering, and memory), hope interweaves with faith, is embedded in God's story and the individual's experience of faith. As well as being a key factor in their spiritual growth, it is integral to the reorientation of their faith. As we listen to these Christians, we become aware of a further dimension of hope—a temporal issue. Their hope is not only for *future* eternal life, but is impacting in transformative ways in the *present*: "I have NOW," Jess writes. This "un-tensed" hope is present-future (and, of course, perfect).[3]

TRANSFORMING HOPE

Coping or Hoping?

Hopefulness is generally acknowledged as being a significant aspect of well-being,[4] but there has been little enquiry into the subjective experience of the impact of the hope of *faith* on those who live with dementia.[5] Elizabeth MacKinlay and Corinne Trevitt's research began to do this, finding spiritual meaning in the experience of dementia.[6] In their model, hope is the *outcome* of persons finding meaning.[7] Trauma brings challenge to discover new life meaning, and this brings opportunity for growth.[8] The resulting transcendence may bring hope, through

> opportunities for reintegration of the person's meaning into a new world-view that may offer hope . . . to incorporate aspects of growth and meaning making and the associated transcendence.[9]

In their research, they were considering a more general question of spiritual growth than is the particular focus here. Others who have explored the questions that dementia brings to committed faith, talk of the transcendence it enables, bringing hope, resulting in the resilience to *cope* with illness. Some have suggested, therefore, that spirituality is "a coping mechanism" that

---

3. See Swinton's discussion of this in *Becoming Friends of Time*, 144–46.
4. For example: Herth, "Fostering Hope."
5. Wolverson (Radbourne) et al., "Remaining Hopeful," 457.
6. See chapter 8, 117–132.
7. MacKinlay and Trevitt, *Finding Meaning*, 154–58.
8. MacKinlay and Trevitt, *Finding Meaning*, 86–90.
9. MacKinlay and Trevitt, *Finding Meaning*, 87.

includes hope.¹⁰ But in Christian faith, hope is the frame,¹¹ and it has a different starting place.

Faith's "Hope" Is Different

Faith's hope is not merely a tool for coping that we can select at will from a resource box. It is different; it is immanent, and it begins with God. Its experience is enabled by the Holy Spirit in the believer—"poured into our hearts" (Rom 5:5)—drawing us into the divine life.¹² For Ron, Matthew, David, Jill, Jess, Bill, Alice, and Rosemary, hope wasn't merely a theological precept that soothed present discomfort; rather, it encompassed and permeated their lived experience, and was motivating them within the temporal context. Enabling their new orientation within dementia's context, this hope was a powerful, key factor in the trajectory of God's story: "in this hope we were saved" (Rom 8:24, NIVUK). As Paul's words in Romans make clear, this "hope of . . . glory" (Rom 5:1–5), founded in Christ and mediated through the Holy Spirit, is the reason why these believers can respond positively to suffering.

The *certainty* of their future with God was liberating them to pursue God's purpose in this new situation, enabling them to feel peaceful—even joyful—in the present. This hope amidst the lived experience of dementia has potential to "radically transform" the Christian's understanding and experience of their suffering in the present: "Our hope amid despair is real because of the life and work of Christ."¹³ Such hope is not just for loved ones of the person living with dementia; this different hope is bringing transformation to the participants' lived experience of faith in the present. Let's listen again to their voices.

"Faith . . . Gives Me Hope"

I asked Jill how faith was important as she came to terms with her diagnosis. There was a thoughtful pause, and then:

> JILL: Well, I couldn't live without it . . . It's the foundation of my life . . . And . . . having . . . dementia with . . . it gives me hope

---

10. For example: Katsuno, "Personal Spirituality"; Beuscher and Grando, "Using Spirituality to Cope."
11. Crowther, *Sustaining Persons*, 112–15.
12. See chapter 3, 42–43.
13. Keck, *Forgetting Whose We Are*, 173.

> ... and a knowledge that God is with me in it ... I can't imagine how awful it would be without ...
> 'TRICIA: Can you say why your sense of knowing God is helping you?
> JILL: Dementia is outside of my control, it's something that has happened ... And the fact that God is with me and knows about it and ... is there is very important ... He is my strength in order to carry on with life with ...

Jill's faith was foundational; its hope was sustaining her in her life as she faced dementia. Her belief that God was with her in this countered what would have been for her the unimaginable awfulness of having no sense of God's presence, both at this stage and as she imagined her future. She recognized that the coming of dementia into her life was outside of her control, yet there was a sense of security because "God ... knows about it." This knowledge gives her strength "to carry on with life." In these earlier years of dementia, it seemed that Jill's faith understanding was already growing, enabled by faith's hope, equipping her for its future development.

"Faith . . . the One Thing That Hangs On"

David's words were also informed by hope as he spoke about his confident faith, both at the present moment and for the future.

> DAVID: As I go on ... dementia gets worse, but that part of me will belong to Jesus ... When you've got that sort of faith, it's there.

Even though David knew that dementia would affect him more, his relationship with Jesus would remain. Past and present faith were both funding his faith for the future.

> DAVID: If we have faith now ... and dementia sets in, I believe ... Jesus will know the dementia ... and just becomes ... he loves me ... yeah ...
> 'TRICIA: So right now, you believe that's safe?
> DAVID: Yes, but ... as ... it gets worse that faith will still be there ... Maybe that's just the one thing that hangs on.

Envisaging his future, David believes that his faith is safe with Jesus. His increasing cognitive incapacity does not affect Jesus' love for him. His faith background is part of who he is and faith will remain in spite of the worsening effects of dementia.

"Not Concerned about the Future"

Ron was also clear about his sense of future hope.

> RON: I am not concerned about the future . . . because I know that I am born again. I know where I'm going without any shadow of doubt . . . and that . . . is what keeps me going . . . I don't know where I'm going in the way that you know where you are going. But I know myself that being a Christian I shall be going . . . to heaven.

Ron's experience of faith was sustaining him in the present and giving him the sense of certain hope for the future, enabling transcendence. His trust in God and hope of heaven were funded by his faith memory, bringing resilience, confident assurance, and contentment in the present.

Hope is not a take-it-or-leave-it option of the faith life; its transcendent presence framed these Christians' experience of life.

Living in God's Story[14]

A powerful and key factor enabling a new orientation for Christians who live with dementia is their participation in God's story characterized by its eschatological hope: "in this hope we were saved" (Rom 8:24, NIVUK). As Paul's words in Romans make clear, this "hope of . . . glory" (see Rom 5:1–5) founded in Christ and mediated through the Holy Spirit is the reason why these believers can respond positively to suffering. "Our hope amid despair is real because of the life and work of Christ."[15]

These disciples of Christ consciously participate in this different story: the purposeful narrative that leads humans from the garden of Eden to the garden of Gethsemane, to resurrection and hope of new creation.[16] Following the resurrection of Christ, God's Spirit came, giving the disciples assurance and indwelling hope of their shared destiny with Jesus.[17] Such confidence was evident in the words of the participants too ("I am going to heaven," Ron). This orientation, which is evident throughout the scriptural narrative and with the New Testament teaching of being in Christ, the image of God, does not end with the Gospel story. God's people are part of the

---

14. Brueggemann, *Texts Under Negotiation*, 57–91; see also chapter 3, 47–48.
15. Keck, *Forgetting Whose We Are*, 173.
16. Grenz, "Social God and the Relational Self," 83.
17. Anderson, *Spiritual Caregiving*, 152.

church eternal, destined for new creation.[18] This "divinely given destiny" is the hope that permeates the experience of those who participate in the life of Christ, and is the experience of the participants in this research:[19] "He has prepared a place for us" (Alice); "That will just be glory!" (Rosemary). It was being in this "counterdrama"[20] that was providing a foundation for these Christians' dynamic and transcendent hope.

The writer of Hebrews uses the scriptural narrative to affirm this certain hope of believers ("faith is the assurance of things hoped for, the conviction of things not seen," Heb 11:1), reminding them of their part in God's story (Heb 11–12:3). He recalls the suffering of Old Testament heroes that led to the suffering of Jesus, to his resurrection, and to the hope of Christ's reign. Counterintuitively, the experience of suffering, throughout the drama of scriptural faith, leads to hope.[21] It is in the light of this particular kind of hope that the writer encourages the endurance of the suffering of fellow believers:

> Run with perseverance the race that is set before us, looking to Jesus . . . who for the sake of the joy that was set before him he endured the cross . . . and has taken his seat at the right hand of the throne of God. (Heb 12:1–3)

It was God's continuing hopeful story[22]—as they are cheered on by the saints—that was providing a foundation for Matthew's, Ron's, Rosemary's, and the others' dynamic, transcendent (surprising) hope. Repeatedly throughout the biblical narrative, it is our brokenness that evokes memory of God's faithfulness and leads to hopefulness.[23] Within this "counterdrama," God's redemptive movement through history means that the present is always informed, as Swinton notes, by "eschatological rhythms and echoes."[24] The Bible—God's story—perceived as redescription of the way in which we see the world, brings hopeful fresh perspectives.

---

18. Grenz, "Social God and the Relational Self," 82.
19. Grenz, "Social God and the Relational Self," 83.
20. Brueggemann, *Texts Under Negotiation*, 57–91.
21. Brueggemann, "Suffering Produces Hope," 97–98.
22. Brueggemann, *Texts Under Negotiation*, 57–91.
23. Brueggemann, "Suffering Produces Hope," 97–99.
24. Swinton, *Raging with Compassion*, 55.

The Hope of Heaven

This hope is not wishful thinking—neither is it only a reassuring (but perhaps convenient) way for those who observe the pain of others to avoid facing their struggles in the present. "We may have a bit of trouble," Ron acknowledges, "but I'm going to heaven... We are content." He recognized his suffering in the present, but I noticed that this was transcended by his confident relationship with God. His assertion "I'm going to heaven" was an expression of his trust and hope in God, which was enabling him to be "contented" in the present. This hope transformed his experience now.

As believers we may struggle with our notions of "heaven"; it is too big and beyond human words; it is holy mystery. Perhaps it is a kind of shorthand used by Christians for talking about our inevitably limited understanding of hope in Christ. The word "heaven," as Tom Wright explores, does not simply indicate "the *ultimate* destination."[25] Our words may fail, but underlying these is a sense that it has to do with my *ongoing relationship* with God.

"I Know Where I'm Going"

For Bill, the certainty of his faith gave a sense of security that was equipping him with resilience for the present as well as hope for the future:

> BILL: This side of heaven that [dementia] is going to be part of my journey. The other side of heaven... Well, that's dealt with then! [chuckles]

His belief in a continuing life after death in heaven put his dementia in the present context of time into eternal perspective. He did not believe that his illness in this temporal context was the end of his story. For him, his hope of heaven resolved difficulties of dementia in the present.

For some of the participants who had been living with dementia for a number of years (for example, Ron and Matthew) there was a sense of calm in the present, in the light of their hope of heaven. In spite of Ron's increasing symptoms of dementia and mobility difficulties, he asserted that he was "happy" and without "worry."

> RON: Where I'm going is to heaven, and ... my God is up there—I know that ... I've got no cares in the world at all ... and I am happy as the day is long ... We don't worry about anything ... All right, we've got a bit of difficulties, but we're all right ...

---

25. Wright, *Surprised by Hope*, 25–26.

> RON: If we know where we're going we cannot help but feel contented . . . By me knowing where I'm going, I've never ever bothered to be so worried about this or worried about that . . . everything falls in its place . . .

His contentment seemed dependent on his hope of heaven and certainty of going to meet with God. His "up there" suggested that *wherever* heaven is, God is there, and Ron was confident that he was going to be with him. It was almost as though the situation of the present time was unimportant in the light of his eternal destiny. His certainty was enabling him not to worry. His confidence in a future with God meant that "everything falls in its place." In the disorientating time that dementia was bringing to him, he was finding reorientation and contentment in spite of "a bit of difficulties," because of his sense of eternal purpose, found in his faith in God.

"I Will Be . . . with the Lord"

As I listened to the words of the research participants, something else became clear. They were not sustained by a vague hope of a *distant* "heaven." It was their sense of relationship with Christ that was transforming their experience in the present, and which, they presumed, would continue into and through eternity. They were making sense of the present confusing experiences of dementia because of their belief in a future with God.

Alice, unperturbed by the future, with faith imagination, saw it as continuing relationship with the God who had always been faithful to her:

> ALICE: God is never going to desert one, he's always there and that he has prepared a place for us.[26]

Such hopeful faith was liberating her in the present for serving others.[27]

Rosemary too was sure of this being with God whatever happened to her as dementia advanced.

> ROSEMARY: I don't think God judges us on . . . if our brains . . . He created us like this . . . so . . . I don't have to worry about that. I believe in my heart and soul that just saying the name of Jesus or just being able to join in a hymn or sing it because I know it still . . . Of course, you do get to a point sometimes when there's absolutely . . . Well, maybe I won't recognize things, matters like that. It matters not. What does matter is that I will be, at the

---

26. See John 14:1–4.
27. Alice has been active in her work with others who live with dementia.

right time, with the Lord. That will just be glory we can't begin to imagine . . . Amen.

Historical time seemed, in a sense, unimportant for Rosemary's earthly life. Yet the "right time" suggested her sense of God's control over her life. She expected one day to be "with the Lord" and she imagined with confidence that the "glory" of that experience would be beyond earthly imagination. Her instinctive "Amen" seemed to address God, rather than me—and brought our conversation to a close.

Hope in Christ

As we talked about fear and hope, Matthew's words pointed me back to the center of God's story: "Jesus went up to Calvary . . . and on the third day . . . he rose." Hopeful transformation centers on Christ—his coming, his crucifixion, his resurrection and glorification. It is in the encounter between Christ and our experience that our lives are transformed by the hope which he brings.[28] As we try to take in the scope of God's big story, we remember that back at the beginning when sin spoilt God's creation, even then, there was this whisper of hope in the coming Christ: "And I will put enmity between you and the woman, and between your offspring and hers; he will crush your head, and you will strike his heel" (Gen 3:15). And later, through his prophets, God the Spirit keeps our thinking tuned to the hope of sin and suffering that's dealt with, and its resolution in the light of the risen Christ: "Surely he took up our pain and bore our suffering . . . But he was pierced for our transgressions, he was crushed for our iniquities; the punishment that brought us peace was on him, and by his wounds we are healed . . . and though the LORD makes his life an offering for sin, he will see his offspring . . . He will see the light of life and be satisfied" (Isa 53:4, 5, 10–11, NIVUK). It is with the incarnation, crucifixion, and resurrection of Jesus that this story brings us to the hope that we find in him now:

> Therefore, since we have been justified through faith, we have peace with God through our Lord Jesus Christ, through whom we have gained access by faith into this grace in which we now stand. And we boast in the hope of the glory of God. (Rom 5:1–2, NIVUK)

The research participants' words took me to the reason for their hope. Some were close to tears as they spoke of forgiveness: this is the reason for the

---

28. Root, *Christopraxis*, 35–52. See Root's exploration of the experience of transformative encounter with Christ.

confidence that the hope of faith is bringing for the future, and their reason for feeling at peace even in the face of dementia.

"I Feel I Have Been Forgiven . . ."

The salvific work of Jesus was often an unspoken assumption of participants, underlying their confidence of forgiveness and heaven. Bill expressed this sense of forgiveness and future hope in this way:

> BILL: God the Father, God the Son, God the Holy Spirit—and they are here for me . . . Yes, I have sinned, I have caused a lot of problems with people in the past, but all that is in the past and I just want to be a follower of you for the rest of my life, and when that life finishes, I shall be with you for ever.

As he asserted his resolution to follow Jesus, his words became a prayer: "I just want to be a follower of you." Freedom from a sense of the guilt of sin was an important issue for these Christians as they faced the future with dementia. Jess also expressed her sense of freedom from guilt when I asked why she thought Jesus died.

> JESS: For our sins . . . yeah. So that we can be sin-free . . . but we do sin . . . but when I recognize that and I say, "Oh God, I'm sorry, I didn't mean to do that," I feel I have been forgiven . . . I don't think we have to carry a burden. We can dump it, can't we? . . . And that's why the fact that I can't remember, my memory loss, doesn't matter.

Jess recognized her human sinfulness, but didn't feel this was a "burden" because "we can dump it." She understood that the death of Jesus had made this possible. The fact that she felt accepted by God through Jesus enabled her to say that her memory loss "doesn't matter." She seemed to be peaceful because of her confident belief and trust in God.

Matthew also chose to talk about forgiveness in response to his recent Scripture reading:

> MATTHEW: One of the readings I read recently was about the centurion who stood in the temple and put his hand on his chest and said "I am a good man . . . I fast twice a week . . . I'm not like this tax collector." And Jesus said to his disciples, "Which of these two men, who do you think had the strongest faith?" And they said, "The one who said, 'God be merciful to me a

sinner.'" Because whatever we do, we've all sinned in some way or another . . .[29]

Matthew, as he imagined himself in the story of the tax collector, expressed his recognition of his own sinfulness, and implied his confidence that he was forgiven. This was enabling his hopefulness and an experience of its transforming peace.

"We Shall All Be Changed"

Matthew then spoke about his confident hope for the future in the following way:

> 'TRICIA: . . . Do you have any worries or fears about your future with God?
> MATTHEW: *No!* [very definite] . . . I wouldn't be afraid to die . . . if I had to! [loudly and firmly]
> 'TRICIA: Why do you say that so firmly?
> MATTHEW: [long pause, struggling with tears] Because . . . Jesus went up to Calvary . . . and on the third day . . . he [voice breaking] he rose . . . "And we shall all be changed . . ."[30]

Matthew was tearful. I reached out my hand and he responded, holding onto my hand very firmly. His definite response made clear that he was not afraid of the future because of his dementia. As he spoke, he was drawing on words from 1 Corinthians 15:50–57. His assertion was grounded in his hope of resurrection. His hope was firm because of the death and resurrection of Jesus. This seemed to be giving him hope that his own physical condition would be transformed: "We shall all be changed." The importance of this for him brought him to the edge of tears.

In response to Matthew's reference to the Bible verses, I asked him if I could read this passage to him. Matthew agreed and at the end of the reading, he was looking and sounding moved. A former, keen choral singer, the Bible text reminded him of words he had sung from Elgar's "The Dream of Gerontius," which is based on the prayer of a dying man.

> MATTHEW: I know where it comes from! . . . "The Dream of Gerontius" . . .[31] Those words are wonderful!

29. See Luke 18:9–14, the parable of the Pharisee and the Tax Collector.

30. See 1 Corinthians 15:51: "Listen, I will tell you a mystery! We will not all die, but we will all be changed."

31. "The Dream of Gerontius," Edward Elgar, 1900. A work for orchestra and voices, which uses the text of a poem by John Henry Newman (1890), the prayer of a dying man.

Here, Matthew's words provided another example of the hopeful clues brought by music and words. His memory of the music, and the words we had read from Scripture, brought thoughts of resurrection and transformation. They clearly brought him great comfort.

Then, looking out on his garden, Matthew's words moved from the subliminal thoughts of resurrection to his delight in the birds of the earth, and back to heaven again.

> 'TRICIA: Why do they give you such comfort and strength?
> MATTHEW: Does it matter? Because, I can look at a bird. What will I do in heaven? I might see a bird first thing . . . before I see the Lord.

I noticed that Matthew's mixing of ideas of heaven and earth foresaw the certainty of heaven as an *embodied* experience ("I can look"; "I see the Lord"). He seemed to find my question "Why do they . . . ?" irrelevant ("Does it matter?"). He was unconcerned about understanding *how* things will happen. The question suggested that he was content to trust God. The confidence of his belief expressed through his faltering speech was deeply moving for both of us. As researcher in this quiet room, I was mindful of these words: "No matter what the condition of any human being, his or her personhood in God requires that pastor and care giver come before that person in reverence."[32]

PRESENT-FUTURE HOPE

This drama of God's story of hope is ongoing through the liminal era of church and our earthly lives—it is surely seen as we witness God's transforming love at work in Matthew and the others. Suffering and sadness, including that of dementia, are part of our historical, temporal lives. Yet, God's promises of hope—being with him—made possible through the saving death and resurrection of Christ, were transforming the lives of the Christians in this research as they were living with dementia in the present moment ("If we know where we're going we cannot help but feel contented," Ron). The well-rehearsed story of faith and its immanence, mediated through Christ's Spirit, was bringing to them an evident calm, even joyful confidence. Their hope, arising in the present time from their trust in God, was bringing peace for living now and assurance of eternal security with God.

More than this, the *lived experience* of dementia nudges us towards new perceptions of what hope means theologically (as well as in practice),

---

32. Shamy, *Guide to the Spiritual Dimension of Care*, 129.

not just for those who live with dementia, but for all of us. God's hopeful story isn't just about a temporal future, but, as Jesus says, "The kingdom of God is in your midst" (Luke 17:21). Paul's "endurance" of present suffering (Rom 5:1–2) is framed in the light of this hope in Christ, who is "the same yesterday and today and for ever" (Heb 13:8, NIVUK). As Wright reminds us, "God's future has arrived in the present in the person of the risen Jesus."[33] When we think about hope and its experience in dementia we cannot help but think about eternity's embrace.

Future-Present Being

This realization of present time being within eternity isn't a new theological understanding. Augustine in the fourth century wrote about "the simultaneity of eternity" and "the Word coeternal with yourself."[34] Perhaps the Enlightenment and its resulting rational habits that have informed our era and faith have clouded our awareness of the presence of the risen Jesus, here with us now. Contemporary theologians are bringing fresh insight into this biblical reality.[35] John Swinton's profound thinking about dementia and intellectual disability confronts us with the realization that as believers, we are within God's time, we are *in Christ*:[36]

> There is no before and after, at least not in the way we assume it to be in the world of sequential clock time. If we have died and been raised in Christ, we reside in a quite different kind of time.[37]

Augustine's "Your Today is eternity"[38] melds our notions of future and present in untensed time reflected in the sense of continuing flow of both in the moment of now. Dementia is "part of the journey" (Bill); there is "No fear . . . in Jesus" (David); "We are content" (Ron); Rosemary, in spite of temporal fears, is filled with joy in her relationship with Christ as she heads towards her imagined life beyond: "I will be, at the right time, with the Lord. That will just be glory!" Such hopefulness is a mode of being for these Christians.[39]

---

33. Wright, *Surprised by Hope*, 300.
34. Augustine, *Confessions* XI.vii (9).
35. Wright, *Surprised by Hope*.
36. See chapter 3, 47.
37. Swinton, *Becoming Friends of Time*, 180.
38. Augustine, *Confessions* XI.xiii (16).
39. See Romans 5:1–5.

Of course, this future beyond temporal life *is* a mystery. We live, as Crowther has highlighted in her pastoral writing, with this tension between the "present and not yet." Christ's reign of love is both "present and a foretaste" of his ultimate victory over suffering. More than this, through the assurance of relationship with Christ and in "solidarity" with the community of faith, this hope is becoming "a present and personal hopefulness as it is received objectively."[40] We glimpse this in the experience of the research participants, and see how it begins to explain their insistent, hopeful positivity in the present. Just as the memory of God's *past* faithfulness has informed and funded *present* experience of God; just as the kingdom of God is both present and not yet;[41] so too the participants' trust in God's promises for the *future* fund their eschatological hope, and bring transformation to their *present* lived experience. In some transcendent, mysterious way, the hope of the future is actualized in my participants' experience in the present moment of now. Tom Greggs captures this future-present mode of being in this way:

> God makes his way from his future into our present, allowing the church through the Holy Spirit to anticipate proleptically the coming of his Kingdom as his eschaton impinges on our time.[42]

"I Have Now"

Following my conversation with Jess about the experience of faith as a Christian living with memory loss, she wrote this poem together with her husband.[43] It powerfully captures the significance of the moment of "now" both for the person living with dementia—and for all of us.

> Everybody is in a rush
>
> But I have all the time in the world—
> I have now.
>
> I have to fit into other people's
> "Rush-Push-Busy" world

---

40. Crowther, *Sustaining Persons*, 169.
41. For example: Luke 17:20–21.
42. Greggs, "Introduction," 4.
43. "Everybody is in a rush" ©. The authors of this poem were participants in this research study and have asserted their rights to anonymity.

> But I have all the time in the world—
> I have now.
>
> I only have Now—that's all I have
> all the time
>
> Lost past No Tomorrow
> ONLY NOW.
>
> What a privilege because
> Now is the accepted time
>
> Today is the Day of Salvation.

In their poem, Jess and her husband express the positive qualities that living in this present moment were bringing especially to her life. She saw this as liberating within the confining busyness of the world's pressured time focus;[44] her thoughts reflect the freedom that declining memory of the recent past was bringing. As an older person living with dementia, she had no expectations of time on earth. Her faith was bringing a liberty and an awareness of "now" as being a privileged time for which she was thankful. The words "Today is the Day of Salvation" are a reference to the words of 2 Corinthians 6:2 ("See, now is the acceptable time; see, now is the day of salvation!"), and affirm her sense of the importance and the significance of the present moment for life and relationship with God, and trust in his promise of help.[45] This moment of "now" described in this way helps us draw close to the faith-ed experience of dementia. This hope transcends chronological time and puts life in the context of eternal significance and God's *Kairos* time.

PRESENT-FUTURE HOPE . . .

In the midst of the uninvited experience of dementia—for Jess, Matthew, Ron, Rosemary, Alice, Jill, David, and Bill—their hope in Christ was bringing transformation and reorientation in their lives. We have seen in their lived experience, as Brueggemann writes, this movement of God's people

---

44. See Swinton's reflection on God's slow time, *Becoming Friends of Time*, 67–83.

45. 2 Corinthians 6:2: "For he says, 'At an acceptable time I have listened to you, and on a day of salvation I have helped you.' See, now is the acceptable time; see, now is the day of salvation!"

"from plea to praise," "from wretchedness to joy."[46] There is no going back for them, but mysteriously they seemed to be finding resolution in their experience of faith in the light of their hope in Christ.[47] As we have reflected on their situations through the lens of Scripture, we have seen in this chapter that their hope of faith was grounded in the work of Christ on the cross and his resurrection, giving them assurance of forgiveness and hope in him of continuing life with God. Their belief in eternal time was putting the events and struggles of earthly time in fresh perspective, and bringing a sense of calm, contentment—even joy—in the present; their belief in God's eternal remembering of individuals was providing a sense of safety in the face of their present forgetfulness.[48] And lastly, this sense of God's eternal "now," experienced through faith, was enabling transcendence of the temporal present.

Faith's hope *is* mysterious. Whilst it cannot be explained, the effects of faith were, nevertheless, bringing transformation to the lives of these courageous people who were living with dementia. In his exploration of the movement of God's people from disorientation to new orientation, Brueggemann suggests that whilst we "can narrate, recite and testify [to]" the lived experience of God's people, *how* this newness happens cannot be explained. It's as mysterious as how a "leper is cleansed, or how a blind person can see (Luke 7:22)."[49] Yet, in the lived experience of faith, there were *clues* to how such a reorientation was happening: faith, disclosed through the expression of trustful hope in God, was bringing spiritual growth as these disciples of Christ walked through the shadows of dementia;[50] eschatological hope and its imagining reframed the experience of dementia and sustained its endurance in transformative ways in the present. Brueggemann suggests that such

> hope in the midst of loss . . . is not a psychological trick. It is a massive theological act . . . a statement about the fidelity of God who is the key player in the past and in the future.[51]

In the final chapter, we turn to the possible implications of the conversations with these Christians who were living with dementia, and the resulting reflections which have arisen from them. In the light of their experience,

---

46. Brueggemann, *Spirituality of the Psalms*, 47–49.
47. Swinton, *Finding Jesus*, 108.
48. See also chapter 8, 126–127.
49. Brueggemann, *Spirituality of the Psalms*, 47–48.
50. See also chapter 8, 117–132.
51. Brueggemann, "Suffering Produces Hope," 99.

in the light of Scripture, how can the community of Christ's body live "in solidarity"[52] with these fellow disciples of Jesus?

For Further Reflection . . .

- Reflect on the words of Hebrews 11:1 and Hebrews 12:1–3. How might we help one another in this hope as, together, we fix our eyes on Jesus (12:2, NIVUK)?
- Read Jess's poem again. How do you think this hope of faith has potential to transform the Christian's experience in the present, even as they live with dementia?
- How might we and our local churches practically encourage those living with dementia in their hope in Christ?

---

52. Crowther, *Sustaining Persons*, 167.

10

Walking Together

"They must remind me."

So what "now"? We have walked and talked with Jess, Alice, Matthew, David, Rosemary, Bill, Ron, and Jill. We have listened to their faithful testimonies of God's grace in their lives and reflected on their words in the light of Christ. How then should we walk with Christians such as these—and those who are further along this path? How might we continue to remind them of the God who has not forgotten any one of us?

In this book I have set out to explore and deepen understanding of the faith experience and practice of Christians from an evangelical tradition who are living with dementia. We have reflected on human identity, relationship with God, faith practice, Bible reading and prayer, the nature of church and its faith community, memory, spiritual growth—and the all-encompassing hope found in Christ. Out of the disorientating shadows of dementia, we have glimpsed a new orientation enabled within faith's light. Now, in this final chapter we reflect on ways in which this work—as we have listened to the voices of Christians living with dementia and reflected on Scripture and theology—has begun to suggest implications for practical ministry, theology, and strategies for the fulfilling of these. Reflecting on what we have heard, in this closing chapter we consider possibilities for how these voices might contribute to transforming our faith practice and experience. What have we learnt from these disciples of Christ who live with dementia?

Surprising Discoveries

In contrast to the expectations of onlookers, and the understandable fears and grief of loving families, we might be surprised by the positive nature of the participants' experience of their illness in the light of faith in Christ. In the midst of the uninvited experience of dementia that has threatened the stable orientation of their lives, these Christians seemed to be finding transformation and reorientation in their faith: "Lord, this is your gift for here . . . with your help I will do what I can in order to reflect your glory in it" (Alice). In their experience, we can identify with Brueggemann's reflection on the movement of God's suffering people—through unexpected disruption towards faithful reorientation.[1] As Bill said: "There is no going back . . . [Dementia will] always be with me now until the day I die . . . This side of heaven that is going to be part of my journey." Even amidst the shadows of their dementia, their transforming faith was lightening the way ahead.

Whilst we might have expected that the "sacred canopy" of belief would be in jeopardy within this experience of dementia,[2] the testimonies we have heard in this book have suggested that this was not the case for these particular disciples of Christ.[3] Surprisingly, their experience reveals paradox. In "decline and loss" there was a more intense sense of "this is who I am!" Memory was funding faith despite the loss of memory. Notwithstanding the sadness and struggles of living with dementia, there was purpose, not meaninglessness; closeness to God, not distance; hope, not despair. Encapsulating it all, is the paradox of God himself who is *Emmanuel* (God with us), accompanying his people through the valley of their shadows in the presence of *Logos* (Christ the Word) who has chosen to live among us (Matt 1:23; Isa 7:14; John 1:14). Surprisingly, the disorientation of dementia was inevitably bringing a reorientation: "even when my brain falls apart" (Alice). Such "newness"[4] may seem inexplicable, apart from perceptions of a sovereign and loving God. Paradoxically, such characteristics are the opposite of the troubling questions that theodicy (God and suffering)

---

1. Brueggemann, *Spirituality of the Psalms*, 47–49.
2. Brueggemann, *Spirituality of the Psalms*, 47.
3. See, for example: Beuscher and Grando, "Using Spirituality to Cope," 584–85; Katsuno, "Personal Spirituality."
4. Brueggemann, *Spirituality of the Psalms*, 48.

brings to God's omnipotence and love.⁵ The believing individual and their community often find themselves "surprised by grace."⁶ So, what have these different voices disclosed about faith in the context of dementia (and about our own walk with God)?

THE EXPERIENCE AND PRACTICE OF FAITH IN DEMENTIA

The faith of these Christians—as Alice reminded me—is founded in *relationship* with God; it's not "a doing." This relationship was enabling them to see their dementia differently from expectations that, as the researcher, I might have brought to my conversations with them. Counterintuitively, the experience of dementia was bringing an increasing sense of closeness to God. In spite of moments of darkness and struggle, an underlying assurance of trust in God remained and was sustaining them in their faith. Even when we are no longer able to communicate our thoughts, their words and hope resonate with Scripture, which tells us that the Holy Spirit will speak for us, and that nothing can separate us from the love of God the Father revealed in Jesus his Son (Rom 8:38–39). Here are some key aspects of what these Christians living with dementia have shown us.

- *Faith and its sense of relationship with God* remain central to identity ("The core is . . . knowing Jesus," David). The sense of being in relationship with God has precedence over the doing of faith practices. Feelings—"overwhelmed with peace"—were becoming more significant as the illness was progressing.[7]

- *Faith in practice.* Traditional approaches to Bible engagement, prayer, participation in worship, and other activities were becoming more difficult as a result of the ongoing development of their dementia.[8] However, these practices, perhaps in different ways, remained central and significant as means of sustaining faith and expressing relationship with God and other believers.[9] The participants in the research were recognizing these difficulties and finding other ways of using resources of faith.

---

5. See chapter 6, 84–87.
6. Brueggemann, *Spirituality of the Psalms*, 47.
7. McFadden et al., "Actions, Feelings, and Values," 76–78.
8. Davis, *My Journey into Alzheimer's Disease*, 57.
9. Hoggarth, *Seed and the Soil*, 145–47.

- *Belonging in the community of faith.*

    - *The identity* of Christians living with dementia is highlighted by the nature of their part in the body of Christ. As attendance at church activities becomes more challenging, dementia asks questions about how their belonging is expressed in the local congregation, and also how their giftedness is recognized.

    - *Stigmatization.* Conversations with the research participants also posed questions about how the person living with dementia is regarded (perhaps by implication) or treated within their community of faith. Some conversations revealed the felt effects of subtle stigmatization (for example, Jess said: "My memory loss has interfered with my being somebody"). Some had even experienced a kind of *spiritual* stigmatizing that communicated a doubt of their faith ("They nullify my Christian walk!," Alice).[10] And sometimes it was not always easy for them to feel welcome in a local congregation ("I can't . . . join a congregation," Rosemary). In spite of this, our conversations also revealed warm appreciation of loving support from their local churches.

    - *Naming dementia.* As my conversations and theological reflections on these have disclosed, some of those living with dementia may find it difficult to acknowledge its impact in their lives. Other believers may not notice, understand, or wish to recognize the struggles and sadness that it is bringing.

    - *Relationships with others.* These were clearly important in the faith activities in which participants were involved, and were a means of providing mutual support, for example: church services and other activities, "home groups" for prayer and Bible engagement. For those who were married, this partnership was providing significant spiritual support. For those who lived alone, there are issues to be resolved about how the support of the community of faith might be enabled.

- *Faith memory* was an important resource for funding faith, shaping participants' experience of faith in the present moment of their lives, and in bringing hopefulness for the future. Experiences of God's past faithfulness were important for the present experience of God's dependability and love for them.

10. See Barclay, "Psalm 88," 90. See also chapter 6, 92–94.

- *Spiritual growth* was evident in the lives of the participants within the context of dementia. It is also shown in biographical writing, such as that of Bryden and Davis,[11] and in the unique experience described in this research. Other pastoral writing has also begun to address this issue, for example, that of Collicutt, Crowther, and Dunlop.[12]

- *Disorientation to reorientation.* Whilst the descriptions of lived experience recounted here revealed the strong faith commitment and experience of the participants, these also disclosed the struggles and darkness that dementia was bringing to their lives. Their transforming faith was being enabled and characterized through the resources of their faith memory, through perception and acceptance of God's purpose, trust in him, and in the light of hopeful, eschatological imagination. Their new orientation was being enabled by a sense of God's presence with them, within the context of the community of faith.

- *Reframing of purpose*, rather than search for meaning, was evident in their lives. The significance of this for spiritual well-being has been shown in other writing too, such as that of Christine Bryden and Jennifer Bute.[13] Those whose voices we have heard in this book were motivated to take part in the research by their desire to bring their unique insights towards transforming practice in the service of God and others. Their discovery of purpose in living with dementia questions the understanding and recognition of this within the community of faith.

- *Being hopeful.* A distinctive quality of Matthew, Rosemary, Bill, and the others' experience of dementia was hopefulness. Such hope was founded in the theological understandings of their Christ-centered faith. For them this was bringing assurance of forgiveness and trust in their continuing life with God. This hopefulness, evident in their accounts, was sustaining faith and transforming the lived experience of dementia in the present. In some ways, this resonates with other research that explores the finding of hope in dementia.[14] The voices of these Christians enable specific focus on the lived experience of committed faith of the evangelical tradition.

As I write this, I recognize that the experience of faith—and faith in dementia—is mysterious. Yet, even though it can't be explained, its effects

---

11. Bryden, *Dancing with Dementia*; Davis, *My Journey into Alzheimer's Disease*.
12. Collicutt, *Thinking of You*; Crowther, *Sustaining Persons*; Dunlop, *Finding Grace*.
13. For example, Bryden and MacKinlay, "Dementia: A Journey Inwards to a Spiritual Self"; Bute, "My Glorious Opportunity."
14. MacKinlay and Trevitt, *Finding Meaning*, 151–70.

were evident and bringing transformation to the lives of these Christians who were living with dementia. Their lived experience, together with theological reflection, brings both insight and implications for how pastoral and ministerial practice, and theology, might find their own reorientation in the light of dementia.

ORIENTING TO THE TASK

In the light of what we have heard (and in the light of God's Word), practical theology now asks: How might we respond practically to what this research discloses and brings attention?[15] What might it mean for the church to "participate faithfully in God's mission" in order to serve and bring Christ's love to Christians who are living with dementia?[16]

The deeper understanding of the experience of Christians living with dementia reveals new perspectives and challenges for practice and theology. In the following, I highlight three areas where I hope the voices of these Christians, the research, and this book might contribute to transforming understanding and care in this area of faith and dementia:[17] the church's response to those who live with dementia; the challenge concerning their pastoral care and spiritual nurture; the potential for fresh theological understanding of Christian faith in the light of dementia.

The Response of the Church

Paul writes to the Corinthian church: "If one member suffers, all suffer together with it" (1 Cor 12:26a). Dianne Crowther, reflecting on this, speaks of the necessity of *solidarity* with one another as we suffer:

> If our Christian convictions are to mean anything in suffering, it will be as they help us to see our lives, our narratives, located in God's narrative and community.[18]

Whilst such solidarity was apparent in the experience of some of the research participants, all of their accounts revealed, in different ways, incipient difficulties resulting from their dementia in some areas of the shared life of faith ("they don't understand," Rosemary). How, then, might the church

---

15. Osmer, *Practical Theology*, 4.
16. Swinton and Mowat, *Practical Theology*, 27.
17. See Introduction, xvi; chapter 1, 1–2.
18. Crowther, *Sustaining Persons*, 167.

respond to their members who live with early to moderate dementia—and to those who are further on in their journey?[19]

The Local Church

The research with these Christians who live with dementia, and the theological reflections arising from their words, have highlighted the need for a reframing and reorientating of practice within the community of faith, in the light of dementia. As the issues of dementia are being increasingly recognized, perhaps the "climate" of believing communities—which may unintentionally stigmatize, objectify, and exclude—might be challenged.

> The key is, then, to create places of belonging where people with dementia and those who offer care and support to them can find a place that is truly theirs and within which they can express the full experience of dementia—its pain, its affliction, and its lament as well as its joys and its possibilities.[20]

This issue might be addressed practically in some of the following ways.

- *Training and education* about faith in dementia, encouraging a positive perception of those living with this illness, and seeking ways of recognizing and enabling the expression of the gifts that they bring to the life of the church.

- *Advocacy* by those who live with dementia. In these early to moderate stages of dementia, some are willing and able to tell their stories (as participants in this research have done here, and as seen in the work of Bryden and Bute[21]). This can bring understanding, affirm those who are living with dementia in a community of faith, and motivate loving, responsive action. Whilst participants in this particular study were positive about their faith experience in living with dementia, I am aware that there is a need to find ways of hearing the voices of those for whom their illness *is* bringing doubt in faith and ongoing distress—both for them and their families.

- *Practical theological engagement* in local churches, with focus on the nature of being a Christian who lives with dementia and being a community of faith to which those with dementia belong. How, for example, does a community's theology of *belonging* work out in practice?

---

19. Adams also begins to address this issue in *Developing Dementia-Friendly Churches*.
20. Swinton, *Dementia*, 278.
21. Bryden, *Dancing with Dementia*; Bute, "My Glorious Opportunity."

- *Recognition of the sadness and struggle* that dementia is bringing to some members of a congregation. Learning to name and express this grief, and to lament as a community "in solidarity" with the person with dementia and their families. John Swinton and Dianne Crowther both bring further insight to the question of lamenting together with those who are suffering.[22] Crowther writes: "At times, the depth of suffering may be inexpressible. Where words are no longer accessible to the person with dementia, the feelings are no less present."[23] Crowther suggests an intentional corporate reading of psalms of lament (e.g., Psalm 88), which may both validate and recognize the suffering that some are currently experiencing—and help towards changing the "climate": creating a situation "where sufferers experience a sense of belonging and kinship rather than alienation and aloneness."[24]

- *Addressing specific practical difficulties* that are affecting individuals' active participation in various ways. For example, not remembering where you were sitting after going to the front for communion (for example, Rosemary[25]); arranging transport for someone who lives independently but still wants to come to a church service (for example, Alice can no longer drive); remembering those who are increasingly affected by issues of dementia, and whose absence from church activities may not be noticed.[26] There will be context-specific issues for which imaginative thinking and awareness can find solutions.

The Wider Community of Faith

- *Ministerial and leadership training* are needed that bring attention to the issue of spiritual care for those who are living with dementia, and enables development of strategies towards this end. Already different denominations, chaplains, and Christian charities are working together to facilitate and grow their ministry in this area.[27]

---

22 Swinton, *Dementia*, 261–64; Swinton, *Finding Jesus*, 86–88.

23. Crowther, *Sustaining Persons*, 163.

24. Crowther, *Sustaining Persons*, 164–65.

25. Chapter 5, 74–75.

26. Mast, *Second Forgetting*, 105.

27. For example, Anna Chaplaincy. Find out more at https://www.annachaplaincy.org.uk.

Faith Nurture in the Context of Dementia

As we saw in chapter 8, Peter's encouragement to keep on growing "in the grace and knowledge of our Lord and Saviour Jesus Christ" (2 Pet 3:18) brings the question of ongoing faith nurture for believers who live with dementia ("I long to know him more in my illness," Jill). There is also then the challenge to other members of the church about their own growth in faith as we learn to walk with those who live with dementia. What do I learn from my brothers and sisters in Christ who live with dementia?

Christine Bryden's work has highlighted the need for this mutuality of care that enables the spiritual growth of those living with dementia. A passionate advocate of growing faith throughout her journey with dementia, she has recognized her dependence on others in the body of Christ ("I need you to minister to me"[28]). Dianne Crowther makes an important point about spiritual companionship: it is about "care *partnerships* rather than care *being done to* the person."[29] Such a view helps us to see what it might mean, in practice, that all parts of the body of Christ should have equal concern for one another (see 1 Cor 12:25).

In the light of the conversations explored in this book—the experience of Christians living with dementia, the theological reflections, and Scripture—how then might the church disciple believers who live with dementia, and nurture their continuing spiritual growth? Imaginative, empathic, and creative response might enable some of the following:

In the Local Church and Faith Communities

- *Loving, purposeful accompaniment of individuals* who are encountering the disorientation of dementia. For example: through deliberate friendship (as illustrated in the co-working of MacKinlay and Bryden[30]); while spiritual mentoring may also be a means of spiritual growth for those who are beginning this journey. These could enable, for example, an ongoing working and talking through of the issues of faith growth and reorientation, as discussed in chapters 8 and 9. How might we accompany one another in our perception of God's purpose; in developing our relational trust in God; endurance under

---

28. Bryden and MacKinlay, "Dementia: A Spiritual Journey Towards the Divine," 74.

29. Crowther, *Sustaining Persons*, 182.

30. Bryden and MacKinlay, "Dementia: A Journey Inwards to a Spiritual Self."

this pressure, and in our shared eschatological hope?[31] Crowther's work about pastoral caring for those with dementia has developed this idea of being a pastoral companion in more detail, seeing this as complementing the care of a supportive community.[32] As dementia progresses, here is a quiet, unassuming ministry of being with one another, knowing that together you are remembered by God.

- *Bible reading and prayer* with those who are living with dementia and no longer finding these practices easy to do individually. The development of the *Being with God*[33] books were an attempt to provide a resource to encourage and enable this. There are others now available—search the internet for suggestions. Or simply commit to reading a passage of Scripture and praying regularly with a Christian who lives with dementia.

- *Development of creative ways of using and building memories* as a resource for faith in the present, and in preparation for the future. For example, share stories of coming to faith, intentionally encourage Scripture engagement, sing Christian songs and hymns that bring into the present moment Christian teaching and experience ("Music, songs . . . brings you into that peaceful sense of joy and happiness," Rosemary).

- *Being hopeful* was characteristic of the participants' faith in dementia. Enabling expressions of this hopeful faith can bring, and strengthen, faith experience in the present moment. Remember the joyful tears of Matthew as he imaginatively thought about the resurrection of Jesus (and his welcome in heaven!).[34]

- *Encouragement and recording of the telling of faith stories* and experience, both as a resource for the person living with dementia, and as a resource for encouraging fellow believers in their own faith, and in the ongoing support they are seeking to give.

- *Development of discipleship groups* in churches (or in a local area) that intentionally welcome those living with dementia. These would give opportunity for sharing of faith experiences, enable Bible engagement and prayer for one another, and facilitate mutual learning in a supportive community. Such meetings could contribute to the journey of growth and reorientation discussed in chapter 8.

---

31. For a fuller discussion of the significance of hope in dementia, see chapter 9.
32. Crowther, *Sustaining Persons*, 182.
33. See Williams, *Words of Faith*; *Words of Hope*; *Words of Peace*.
34. See chapter 9, 143.

The Wider Community of Faith, Denominational, Faith Organizations, Chaplaincy Teams

- *Development of pastoral expertise* that understands and can focus on the particular needs of Christians who are beginning to live with dementia in a local community of faith. Increasingly, this is being achieved through ministerial, church leadership, and chaplaincy training.
- *Ongoing development of Bible, prayer, and faith resources* that aim to enable the person living with dementia to continue to spend intentional time with God.[35] Also important are resources aimed at facilitating individual devotional practice and development of group faith resources that enable the participation of those living with dementia in corporate faith activities. Recognition of this ministerial need requires ongoing commitment of Christian publishers and organizations to develop, and to find ways to fund such projects.

New Perspectives for Theology

Alongside the pastoral concerns, the experience of the research participants and theological reflection on these have also highlighted significant theological issues and questions. As Andrew Root has recognized, the lived nature of our practice cannot be separated from theology.[36] The two are interwoven.

One of the hoped-for outcomes envisaged at the beginning of my research was that it would bring further understanding to the theological issues raised by dementia. In particular, I have been concerned to show how this illness questions theological (and cultural) issues within the evangelical tradition. Addressing theological implications is important because theological assumptions inform our practice (for example, the nature of personal faith, the church, hope). This book has been exploring a *newly recognized* context within the community of faith. Lack of fresh theological engagement with its arising questions has potential to cause pain and bring discouragement to those facing the challenges of living with dementia (both the person with the illness and their loved ones).

---

35. For example, Williams, *Words of Faith*; *Words of Hope*; *Words of Peace*.
36. Root, *Christopraxis*, 34.

Building on the work of other theologians of dementia,[37] committed exploration of its theology, emerging from lived experience of this disease, can contribute to the faith experience of those who live with this illness—and also to that of their communities of faith (this is one of the gifts that dementia brings). These issues are not only relevant to the spiritual support of those who live with dementia, but have wider significance for how the evangelical community understands its faith. Whether or not an individual lives with dementia, what is the nature of our faith and discipleship? How does dementia challenge our understanding? In the light of dementia, how can transformative, new theological understanding be brought to the church? Here are some possibilities and questions:

- *Development of practical theological expertise,* pertaining to the new insights into faith brought by dementia, for example, through ministerial training and university research.

- *Development of theological education and training* that responds to the profound theological questions that dementia asks of evangelical theology, and of its resulting practice. For example, in the light of dementia and its impact on believers . . .

    - What does it mean to be human, created by a loving and sovereign God?
    - What is the nature of "saving faith" and the Christian believer's reason for assurance of this?
    - What does it mean to be a disciple of Christ, whatever my particular capacities?
    - What does it mean to be a participant in the body of Christ?
    - What are the implications of collective memory of Scripture for the community of faith and its practices?
    - What is the nature of the Christian believer's hope and its impact in the present?

- *Development of ministerial and leadership training* to enable practical thinking about the above theological questions, in the light of the experience of dementia.

- *Provision of accessible theological education* at a local level for the community of faith (for example, through cross-city initiatives). Dialogical

---

37. For example, Keck, *Forgetting Whose We Are*; Swinton, *Dementia*.

approaches to learning (for example, small group study and workshops) have potential to bring theological and biblical understanding of these issues.

Further understanding of such issues as these, deliberately pursued in the light of dementia, has potential to affect pastoral practice in ways that will be significant for those who live with dementia, and for their communities of faith.

MORE TO BE DONE . . .

Of course, there is more to be done. The focus of my research and this book is inevitably limited. Yet, I hope that its limitations will have brought, in some way, deepening focus. My aim has been to further *understanding* of the faith experience of Christians living with dementia, "rather than to *explain* the experience."[38] I hope that the words of the participants recorded in this book and the theological reflection on these may have contributed towards this. I am aware that the reader's own situation and experience may be different from that which has been discussed here. Even so, I hope that they will have discovered helpful senses of identification and resonance.

As I have met with these disciples of Jesus, I am aware that their words and my reflections will have brought to mind other issues which prompt further questioning, thought, and action. So, I hope that this book may inspire further investigation, for example:[39]

- Reflection on the implications of this study for evangelical theology and biblical hermeneutics.

- Development of strategy to enable research with Christians for whom dementia has had a negative impact on their faith.

- Exploration of the difference that "couplehood"[40] brings to the faith experience for Christian believers who are living with dementia, in comparison to those who are living alone.

- The ongoing development of pastoral practices and faith resources that can support the spiritual lives of Christians living with dementia. For example, new approaches to Bible engagement and prayer, the development of spiritual mentoring of those in early to moderate stages of dementia.

38. Swinton and Mowat, *Practical Theology*, 121.
39. Patton, *Qualitative Research and Evaluation Methods*, 46.
40. Hellström, "'I'm His Wife Not His Carer!'"

- Creation of strategies that enable the Christian living with early to moderate dementia to be prepared and resourced spiritually for the more advanced stages of their illness.
- Exploration of the resonance between the spiritual experience of other faiths and that of the Christian faith whilst living with dementia. What mutual learning might be possible?
- Investigation into how the significance of the spiritual dimension for those living with dementia is acknowledged in public policy and professional practice documents.

"God Has Not Forgotten Me"

Through these conversations with Matthew, Bill, Alice, Ron, Rosemary, Jess, David, and Jill and my subsequent reflections, I have sought deeper understanding and fresh insights into the experience and practice of faith in dementia. Their words have challenged my understandings and, maybe, questioned our presuppositions about faith. They will hopefully inspire our search for ways in which to nurture their faith and receive the gifts which they are bringing to the church. Their voices affirm the crucial importance of being attentive to the faith experience of those who live with dementia—and bring significant questions in the light of this—to our theological and biblical understanding of faith. As we come to the closure of this particular conversation, there is a moment of stillness . . . Then, these reflections bring us to the pragmatic questions about the implications of what we have heard.[41] I am challenged and moved as I recollect words from Jess's poem:

> I only have Now . . . Lost past, No tomorrow, ONLY NOW . . .
> What a privilege because . . . Today is the day of salvation.[42]

Some of those with whom it has been my privilege to meet and talk with have now sadly passed away. Their lives and words continue to remind us, inevitably, of those we walk with *now* through the shadows of dementia—and bring challenge to our own faithfulness in our walk with God. So, how might we respond in "lived-out" ways that have potential to bring transformation, as we participate in the loving and purposeful mission of God? How might we *now* set about this walking together, responding to Alice's desire for others to remind her about her relationship with God: "They must remind me"?

41. See Osmer, *Practical Theology*, 4.
42. See chapter 9, 146–147, n43.

God has not forgotten his people, especially not those with dementia—or those who faithfully care and love. Lord Jesus, help us to remember you. Amen.

For Further Reflection . . .

- Thinking of those you know and love who live with dementia, reflect on the words of 1 John 4:7–12.
- Choose one or two ideas from this chapter. How could you and others in your community of faith respond in practice? How might the experience of dementia challenge your theology?
- Pause to reflect on what you have heard through this book. What do you think might be the most important or helpful things for you, your loved ones, and your faith community?

"I will not forget you! See, I have engraved you on the palms of my hands" (Isa 49:15–16, NIVUK).

Bibliography

Adams, Trevor. *Developing Dementia-Friendly Churches*. Cambridge: Grove, 2018.
Allen, F. Brian, and Peter G. Coleman. "Spiritual Perspectives on the Person with Dementia: Identity and Personhood." In *Dementia: Mind, Meaning, and the Person*, edited by Julian C. Hughes et al., 205–21. Oxford: Oxford University Press, 2006.
Alzheimer's Association. "Alzheimer's Disease Facts and Figures." https://www.alz.org/alzheimers-dementia/facts-figures.
———. "Stages of Alzheimer's." https://www.alz.org/alzheimers-dementia-stages.
Alzheimer's Disease International. "Dementia Statistics." https://www.alzint.org/about/dementia-facts-figures/dementia-statistics/.
———. "Numbers of People with Dementia Worldwide: An Update to the Estimates of the World Alzheimer Report in 2015." https://www.alzint.org/resource/numbers-of-people-with-dementia-worldwide.
Alzheimer's Research UK. "Facts and Stats." http://www.alzheimersresearchuk.org/about-dementia/facts-stats.
Alzheimer's Society. "End of Life Care." https://www.alzheimers.org.uk/info/20091/position_statements/139/end_of_life_care.
———. "The Progression of Alzheimer's Disease." https://alzheimers.org.uk/about-dementia/symptoms-and-diagnosis/how-dementia-progresses/progression-alzheimers-disease.
———. "Types of Dementia." https://www.alzheimers.org.uk/info/20007/types_of_dementia.
Anderson, Ray S. *On Being Human: Essays in Theological Anthropology*. Grand Rapids: Eerdmans, 1982.
———. *Spiritual Caregiving as Secular Sacrament: A Practical Theology for Professional Caregivers*. London: Jessica Kingsley, 2003.
Aquinas, Thomas. *The Summa Theologica*. Translated by Fathers of the English Dominican Province. 2nd and rev. ed. London: Burns, Oates and Washbourne, 1922.
Augustine, Saint. *The City of God*, 20.20. "Documenta Catholica Omnia." http://www.documentacatholicaomnia.eu/03d/03540430,_Augustinus,_De_Civitate_Dei_Contra_Paganos,_EN.pdf.
———. *Confessions*. Translated by Henry Chadwick. London: Oxford University Press, 2008.
———. *Enchiridion: On Faith, Hope, and Love*. Translated by Albert C. Outler. Philadelphia: Westminster, 1955. http://www.tertullian.org/fathers/augustine_enchiridion_02_trans.htm.

———. *On Genesis: Two Books on Genesis: Against the Manichees and on the Literal Interpretation of Genesis: An Unfinished Book*. Translated by Roland J. Teske. Washington, DC: Catholic University of America Press, 2001.

Barclay, Aileen. "Psalm 88: Living with Alzheimer's." *Journal of Religion, Disability & Health*, 16.1 (2012) 88–101. https://doi.org/10.1080/15228967.2012.645607.

Barth, Karl. *Church Dogmatics*. Edited by G. W. Bromiley and T. F. Torrance. Translated by G. W. Bromiley et al. Edinburgh: T. & T. Clark, 1936–62.

Bartlett, Helen, and Wendy Martin. "Ethical Issues in Dementia Care Research." In *The Perspectives of People with Dementia: Research Methods and Motivations*, edited by Heather Wilkinson, 47–61. London: Jessica Kingsley, 2002.

Bayley, John. *Iris: A Memoir of Iris Murdoch*. London: Duckworth, 1998.

Bebbington, David W. *Evangelicalism in Modern Britain: A History from the 1730s to the 1930s*. London: Routledge, 1988.

———. "Evangelical Trends, 1959–2009." *Anvil* 26.2 (2009) 93–106.

Beuscher, Linda, and Victoria E. Grando. "Using Spirituality to Cope with Early-Stage Alzheimer's Disease." *Western Journal of Nursing Research* 31.5 (2009) 583–98. https://doi.org/10.1177/0193945909332776.

Bonhoeffer, Dietrich. *The Cost of Discipleship*. London: SCM, 1959.

Bosch, David J. *Transforming Mission: Paradigm Shifts in Theology of Mission*. Maryknoll, NY: Orbis, 1991.

Briggs, Richard. S. "The Bible Before Us: Evangelical Possibilities for Taking Scripture Seriously." In *New Perspectives for Evangelical Theology: Engaging with God, Scripture and the World*, edited by Tom Greggs, 14–28. London: Routledge, 2010.

Brockmeier, Jens. "Questions of Meaning: Memory, Dementia, and the Postautobiographical Perspective." In *Beyond Loss: Dementia, Identity, and Personhood*, edited by Lars C. Hydén et al., 69–90. Oxford: Oxford University Press, 2014.

Brueggemann, Walter. *Praying the Psalms: Engaging Scripture and the Life of the Spirit*. 2nd ed. Eugene, OR: Cascade, 2007.

———. *Redescribing Reality: What We Do When We Read the Bible*. London: SCM, 2009.

———. *Spirituality of the Psalms*. Minneapolis: Augsburg Fortress, 2002.

———. "Suffering Produces Hope." *Biblical Theology Bulletin: Journal of Bible and Culture* 28.3 (1998) 95–103. https://doi.org/10.1177/014610799802800302.

———. *Texts Under Negotiation: The Bible and Postmodern Imagination*. Minneapolis: Fortress, 1993.

———. *An Unsettling God: The Heart of the Hebrew Bible*. Minneapolis: Fortress, 2009.

Bryden, Christine. *Dancing with Dementia: My Story of Living Positively with Dementia*. London: Jessica Kingsley, 2005.

———. "A Spiritual Journey Into the I-Thou Relationship: A Personal Reflection on Living with Dementia." *Journal of Religion, Spirituality & Aging* 28.1–2 (2016) 7–14. https://doi.org/10.1080/15528030.2015.1047294.

Bryden, Christine, and Elizabeth MacKinlay. "Dementia: A Journey Inwards to a Spiritual Self." In *Ageing, Disability and Spirituality*, edited by Elizabeth MacKinlay, 134–44. London: Jessica Kingsley, 2008.

———. "Dementia: A Spiritual Journey Towards the Divine: A Personal View of Dementia." *Journal of Religious Gerontology* 13.3–4 (2003) 69–75. https://doi.org/10.1300/J078v13n03_05.

Buber, Martin. *I and Thou*. Edinburgh: T. & T. Clark, 1958.

Bute, Jennifer. "My Glorious Opportunity: How My Dementia Has Been a Gift." *Journal of Religion, Spirituality and Aging* 28 (2016) 15–23. https://doi.org:10.1080/1552 8030.2015.1047295.

Bute, Jennifer, with Louise Morse. *Dementia from the Inside: A Doctor's Personal Journey of Hope*. London: SPCK, 2018.

Childs, Brevard S. *Memory and Tradition in Israel*. London: SCM, 1962.

Collicutt, Joanna. *Thinking of You: A Resource for the Spiritual Care of People with Dementia*. Abingdon, Oxon: Bible Reading Fellowship, 2017.

Congdon, David W., and W. Travis McMaken. "Ten Reasons Why Theology Matters." *Christianity Today*, October 27, 2016. https://www.christianitytoday.com/ct/2016/october-web/only-ten-reasons-why-theology-matters.html.

Cranfield, C. E. B. *Romans: A Shorter Commentary*. Edinburgh: T. & T. Clark, 1985.

Crowther, Dianne. *Sustaining Persons, Grieving Losses: A Fresh Pastoral Approach for the Challenges of the Dementia Journey*. Eugene, OR: Cascade, 2017.

Dalby, Padmaprabha, et al. "The Lived Experience of Spirituality and Dementia in Older People Living with Mild to Moderate Dementia." *Dementia* 11 (2012) 75–94. https://doi.org/10.1177/1471301211416608.

Davis, Robert. *My Journey into Alzheimer's Disease: Helpful Insights for Family and Friends*. Carol Stream, IL: Tyndale House, 1989.

Dementia Australia. "Dementia Statistics." https://www.dementia.org.au/statistics.

Dunlop, John. *Finding Grace in the Face of Dementia*. Wheaton, IL: Crossway, 2017.

Dunn, James D. G. *Romans 1–8*. Volume 38A: Word Biblical Commentary. Nashville, TN: Thomas Nelson, 1988.

Eastman, Susan. "Double Participation and the Responsible Self in Romans 5–8." In *Apocalyptic Paul: Cosmos and Anthropos in Romans 5–8*, edited by Beverly Roberts Gaventa, 93–110. Waco, TX: Baylor University Press, 2013.

Erikson, Erik. *The Life Cycle Completed*. Extended Version. New York: W. W. Norton, 1997.

Fitzmyer, Joseph. *Romans: A New Translation with Introduction and Commentary*. New Haven, CT: Yale University Press, 1993.

Fowler James W. *Stages of Faith: The Psychology of Human Development and the Quest for Meaning*. San Francisco: Harper, 1981.

Frankl, Viktor E. *Man's Search for Meaning*. New York: Washington Square, 1984.

Gaventa, Beverley R. "Which Human? What Response? A Reflection on Pauline Theology." *Ex Auditu: An International Journal of Theological Interpretation of Scripture* 30 (2014) 50–64.

Genova, Lisa. *Still Alice*. London: Simon & Schuster, 2009.

Gerrard, Nicci. *What Dementia Teaches Us about Love*. London: Allen Lane, 2019.

Giddens, Anthony. *Modernity and Self Identity: Self and Society in the Late Modern Age*. Cambridge: Polity, 1991.

Goffman, Erving. *Stigma: Notes on the Management of Spoiled Identity*. New York: Simon & Schuster, 1963.

Goldsmith, Malcolm. "Dementia: A Challenge to Christian Theology and Pastoral Care." In *Spirituality and Ageing*, edited by Albert Jewell, 125–35. London: Jessica Kingsley, 1998.

———. *In a Strange Land . . . People with Dementia and the Local Church*. Southwell, Notts: 4M, 2004.

———. "Through a Glass Darkly." *Journal of Religious Gerontology* 12.3–4 (2002) 123–138. https://doi.org/10.1300/J078v12n03_10.

———. "Tracing Rainbows through the Rain: Addressing the Challenge of Dementia in Later Life." In *Ageing, Disability and Spirituality: Addressing the Challenge of Disability*, edited by Elizabeth MacKinlay, 118–33. London: Jessica Kingsley, 2008.

Gooder, Paula. *Body: Biblical Spirituality for the Whole Person*. London: SPCK, 2016.

Greggs, Tom. "Beyond the Binary: Forming Evangelical Eschatology." In *New Perspectives for Evangelical Theology: Engaging with God, Scripture and the World*, edited by Tom Greggs, 153–67. Abingdon, Oxon: Routledge, 2010.

———. "Introduction—Opening Evangelicalism: Towards a Post-critical and Formative Theology." In *New Perspectives for Evangelical Theology: Engaging with God, Scripture and the World*, edited by Tom Greggs, 1–13. Abingdon, Oxon: Routledge, 2010.

———. *New Perspectives for Evangelical Theology: Engaging with God, Scripture and the World*. Abingdon, Oxon: Routledge, 2010.

Grenz, Stanley J. "The Social God and the Relational Self." In *Personal Identity in Theological Perspective*, edited by Richard Lints et al., 70–92. Grand Rapids: Eerdmans, 2006.

Gutiérrez, Gustavo. *A Theology of Liberation*. British ed. London: SCM, 1985.

Harris, Brian. "Beyond Bebbington: The Quest for Evangelical Identity in a Postmodern Era." *Churchman* 122.3 (2008) 201–19.

Hauerwas, Stanley. *A Community of Character: Toward a Constructive Christian Social Ethic*. Notre Dame, IN: University of Notre Dame Press, 1991.

———. *Cross-Shattered Christ: Meditations on the Seven Last Words*. Grand Rapids: Brazos, 2011.

———. *Naming the Silences: God, Medicine, and the Problem of Suffering*. London: T. & T. Clark International, 2004.

———. *The Peaceable Kingdom: A Primer in Christian Ethics*. Notre Dame, IN: University of Notre Dame Press, 1983.

———. "Seeing Darkness, Hearing Silence: Augustine's Account of Evil." In *Naming Evil, Judging Evil*, edited by Ruth W. Grant, 35–52. Chicago: University of Chicago Press, 2006.

Heidegger, Martin. *Being and Time*. Translated by John Macquarrie and Edward Robinson. Oxford: Blackwell, 1962.

Hellström, Ingrid. "'I'm His Wife Not His Carer!'—Dignity and Couplehood in Dementia." In *Beyond Loss: Dementia, Identity and Personhood*, edited by Lars C. Hydén et al., 53–66. Oxford: Oxford University Press, 2014.

Herth, Kaye. "Fostering Hope in Terminally-ill People." *Journal of Advanced Nursing* 15 (1990) 1250–59.

Heuser, Stefan. "The Human Condition as Seen from the Cross: Luther and Disability." In *Disability and the Christian Tradition*, edited by Brian Brock and John Swinton, 184–215. Grand Rapids: Eerdmans, 2012.

Higgins, Patricia. "The Spiritual and Religious Needs of People with Dementia." *Catholic Medical Quarterly* 61.4 (November 2011) 24–29.

Hoggarth, Pauline. *The Seed and the Soil: Engaging with the Word of God*. Carlisle, Cumbria: Langham Global Library, 2011.

Hudson, Rosalie. "God's Faithfulness and Dementia: Christian Theology in Context." *Journal of Religion, Spirituality and Aging* 28 (2016) 50–67. https://doi.org/10.1080/15528030.2015.1041669.

Hughes, Julian C. "A Situated Embodied View of the Person with Dementia." In *Spirituality and Personhood in Dementia*, edited by Albert Jewell, 198–206. London: Jessica Kingsley, 2011.

Hughes, Julian, C., ed. *Dementia: Mind, Meaning, and the Person*. Oxford: Oxford University Press, 2006.

Hull, John. "Spiritual Development: Interpretations and Applications," *British Journal of Religious Education* 24.3 (Summer 2002) 171–82. https://doi.org/10.1080/0141620020240302.

Jenson, Robert. "Nihilism: Sin, Death, and the Devil." *Newsletter: Report from the Center for Catholic and Evangelical Theology*, Summer 1998, 4.

Jewell, Albert. *Ageing, Spirituality and Well-being*. London: Jessica Kingsley, 2004.

———. *Spirituality and Ageing*. London: Jessica Kingsley, 1998.

———. *Spirituality and Personhood in Dementia*. London: Jessica Kingsley, 2011.

Katsuno, Towako. "Personal Spirituality of Persons with Dementia: Is it Related to Perceived Quality of Life?" *Dementia* 2.3 (2003) 315–35. https://doi.org/10.1177/14713012030023003.

Keck, David. *Forgetting Whose We Are: Alzheimer's Disease and the Love of God*. Nashville, TN: Abingdon, 1996.

Kent, Elizabeth. "Embodied Evangelicalism: The Body of Christ and the Christian Body." In *New Perspectives for Evangelical Theology: Engaging with God, Scripture and the World*, edited by Tom Greggs, 108–37. Abingdon, Oxon: Routledge, 2010.

Kevern, Peter. "Alzheimer's and the Dementia of God." *International Journal of Public Theology* 4 (2010) 237–53. https://doi.org/10.1163/156973210X491895.

———. "Dementia and Spirituality: The Current State of Research and its Implications." Royal College of Psychiatrists 6 (2013). https://www.rcpsych.ac.uk/pdf/Peter%20Kevern%20Dementia%20and%20Spirituality.pdf.

———. "I Pray that I Will Not Fall over the Edge." *Practical Theology* 4.3 (2011) 283–294. https://doi.org/10.1558/prth.v4i3.283.

———. "Sharing the Mind of Christ: Preliminary Thoughts on Dementia and the Cross." *New Blackfriars* 91.1034 (2010) 408–22. https:/doi.org/10.1111/j.1741-2005.2009.01317.x.

———. "The Spirituality of People with Late-Stage Dementia: A Review of the Research Literature, a Critical Analysis and some Implications for Person-centred Spirituality and Dementia Care." *Mental Health, Religion & Culture* 18.9 (2015) 765–776. https://doi.org/10.1080/13674676.2015.1094781.

———. "What Sort of a God is to Be Found in Dementia? A Survey of Theological Responses and an Agenda for Their Development." *Theology* 113.873 (May 2010) 174–84. https://doi.org/10.1177/0040571X1011300303.

Kilby, Karen. "Perichoresis and Projection: Problems with Social Doctrines of the Trinity." *New Blackfriars* 81.956 (2000) 432–45. https://doi.org/10.1111/j.1741-2005.2000.tb06456.x.

Kitwood, Tom. *Dementia Reconsidered: The Person Comes First*. Maidenhead: Open University Press, 1997.

Kontos, Pia C. "Alzheimer Expressions or Expressions despite Alzheimer's? Philosophical Reflections on Selfhood and Embodiment." *Occasion: Interdisciplinary Studies in the Humanities* 4 (May 2012) 1–12.

Kontos, Pia C., and Gary Naglie. "Expressions of Personhood in Alzheimer's Disease: An Evaluation of Research-Based Theatre as a Pedagogical Tool." *Qualitative Health Research* 17.6 (2007) 799–811. https://doi.org/10.1177/1049732307302838.

———. "Tacit Knowledge of Caring and Embodied Selfhood." *Sociology of Health & Illness* 31.5 (2009) 688–704. https://doi.org/10.1111/j.14679566.2009.01158.x/full.

Kuhse, Helga, and Peter Singer. *Should the Baby Live?: The Problem of Handicapped Infants*. Oxford: Oxford University Press, 1985.

Lartey, Emmanuel. "Practical Theology as a Theological Form." In *The Blackwell Reader in Pastoral and Practical Theology*, edited by James Woodward and Stephen Pattison, 128–34.Oxford: Blackwell, 2000.

Lennon, Dennis. *The Eyes of the Heart: A Spirituality of the Senses*. London: SPCK, 2000.

Locke, John. *Essay concerning Human Understanding*, II.xxvii.9 (1689). http://www.earlymoderntexts.com/assets/pdfs/locke1690book2.pdf.

MacKinlay, Elizabeth. *Ageing, Disability and Spirituality: Addressing the Challenge of Disability in Later Life*. London: Jessica Kingsley, 2008.

———. "The Spiritual Dimension of Ageing." In *Ageing, Spirituality and Well-being*. Edited by Albert Jewell, 72–85. London: Jessica Kingsley, 2004.

———. *The Spiritual Dimension of Ageing*. 2nd ed. London: Jessica Kingsley, 2017.

———. "Walking with a Person into Dementia: Creating Care Together." In *Spirituality, Personhood and Dementia*, edited by Albert Jewell, 42–51. London: Jessica Kingsley, 2011.

MacKinlay, Elizabeth, and Corinne Trevitt. *Finding Meaning in the Experience of Dementia: The Place of Spiritual Reminiscence Work*. London: Jessica Kingsley, 2012.

MacKinlay, Karen. "Listening to People with Dementia: A Pastoral Care Perspective." *Journal of Religious Gerontology* 13.3–4 (2003) 91–106. https://doi.org/10.1300/J078v13n03_07.

Magnusson, Sally. *Where Memories Go: Why Dementia Changes Everything*. London: Hodder & Stoughton, 2014.

Manen, Max van. *Researching Lived Experience: Human Science for an Action Sensitive Pedagogy*. Albany, NY: State University of New York, 1990.

Mast, Benjamin. *Second Forgetting: Remembering the Power of the Gospel During Alzheimer's Disease*. Grand Rapids: Zondervan, 2014.

Matthews, Eric. "Dementia and the Identity of the Person." In *Dementia: Mind, Meaning, and the Person*, edited by Julian C. Hughes et al., 163–77. Oxford: Oxford University Press, 2006.

McFadden, Susan, et al. "Actions, Feelings, and Values: Foundations of Meaning and Personhood in Dementia." *Journal of Religious Gerontology* 11.3–4 (2001) 67–86. https://doi.org /10.1300/J078v11n03_0.

McFadyen, Donald. "Embodied Christianity." In *New Perspectives for Evangelical Theology: Engaging with God, Scripture and the World*, edited by Tom Greggs, 123–37. Abingdon, Oxon: Routledge, 2010.

McGrath, Alister. *Evangelicalism and the Future of Christianity*. London: Hodder & Stoughton, 1995.

Merleau-Ponty, Maurice. *Phenomenology of Perception*. Translated by Colin Smith. London: Routledge and Kegan Paul, 1962.

Moltmann, Jürgen. *The Crucified God*. London: SCM, 1974.

———. *The Trinity and the Kingdom of God*. London: SCM, 1981.

Osmer, Richard R. *Practical Theology: An Introduction*. Grand Rapids: Eerdmans, 2008.

Pattison, Stephen. "Some Straw for the Bricks: A Basic Introduction to Theological Reflection." In *The Blackwell Reader in Pastoral and Practical Theology*, edited by James Woodward and Stephen Pattison, 139–40. Oxford: Blackwell, 2000.

Patton, Michael Q. *Qualitative Research and Evaluation Methods*. 3rd ed. Thousand Oaks, CA: Sage, 2002.

Peace, Richard V. *Conversion in the New Testament: Paul and the Twelve*. Grand Rapids: Eerdmans, 1999.

Post, Stephen G. *The Moral Challenge of Alzheimer Disease: Ethical Issues from Diagnosis to Dying*. 2nd ed. Baltimore: Johns Hopkins University Press, 2000.

———. "*Respectare*: Moral Respect for the Lives of the Deeply Forgetful." In *Dementia: Mind, Meaning, and the Person*, edited by Julian C. Hughes et al., 223–34 Oxford: Oxford University Press, 2006.

Reinders, Hans S. *Disability, Providence, and Ethics: Bridging Gaps, Transforming Lives*. Waco, TX: Baylor University Press, 2014.

———. *Receiving the Gift of Friendship: Profound Disability, Theological Anthropology, and Ethics*. Grand Rapids: Eerdmans, 2008.

Root, Andrew. *Christopraxis: A Practical Theology of the Cross*. Minneapolis: Fortress, 2014.

Sabat, Steven R. *The Experience of Alzheimer's Disease: Life through a Tangled Veil*. Oxford: Blackwell, 2001.

———. "Mind, Meaning, and Personhood in Dementia: The Effects of Positioning." In *Dementia: Mind, Meaning, and the Person*, edited by Julian C. Hughes et al., 287–302. Oxford: Oxford University Press, 2006.

SAGA. "Dementia more feared than Cancer." May 14, 2016. https://newsroom.saga.co.uk/news/dementia-more-feared-than-cancer-new-saga-survey-reveals.

Sapp, Stephen. "Living with Alzheimer's: Body, Soul and the Remembering Community." *The Christian Century*, January 21, 1998, 54–60.

———. "Spiritual Care of People with Dementia and their Carers." In *Supportive Care for the Person with Dementia*, edited by Julian C. Hughes et al., 199–206. Oxford: Oxford University Press, 2010.

Saunders, James. *Dementia: Pastoral Theology and Pastoral Care*. Cambridge: Grove, 2002.

Schacter, Daniel. *Searching for Memory: The Brain, the Mind, and the Past*. New York: Basic, 1996.

Scripture4All. "2 Corinthians." Greek Interlinear Bible. https://www.scripture4all.org/OnlineInterlinear/NTpdf/2co1.pdf.

———. "Romans 5." Greek Interlinear Bible. https://www.scripture4all.org/OnlineInterlinear/NTpdf/rom5.pdf.

Scripture Union International Council (SUIC). "Aims, Beliefs and Working Principles of Scripture Union." January 12, 2011. https://issuu.com/scripture_union_australia/docs/aims_beliefs_working_principles.

Shamy, Eileen. *A Guide to the Spiritual Dimension of Care for People with Alzheimer's Disease and Related Dementia: More than Body, Brain and Breath.* London: Jessica Kingsley, 2003.

Singer, Peter. *Practical Ethics.* 2nd ed. Cambridge: Cambridge University Press, 1993.

Spaemann, Robert. *Persons: The Difference between "Someone" and "Something."* Translated by Oliver O'Donovan. Oxford: Oxford University Press, 2017.

Stott, John. "The Age of Dependence." *Christianity Magazine,* January 2010. https://www.premierchristianity.com/Past-Issues/2010/January-2010.

———. *The Message of Romans.* The Bible Speaks Today. Nottingham: Inter-Varsity, 1994.

Strong, James. "3820 *Leb.*" In *Strong's Exhaustive Concordance of the Bible.* Nashville, TN: Abingdon, 1890. https://biblehub.com/hebrew/3820.htm.

Stuckey, Jon C., and Lisa P. Gwyther. "Dementia, Religion, and Spirituality." *Dementia* 2.3 (2003) 291–97. https://doi.org/1177/14713012030023001.

Summa, Michela, and Thomas Fuchs. "Self-experience in Dementia." *Rivista Internazionale di Filosofia e Psicologia* 6:2 (2015) 387–405. https://doi.org/10.4453/rifp.2015.0038.

Swinton, John. *Becoming Friends of Time: Disability, Timefullness and Gentle Discipleship.* London: SCM, 2017.

———. *Dementia: Living in the Memories of God.* Grand Rapids: Eerdmans, 2012.

———. *Finding Jesus in the Storm: The Spiritual Lives of Christians with Mental Health Challenges.* Grand Rapids: Eerdmans, 2020.

———. *Raging with Compassion: Pastoral Responses to the Problem of Evil.* Grand Rapids: Eerdmans, 2007.

———. "Reforming, Revisionist, Refounding: Practical Theology as Disciplined Seeing." Reforming Practical Theology: The Politics of Body and Space, International Academy of Practical Theology Conference Series 1 (2019) 5–12. https:// doi.org/10.25785/iapt.cs.v1i0.46.

———. *Spirituality and Mental Health Care: Rediscovering a Forgotten Dimension.* London: Jessica Kingsley, 2001.

———. "What the Body Remembers: Theological Reflections on Dementia." ABC Religion and Ethics, June 26, 2013. http://www.abc.net.au/religion/articles/2013/06/26/3790480.htm.2013.

Swinton, John, and Harriet Mowat. *Practical Theology and Qualitative Research.* London: SCM, 2006.

Vanhoozer, Kevin J. *Is There a Meaning in This Text?* Grand Rapids: Zondervan, 1998.

Wallace, Daphne. "Maintaining a Sense of Personhood." In *Spirituality and Personhood in Dementia,* edited by Albert Jewell, 24–30. London: Jessica Kingsley, 2011.

Weil, Simone. *Waiting on God.* London: Routledge and Kegan Paul, 1951.

Westminster Assembly. "Westminster Shorter Catechism." July 28, 1648. Centre for Reformed Theology and Apologetics. https://www.reformed.org/documents/wsc/index.html.

Whitman, Lucy, ed. *People with Dementia Speak Out.* London: Jessica Kingsley, 2016.

Williams, Patricia S. "Knowing God in Dementia: What Happens to Faith When You Can No Longer Remember?" *Journal of Health and Social Care Chaplaincy* 4.2 (2016) 1–16. https://doi.org/10.1558/hscc.v4i2.30960.

———. "What Happens to Faith When Christians Get Dementia? A Critical Exploration of How Dementia Affects the Faith Experience and Practice of Christians from the

Evangelical Tradition Living with Mild to Moderate Symptoms of Dementia." PhD diss., University of Aberdeen, 2018.

Williams, Rowan. *Being Disciples: Essentials of Christian Life*. London: SPCK, 2016.

———. "The Person and the Individual: Human Dignity, Human Relationships and Human Limits." Annual Lecture 2012. London: Theos, 2013. https://www.theosthinktank.co.uk/research/2012/10/01/the-person-and-the-individual-human-dignity-human-relationships-and-human-limits.

Williams, 'Tricia. "Growing Faith in Dementia: A Theological Reflection on Lived Experience." *Global Anglican* 135.2 (2021) 115–32.

———. *What Happens to Faith When Christians Get Dementia? The Faith Experience and Practice of Evangelical Christians Living with Mild to Moderate Dementia*. Eugene, OR: Pickwick, 2021.

———. *Words of Faith*. Being with God: A Bible and Prayer Guide for People with Dementia. Milton Keynes: Scripture Union, 2010.

———. *Words of Hope*. Being with God: A Bible and Prayer Guide for People with Dementia. Milton Keynes: Scripture Union, 2010.

———. *Words of Peace*. Being with God: A Bible and Prayer Guide for People with Dementia. Milton Keynes: Scripture Union, 2010.

Wilkinson, Heather. *The Perspectives of People with Dementia: Research Methods and Motivations*. London: Jessica Kingsley, 2002.

Wolverson (Radbourne), Emma L., et al. "Remaining Hopeful in Early-stage Dementia: A Qualitative Study." *Aging & Mental Health* 14.4 (2010) 450–60. https://doi.org/10.1080/13607860903483110.

Woodward, James, and Stephen Pattison, eds. *The Blackwell Reader in Pastoral and Practical Theology*. Oxford: Blackwell, 2000.

Wright, N. T. "Mind, Spirit, Soul and Body: All for One and One for All: Reflections on Paul's Anthropology in his Complex Contexts." Paper given at Society of Christian Philosophers. Fordham University, March 18, 2011. https://ntwrightpage.com/2016/07/12/mind-spirit-soul-and-body.

Wright, Tom. *Surprised by Hope*. London: SPCK, 2007.

Zahl, Simeon. "Reformation Pessimism or Pietist Personalism?: The Problem of the Holy Spirit in Evangelical Theology." In *New Perspectives for Evangelical Theology: Engaging with God, Scripture and the World*, edited by Tom Greggs, 78–92. Abingdon, Oxon: Routledge, 2010.

Zizioulas, John D. *Being as Communion: Studies in Personhood and the Church*. New York: St. Vladimir's Seminary Press, 1985.

———. *Communion and Otherness: Further Studies in Personhood and the Church*. London: T. & T. Clark International, 2006.

Index

acceptance, 54, 62, 120–23, 126, 132, 154
accompaniment of those living with dementia, 158–59
affliction, 89–90, 98
Adams, Trevor, 156
adversity, 84–89, 112, 128–30
advocacy, 156
ageing, tasks of, 23–24, 128
Alzheimer's Association, 2–3
Alzheimer's disease, 2–4, 103
Alzheimer's Disease International, 2
Alzheimer's Research, UK, 2
Alzheimer's Society, 2, 11, 20
Allen, F. Brian, and Peter G. Coleman, 22
Anderson, Ray S, 36–40, 45, 137
Aquinas, Thomas, 37
Augustine, St., 28, 37, 39, 41–42, 86, 145
autobiographical accounts, 30, 48

Barclay, Aileen, 89, 92–94, 97, 153
Barth, Karl, 37, 45, 86
Bartlett, Helen, and Wendy Martin, 12
Bayley, John, 19
Bebbington, David W., 4, 6–7, 107
belonging to a faith community, 72–80
Beuscher, Linda, and Victoria E. Grando, 22, 54, 135, 151
Bible (biblical),
  agenda and boundaries, 10, 14
  authority, 7, 10
  central role of, 7–8
  engagement, 1, 68, 80, 152–53, 159, 162, see also faith practice
  and interpretation, 10, 46
  and memory, 15, 104–106
  perspective(s), 10, 14, 19, 32–50, 95, 104–6, 138
  reading, 7, 15, 18, 64, 66–72, 80, 91, 159
  as story or narrative, ix, 15, 38–41, 44, 47–50, 94–95, 99, 101, 104, 117, 121–22, 124, 135, 137–38, 141–42, 144–45, 155
  see also Scripture
Bible Society, xi
blame, 84–86, 93
body of Christ, 6, 9, 14, 19, 30, 33, 41, 47–50, 67, 72–73, 114–15, 120, 128–30, 153, 158, 161, see also belonging to a faith community
Bonhoeffer, Dietrich, 97
Bosch, David J., 7, 87
brain(s), xv, 2, 21, 29, 33, 40, 47, 55, 64, 70, 74, 98, 104, 140
Briggs, Richard. S., 7, 68
Brockmeier, Jens, 28, 102, 117
Brueggemann, Walter, 10–11, 19, 33n, 36n, 82n, 87–88, 90–91, 95, 101, 104n, 106, 118–19, 124–26, 137–38, 147–48, 151–52
Bryden, Christine, 26, 30, 31, 33, 40, 67, 77, 92, 94, 121, 125, 154, 156
Bryden, Christine, and Elizabeth MacKinlay, 3, 11, 35, 129, 154, 158
Buber, Martin, 27, 37, 40, 67
Bute, Jennifer, 20, 30, 129n, 154, 156
Bute, Jennifer, with Louise Morse, 20

INDEX

care,
  care home(s), 2, 29, 86
  (supportive) community of care, 128–29, 159
  God's care, 58
  holistic care, 20–21
  medical, 20, 21, 33–35, 77
  pastoral care, xi, 16, 21, 25, 83, 154–55, 158–59
  person-centered care, 26–27
  spiritual, ix–x, 4, 21–25, 29–31, 129–30, 155, 157, 158
carer(s), 18, 29, 47, 76–81, 131, 144, 155, 164
chaplain(s), 20, 21, 79, 157
chaplaincy, 2, 157, 160
Childs, Brevard S., 104
Christ,
  being in, 33, 44–47, 133, 137
  commitment to, 108, 109
  on the cross, 54, 60, 88, 91, 95, 97–98, 112, 126, 148
  encounter(s) with (and Jesus), 9, 52, 108, 141, *see* also encounter(s) with God
  faith in, 30, 35, 44, 46, 151
  incarnation of, 47, 60, 141
  identity in, 5, 14, 30, 35, 44–47, 50
  relationship with (and Jesus), 5–6, 37–38, 43, 47, 58–61, 66, 107–10, 117, 136, 140, 145–46
  sacrifice of, 60, 95
  the work of (and Jesus), 9, 135, 137, 142, 148
  see also Jesus
christopraxis, 8–10, 17, 52, 63–64, 107, 141, 160
church('s),
  activities, 64, 66–68, 152–53, 157, 159–60
  eternal, 137–38
  churchgoing, 5, 73–76, 80, 107–109, 111, 114
  response of the, 117, 125, 128, 129–30, 132, 148–49, 155–160, 162–64
  local, 11, 15, 41, 48, 64, 73–74, 77, 80, 94, 99, 125, 129–30, 149, 153, 156–57, 158–60
  see also: belonging to a faith community; Body of Christ
cognitive aspects of belief, 3–4, 6, 35–38, 40, 43, 46–47, 49, 54–56, 61, 64, 86–87, 115–16, 118, 123–24, 127, 128, 131, 136
cognitive capacity (decline *and* loss), xv, 1–3, 6, 21, 26, 29, 38, 40, 43, 46, 49, 52, 54, 64, 102–3, 104, 118, 123–24, 127, 128, 131
Collicutt, Joanna, 154
commitment to God,
  "born again," 5, 45, 63, 100, 107, 109, 137
  converted (conversion), 4, 5–6, 13, 52, 105, 107, 109–1to faith, 13, 110, 112
  to God, 56, 86, 122
  to Christ (Jesus) 107, 108, 109
community(ies) of faith, xvi, 1, 6, 33, 46, 49, 50, 64, 67, 76, 91, 93, 95, 128–30, 146, 153–54, 156–57, 160–62, 164
  as fellowship, 70, 73, 78, 79, 114
  of God's people, 15, 19, 41, 48, 87, 147–48
  as local church (congregation), 11, 15, 48, 73–74, 77, 80, 94
  relationality of, 48–49
  remembering community of faith, 114–15, 128–30
  which trusts, 91
  see also Body of Christ; belonging to a faith community
Congdon, David W., and W. Travis McMaken, 4
context(s),
  changing, 10
  community of faith, 154, 157, 160
  cultural, of suffering, 85, 87–88
  dementia and faith, 4–5, 17–31, 41, 50, 61, 69–70, 71–72, 84, 91, 92, 99, 106, 107, 121, 122, 135, 152, 154, 157, 158–160
  divine mystery, 54

INDEX   177

eternity and time, 135, 139, 147
of God's story, 120, 122
relationship, 42, 68, 83, 110, 112
remembering community of faith,
    128–130
of the research, 2–5, 8–16
of suffering, 84–86
Western, xv, 19, 28, 36, 38, 87
conversation,
    with the Bible, xvi, 15–16
    as image for the research, 8, 10, 14,
        30, 91, 163
conversion,
    belief and, 105
    as "born again," 5, 45, 63, 100, 107,
        109, 137
    and conversionism, 4
    experience of, 5–6, 52, 105, 107,
        109–10
coping, 24, 25, 54, 112, 118–19,
    134–35
couplehood, 78, 162
covenant(al) faithfulness and love,
    122, 124
created
    being human, 38–41
    body-and-soul, 39–40, 115
    by God, 14, 33, 38–41, 115
    in the image of God, 32, 33, 35,
        36–43
Cranfield, C. E. B., 125
cross, the, 6, 9, 46, 54, 83, 84, 88, 91,
    95, 97–99, 112, 121, 126, 138
    Christ on, 60, 88, 91, 95, 97–99,
        126, 148
    shadow of, 97–99
Crowther, Dianne, 48, 117, 129, 130,
    135, 146, 149, 154, 155, 157,
    158, 159

Dalby, Padmaprabha, et al., 116
darkness, 15, 52, 80, 83, 89, 92, 95,
    97–98, 133, 152, 154
Davis, Robert, 30, 52, 89, 96, 97, 121–
    22, 152, 154
dementia,
    as context, 5, 41, 50, 61, 69, 71, 99,
        121, 152, 154, 158

as "deconstruction incarnate,"
    18–19
difficulties, 1, 3, 33, 52, 66, 71, 75,
    77, 83, 89, 91, 114, 122, 129,
    139, 152, 155, 157
as disempowerment, 91
and faith, 2–4
journey with/of, xv, 2–3, 28, 30, 34,
    47, 52, 59, 93, 101–2, 41 25, 28,
    30, 31, 34, 47, 52, 59, 78, 93,
    101–2, 105, 116, 119, 120, 122,
    125, 131, 132, 139, 145, 151,
    156, 158
later stages of, 18–19, 27, 31, 103,
    114, 156
naming, 91, 93, 153
and acknowledging, 83, 90, 93,
    125, 153, 163
and denial, 90
negative impact on faith, 162
questions arising from, xv–xvi,
    3–4, 5, 6, 7, 8, 14, 16, 18–19,
    25–30, 35–38, 44, 48, 49, 57,
    73, 84–88, 101, 122, 134, 151,
    153, 154, 158, 160–62
recognition of, 157, 160
and research, ix, 2, 5, 8, 14, 30–31,
    52n, 156, 162
stages of, xv, 2–4, 11, 18–19, 24–25,
    27, 32, 33, 38, 44, 64, 77, 83,
    90, 92, 103, 113, 156, 162, 163
struggles of, xv, 16, 31, 32, 52, 64,
    82–84, 87, 92, 95–97, 98–99,
    118, 124, 128, 133, 151, 152–
    155, 157
as theological disease, 18
see also suffering
Dementia Australia, 2
dependence,
    on God, 54, 56, 79, 110, 123–24,
        130
    on others, 67, 76–80, 115, 158
Descartes, René, 26
devotional practice(s) 7, 67, 71, 160
diagnosis, the effects of, 12, 20, 28, 31,
    33, 76–77, 92, 119, 125, 135
disability(ies), 24, 93, 120, 145

INDEX

disciple(s), 5, 7, 19, 35, 43, 45, 46, 64–65, 80, 84, 85, 94, 95, 97, 99, 106, 119, 121, 123, 127, 128, 131, 132, 137, 148–49, 151
    disciple(ship), ix, 1, 7, 158–60, 161–162
    follower(s) of Jesus, 7, 23, 43, 48, 52, 121, 128, 142
disorientation, 10–11, 15, 19, 50, 82–99, 118, 119, 120, 148, 151, 154, 158
    walking through shadow, 82–99
    experiencing shadow, 89–99
    responding to adversity, 84–89
doubt, 52, 53, 84–85, 87, 94, 118, 121, 137, 153, 156
Dunlop, John, 123–24, 128, 154
dualism, 39

Eastman, Susan, 49n, 128
embodiment,
    the body's memory 29, 103
    body and soul 39–40, 104, 105, 115
    body language 53
    embodied encounter(s), 83, 102
encounter(s),
    with Christ (Jesus), 9, 17, 52, 108, 141n
    with God, 45, 63, 106–112
endurance,
    enabling endurance, 15, 125, 128–32
    under pressure, 119, 125–27
    hypomone, 125
Enlightenment, 37, 46, 87, 145
    post-Enlightenment, 87
Erikson, Erik, 120n
eschatology (eschatological),
    hope, 33, 127, 137, 138, 146, 148, 159
    imagination, 154
    orientation, 194–96, 204
eternal (eternity), 28, 42, 133, 134, 138, 139, 140, 144, 145, 147, 148
evangelical(ism),
    emphasis(es), 3, 4–7, 19, 46, 37, 61, 87, 124
    and practical theology, 9–10
    and propositional truth(s)/thinking, 3, 37, 46, 123–24
    tradition 2, 3, 4–10, 11–13, 14–15, 18, 35, 37–38, 43, 49, 55, 56, 68, 72, 87, 107, 123, 150, 154, 160
    theology 35–38, 42
evil and suffering, 86–88
experience of faith in dementia, xvi, 1–16, 18, 21, 23–25, 29–31, 120–21, 134–35
    faith practice, 66–81, 152–53, 158–59
    personal experience(s), 51–65, 83–86, 89–99, 100–101, 104, 106, 107–116, 117–19, 121–32, 133–34, 135–38, 139–49, 151–55

faith,
    funding, 15, 31, 100–116, 136, 151, 153
    intrinsic, 5, 11, 44, 46–47, 64, 66, 107n
    and extrinsic religiousness, 5, 23, 66
    the lived experience of, 11, 18, 51–65, 117, 135, 144–45, 148, 154
    memory, 15, 100–116, 137, 144, 146–47, 153, 154
    nature of, xv–xvi, 20–25, 29–30, 36–38, 40–41, 67, 101, 114, 129, 150, 151, 156, 160–61
    remembering, of God, 104
    transcendent (-ing) 9, 22, 35, 52, 55, 59, 62, 66, 103, 120–22, 123, 130, 134, 137–38, 139, 146–48
    transforming, 107–8, 110, 116, 118, 131, 132
faith commitment,
    "born again," 5, 45, 63, 100, 107, 109, 137
    converted, 13, 109
    to faith, 12, 13, 63, 100, 106, 108, 109, 110, 112, 159
    to God, 56, 86, 122
    to Jesus (Christ), 107, 108, 109

INDEX

faith, growing, 15, 52–54, 64, 87, 117–32, 133, 136, 147, 158
  faith nurture in the context of dementia, 7, 16, 18, 21, 77–78, 155, 158–60,
  strengthening faith, 15, 52–54
  transforming faith, 116, 118, 107, 134–141, 143, 144, 151, 154
  see also spiritual growth
faith(ful) imagination, ix, 75, 132, 140–41, 148, 154, 157, 158
  of the future, 38, 39, 44, 59, 98, 116, 136, 145, 154, 159
faith practice(s), 4–5, 15, 22, 29, 64, 66–81, 111, 114, 150–151, 152–56, 160
  Bible reading, 7–8, 15, 18, 64, 66, 67–71, 72, 78, 80, 91, 106, 142, 150, 159
  Bible reading and prayer, 1, 18, 67–68, 70, 72, 80, 150, 159
  communion, 29, 73, 74, 80, 114–115, 157
  difficulties with faith practice, 66–67, 71, 73–74, 74–76, 79, 114, 152–56, 157
  going to church, 70, 73–80, 114
  "home group," 70–71, 77–78, 153
  music, songs and hymns, 29, 51n, 75, 103, 113, 119, 140, 144, 159
  prayer, 1, 15, 29, 64, 71–72, 78, 80, 152
  worship, 23, 29, 36, 58, 64, 66, 103, 152
faith resources, 69, 71, 152, 160, 162
faithfulness,
  of God, 43, 83, 108, 112, 123, 124–25, 126, 132, 138, 146, 148, 153
  to God, 90
fear(s) ix, 2, 26, 45, 93–94, 96, 133, 141, 143, 145, 151
feelings, 15, 47, 52, 61–64, 70, 72, 96, 109, 110, 123, 141–42, 152, 157
Fitzmyer, Joseph, 125n
forgiveness, 46, 86–87, 133, 141–43, 148, 154
Fowler James W., 120n
Frankl, Viktor E., 120n

Gaventa, Beverley R., 6n
Genova, Lisa 19
Giddens, Anthony, 39n
gift(s),
  dementia as, 30, 122, 126–127, 151, 161
  of God (Christ, the Spirit), 37, 43, 45, 46, 49, 58, 123, 128
  of person with dementia, xv, 16, 31, 49, 54, 101, 128, 153, 156, 163
God,
  Creator, 36–41, 44, 57–58, 71
  Father, 5n, 41–43, 47, 54, 56n, 57, 58, 97, 98, 121, 131, 142, 152
  Son, 5n, 34, 42, 43, 54, 56n, 59, 60, 130
  (Holy) Spirit, x, 5, 7, 15, 33, 41, 42, 43, 45, 48–49, 54, 55–56, 57, 61, 73, 78–79, 105, 113, 119, 123, 127, 128, 130–31, 132, 135, 137, 141, 142, 144, 146, 152
  Trinity, 41–43, 57, 98
  being as communion, 42–43
  perichoretic community, 42
God('s) love, x, xv, 30, 34, 43, 64, 69, 119, 123–24, 130
  is love, 43
  loved by God, 32, 34, 41, 45, 61, 63, 79
  loving God, 69, 104
  loving relationship with God, 42–43, 55–58, 66–67, 69, 123
God's sovereignty, 36, 39, 50, 84, 87, 91, 120–121, 124, 126, 151, 161
God's story, 15, 47–48, 50, 99, 101, 114–15, 120, 122, 134, 135, 137–38, 141, 144–45
  see also narrative
Goffman, Erving, 77, 93
Goldsmith, Malcolm, 11n, 16, 22, 23, 25, 90, 91, 95
Gooder, Paula, 39–40
grace, 6, 37, 46–47, 49, 113, 117, 123, 124, 141, 150, 152, 158
Greggs, Tom, 4, 14, 146
Grenz, Stanley J., 48–49, 137–38

grief, 25–26, 84, 90–91, 92, 101, 151
    naming of, 90–91, 157
Gutiérrez, Gustavo, 5

Harris, Brian, 4, 6, 7, 107
Hauerwas, Stanley, 10, 14, 48, 85–89, 98, 123, 128–30
heart(s), ix, x, 6n, 31, 37n, 56, 104–106, 113, 115, 116, 119, 130–31, 135, 140
    kardia, 105
    leb, 104
    and memory, 104–106, 115–16
heaven, hope of, 137, 139–41, 142, 144, 151, 159
Heidegger, Martin,
    Being and Time, 53n
    being-with, 30
Hellström, Ingrid, 78, 162
hermeneutic phenomenology, 30–31, 52n
Herth, Kaye, 134n
Heuser, Stefan, 97n
    Higgins, Patricia, 22n
Hoggarth, Pauline, 7, 152
holiness, 25
Holy Spirit (the Spirit), 5n, 7, 15, 42–43, 45, 48–49, 54, 55–56, 61, 73, 78, 105, 119, 123, 127–28, 130–31, 132, 135, 137, 141–42, 144, 146, 152
hope, 131–132, 133–149, 150, 151, 152,
    eschatological, 33, 127, 137, 146, 148, 159
    being hope-ful(hopefulness), x, 50, 73, 128, 134–46, 153, 154, 159, 161
    hopeful orientation 10, 15, 49
    present-future, 15–16, 133–49
    of resurrection, 9, 36, 143–44, 148, 159
    transforming, 15–16, 134–45
horizon(s), of faith, 30, 131
    Hudson, Rosalie, 43
    Hughes, Julian, C., 22, 24

human being(s), 13, 22, 27, 31, 37, 39n, 40, 43, 53, 60, 87, 89, 101, 144,
    being human, 21, 27, 36–41, 44, 98
    body-and-soul, 39–40, 115
    created, 14, 32–33, 35–40, 161
    made for relationship, 40–41
Hull, John, 22–23
humor, 95, 102,
hypercognitive, 26, 38
hypomone, 125

identity,
    belonging to the community of faith, 6, 15, 72–81, 153, 156, 157
    belonging in the body of Christ, 33, 47–49, 120
    being in Christ, 33, 44–47, 133, 137
    as a couple (couplehood), 78, 162
    and faith, 32–50
    as being in relationship with God, 32, 35, 40–41, 50, 80, 152
    "I-Thou" relationship, 27, 40, 67
    being part of God's story, 47–48, 50, 99, 101, 114–15, 120, 122, 134, 135, 137–138, 141, 144,
    and memory and faith, 100–116
    and knowing who I am, 32–50
    the relational self, 36–38
image of God, 32, 33, 35, 36–41, 43, 44, 48–50, 97, 137
imago Dei, 36–41
implications (of the research), 150–64
    the experience and practice of faith in dementia, 152–55
    faith nurture in the context of dementia, 158–60
    the response of the church, 155–57
    new perspectives for theology, 160–62

Jenson, Robert, 86n
Jesus,
    commitment to, 107

being a disciple/follower of, xii, 5, 7, 23, 43, 52, 115, 121, 123, 128, 161
encounter with, 52, 108
knowing Jesus, 5, 15, 32, 45, 52, 58–61, 64, 103, 108, 152
presence of, 59, 115, 126, 131, 145, 151
relationship with, 38, 58–61, 66, 107, 110, 136
see also Christ
Jewell, Albert, 169
see also Goldsmith, Malcolm; Hughes, Julian C.; MacKinlay, Elizabeth
joy(-ful), ix–x, 15, 62–63, 83, 86, 96, 97, 100, 106, 110, 113, 119, 125–27, 135, 138, 144, 145, 148, 159
in suffering, 126–27, 138, 156

Katsuno, Towako, 25, 126, 134–35, 151
Keck, David, 3, 18–19, 48, 86, 98, 105, 115–16, 135, 137
Kent, Elizabeth, 129
Kevern, Peter, 4, 11, 22, 24–25, 34n, 41, 98, 117n, 121
Kilby, Karen, 41–42
kingdom, the, 145, 146
Kitwood, Tom, 20, 26–27, 34, 35, 93
knowing God, 51–65
Kontos, Pia C., 103
Kontos, Pia C., and Gary Naglie, 27, 46n
Kuhse, Helga, and Peter Singer, 26

lament, 91, 156–57
Lartey, Emmanuel, 8
Lennon, Dennis, 106
listen(ed/ing), to people with dementia, ix, 1, 2, 8, 9, 14–15, 18, 30–31, 38, 54, 64, 67, 75, 80, 83, 107, 112–13, 125, 132, 134, 140, 150
lived experience, 30–31, 47–48, 84, 87–88, 89, 90, 98, 117, 119, 135, 144–48, 154–155

and theology of dementia, 8–9, 14, 17–19, 21, 27, 160–62, *see also* questions, arising from dementia
lived experience, research participants', the experience of faith, 51–65, 152–155
the experience of practice, 66–81, 152–155
finding meaning/purpose in dementia, 120–23, 154
growing faith, 117–132, 154, 158
memory funding faith, 100–103, 106–116, 153, 159
hope, 133–149, 152–154, 159
"walking through shadow," 82–87, 89–99, 151, 154, 157, 163
"who I am," 32–50, 152, 153
Locke, John, 26
Luther, Martin, 37, 97n

MacKinlay, Elizabeth, 3, 24
MacKinlay, Elizabeth and Corinne Trevitt, 22, 23–24, 44–45, 53, 120, 128, 134
MacKinlay, Karen, 96
Magnusson, Sally, 19
Manen, Max van., 83
Mast, Benjamin, 115n, 129, 131, 157
Matthews, Eric, 103
McFadden, Susan, et al., 64n, 152
McFadyen, Donald, 72–73
McGrath, Alister, 7, 107
meaning,
finding, 23–25, 53n, 120n, 128, 134
of memory, 27–28, 63
search(ing) for, 53, 120n, 121, 154
see also purpose
medical,
perspective(s), 20, 21, 35, 55, 77
diagnoses, 33–34
memory,
autobiographical, 28–29, 107, 115–16
building memories, 159
collective 48, 105, 161
embodied, 15, 29, 103, 107
faith(-ed), 100–116, 104, 107–15

memory (*continued*)
    and fragile clues, 28, 101–102, 103, 116
    funding faith, 15, 100–116, 151, 153
    (of) God's faithfulness, 108, 112, 123, 125, 138, 146, 153
    heart (and), 104–106, 115–16
    and identity, 27–30, 101–103
    memory loss, 3, 12, 34, 56–57, 70–71, 76, 79, 92, 95–96, 101, 107, 142, 146, 153
    and remembering God/Jesus, 104, 114
    of Scripture, xv, 104, 106, 144, 161
    and time, 25, 28, 102, 115–16
    of the Word, 106
    zkr, 104–5
Merleau-Ponty, Maurice, 27, 29
methodology and research approach, 31n, 52n
ministry,
    implications for, 150–64
    and practical theology, 8–10, 17–18, 83, 155
mission (missiological),
    church's role, 7,
    God's mission, 7, 8, 9, 64, 121, 155, 163
    missio Dei, 7
    missiological and ministerial impetus, 9–10
Moltmann, Jürgen, 41, 42, 97n
music, songs and hymns, 29, 51n, 75, 103, 113, 119, 140, 144, 159
mystery, 22, 43, 44, 54, 98, 122, 126, 134, 139, 143n, 146

naming,
    acknowledge(ing), 64, 83, 90–91, 93, 125, 153

    dementia, 93, 153
    of grief, 90–91
narrative, biblical *or* scriptural, 48, 49, 50, 87–88, 105n, 122, 137–38, 155

neurons (neurology, neurological), ix, 25, 29, 47, 96, 102
neuroscience, 21

orientation, disorientation and reorientation, 10–11, 14–16, 19, 82n, 118, 119, 151, 154
    orientation: 14, 37, 45, 49, 50, 82, 89, 90, 121
    disorientation 15, 50, 80, 82–99, 119, 120, 158
    reorientation (new orientation) 15–16, 91, 99, 101, 106, 119, 126, 132, 134, 135, 137, 140, 147–48, 150, 151, 154 155, 158, 159
Osmer, Richard R., 9, 155, 163n
other faiths, 163

pastoral
    cycle, 8, 18, 131
    expertise, development of, 160
    practice, 162
    a pastoral theology of suffering, 83–87, 97n
Pattison, Stephen, 8n
Patton, Michael Q., 162
perception, art of, 83
person, the,
    holistic (view/emphases/understanding of), 20–21, 28–29, 39–40
    medical definitions of, 21, 77
    personhood, 3, 19, 20, 24, 25–28, 35n, 40, 41, 44, 144
    self-identity, 25–28
    phenomenology, 30–31, 52n
    see also 83n
Post, Stephen G., 26, 28, 38, 101
power, issues of, x, 91, 92, 106
practical theology, 2, 8–10, 14, 17–18, 83, 155, 162
    and evangelicalism, 9–10
    as redescription (from the perspective of the Bible), 10, 138
prayer, 1, 7, 15, 18, 29, 43, 64, 66, 67, 70, 71–72, 78, 80, 115, 121,

122, 142, 143, 150, 152, 153, 159, 160, 162, *see also* faith practice, Bible and prayer
propositon(al), 3, 37, 46, 123, 124
purpose(s),
    discovery/finding of, 15, 99, 154
    God's, 8, 36, 48, 119, 120–123, 124, 127, 135, 163
    missiological, 9–10
    sense of, 22, 30, 128, 140, 151
    perception of God's, 119, 120–23, 125, 132, 154, 158

qualitative research, ix, *see also* research
questions arising from(about) dementia,
    dementia, xv–xvi, 1–2, 3–5, 7, 8, 24, 26, 32–50, 124, 128, 154
    the community of faith (church), 7, 73, 128, 153, 154
    the experience of faith in dementia, 3–6, 7–8, 14, 16, 17, 18–19, 24, 25, 29–30, 57, 63, 83, 84, 85, 94, 101, 117–18, 122, 126, 133, 134, 153, 154, 158, 163
    identity, 32–50, 67, 153
    memory,
    and identity, 3, 19, 25, 26, 28–29, 30
    and time, 25, 28
    personhood, 19–20, 25–28, 30, 44
    Scripture *and* Bible (biblical understanding), 8, 49, 163
    suffering and evil, 84–87, 89, 93, 151
    theological, 18–19, 21, 32, 35–50, 120, 160–63

rational *and* relational, 3, 6, 22, 26–27, 36–38, 40–42, 145
reason, 26, 37, 38, 42, 87
Reinders, Hans S., 37n, 85, 93
reflection(s), 16, 18, 83, 147n, 153
    for further reflection, questions, 16, 31, 50, 65, 81, 99, 116, 132, 149, 164
relationality, 3, 37, 40–43, 49, 67

relationship,
    with Christ (Jesus), 5–6, 9, 37, 38, 44, 47, 58–61, 66, 107–10, 117
    with God, xv, 3, 5, 6, 9, 11, 13, 15, 23, 24, 27, 30, 32, 34–35, 37, 38, 42, 43, 44, 49, 50, 52–58, 61–65, 66–70, 72, 80, 83, 96–97, 103, 104, 106, 110, 111, 115, 116, 118, 119, 120, 121, 123
    made for, 40–41
    with others, 6, 19, 26–27, 30, 34, 67, 73, 74, 76, 77, 78, 79, 92, 94, 96
    see also community of faith, belonging to the Body of Christ
religion (religious, religiousness),
    extrinsic, 5, 23, 66
    and faith, 14, 22–23, 66
    intrinsic, 23
    practice, 5, 66
    spirituality and, 14, 20, 21–23
remember(ing),
    community, 29n, 48, 114–15, 119, 128–30
    faith, xv, 6, 63, 100–116
    God, 18, 70, 104–105, 115, 119, 124, 131
    God's remembering, 15, 124, 148
    see also memory
reorientation, 10, 82n, 91, 99, 101, 106, 118, 119, 126, 132, 134, 140, 147, 148, 151, 154, 155, 158, 159, *see also* orientation, disorientation
research,
    goals of, 2, 9–10
    implications, 14, 16, 150–64
    qualitative, ix
    the participants (introducing), 11–13
    methodology, 52n
    see dementia and research
resources (faith, spiritual, inner), 1–2, 25, 69, 71, 80, 152, 154, 160, 162
resurrection (hope of), 9, 36, 89, 99, 114, 133, 137–38, 141–42, 143–44, 147–49, 159

Root, Andrew, 8, 9n, 10n, 17–18,
    63–64, 107, 141n, 160

Sabat, Steven R., 20–21, 27, 93–94
sacred(ness), 16, 19, 42, 151
sadness, 67, 74, 76, 87, 89, 90, 99, 102,
    124, 144, 151, 153, 157
SAGA, 2
salvation,
    being saved, 6n, 37n, 46–47, 135,
        137
    saving faith, xvi, 18, 161
    sozo, 46
Sapp, Stephen, 22, 103
Saunders, James, 20, 115
Schacter, Daniel, 28, 29n, 102
Scripture(s), scriptural
    authority of, 10
    as context
    faith, 38
    lens of, 148–49
    memory of, xv, 106, 161, 104, 106,
        161
    narrative, 137–38
    reading, 69, 106, 142–43, 157, 159
    understanding (interpretations) of,
        7, 8, 41, 46, 69–70
    voice(s) of, 14, 38
    see also Bible (biblical)
Scripture4All, 125n
Scripture Union, 68
self, 3, 13, 19, 26, 27, 28–29, 33, 35,
    38–39, 40, 46, 77, 93, 102, 103
    embodied, 27, 29
    identity, 25, 27, 28, 38–39
    medical definitions, 12, 21, 33–34,
        77
    -perception, 92
    sense of, 23, 26, 28, 102
    see also person
Shamy, Eileen, 3, 4, 6, 11, 21, 28, 29,
    35, 47, 103, 144
shadow(s), experiencing 15, 80, 82–84,
    89, 92–99
sin and guilt, 46, 85, 86–87, 141, 142,
    143
Singer, Peter, 26

singing, songs and hymns, 11, 29, 51n,
    75, 90, 103, 113, 119n, 124,
    140, 159
solidarity,
    divine, 97
    of the church, with those living
        with dementia, 130, 146, 149,
        155, 157
soul,
    body-and-soul, 28, 39–40, 104,
        105, 115
    "dark night of the soul," 62, 64,
        82, 96
    heart and, 31, 56, 104, 105, 140
    nephesh, 39
    psuche, 39
    rational, 37
Spaemann, Robert, 27
Spirit, *see* Holy Spirit
spiritual (spirituality), ix, 116
    care, ix, 11, 20, 29, 31, 157
    growth, 7, 25, 83, 117–19, 120, 127,
        128, 132, 134, 148, 150, 154,
        155, 158, *see also* growing faith
    in dementia, 3, 23–25, 31, 35, 54,
        64, 134–35, 163
    needs, 4, 20,
    resources, 25, 163
    support, 76, 78–80, 153, 161, 162
    understandings of, 14, 20, 21–24
stigma,
    becoming a stranger, 95
    cultural stigma, x, 12, 92–94
    experiencing stigma, 92–95
    labelled, 12, 34, 92–93, 100
    malignant social positioning, 21,
        93–94
    malignant spiritual positioning, 94
    stigmatization (-ing), 20–21, 36,
        39–40, 92–95, 99, 153, 156
    see also fear(s)
Stott, John, 80, 125n, 126, 130
Stuckey, Jon C., 52, 118
Stuckey, Jon C., and Lisa P. Gwyther,
    22
suffering, 62, 82–99
    of Christ, 15, 95, 97–99
    evil and suffering, 86–87

experiencing shadow, 89–97
New Testament norm, 88–89
pastoral theology of, 84–86
rejoicing in, 72, 83, 126–27
theodicy, 87, 151–52
transcendence of, 24, 120, 122, 134
see also dementia, struggles; joy in suffering; transcendence
Scripture Union International Council (SUIC), 68
Summa, Michela, and Thomas Fuchs, 29
Swinton, John, 10, 19, 21, 23, 25, 29, 39, 42, 44, 46, 47, 62, 82n, 83, 86, 87, 88, 92n, 93, 94, 95, 103, 113, 118n, 122, 123, 126, 127, 129, 134n, 138, 145, 147n, 156, 157
Swinton, John, and Harriet Mowat, 8, 19, 155, 162

thankfulness, 72, 77, 126, 132
theodicy, 87, 151–52
theological
  questions, xv–xvi, 19, 32–50, 84, 87, 161
  perspectives, 25, 33,
  reflection(s), 8, 16, 18–19, 83, 155
  "soundness," 21
  understanding, 32, 36, 145, 154, 155, 161
theology,
  new perspectives for, 160–162
  pastoral theology of suffering, 84–91, *see also* pastoral; suffering
time,
  autobiographical, 28, 116
  and eternity, 28, 140, 145
  "I have now," 146–47
  past, present and future, 28, 44, 48, 102, 107, 116, 136
  present-future hope, 132, 133–34, 136–38, 139–40, 144–49
  temporality, 53, 53n
  time-transcendent purposes of God, 48
  see also Heidegger; questions, memory and time

training and education, 156, 157, 160, 161
transcendence, 22, 24, 59, 120, 122, 128, 134, 137, 148
transcendent
  experience(s), 9, 62
  hope, 138
  sense of purpose, 22
  sense of relationship with God, 35, 130
  time-transcendent purposes of God, 48
Trinity, 41–43, 57, 98
  trust(s),in Jesus, 46, 59
  trust (in) God, xv, 15, 54, 58, 83, 84, 85, 87, 88, 89, 90, 91, 104, 119, 122, 123–25, 126, 128, 130, 132, 137, 139, 142, 144, 146, 147, 148, 152, 154, 158

University of Aberdeen, x, xi, xvi

Vanhoozer, Kevin J., 10

Wallace Daphne, 25–26
Weil, Simone, 89–90, 93, 97n, 98, 99
"Westminster Shorter Catechism," 36
Whitman, Lucy, 20n
Wilkinson, Heather, *see* Bartlett and Martin, 12
Williams, Rowan, 5, 42
Williams, 'Tricia, xi, xvi, 2, 30, 31, 33, 52, 53, 83, 117, 118, 124, 159, 160
Williams, Patricia S., xi, 27, 29, 41, 46, 86, 103
Wolverson (Radbourne), Emma L., et al., 134
Word, the, 5, 9, 14, 44, 68, 106, 132, 145, 151
worship, *see* faith practices
Wright, N.T., 105
Wright, Tom, 133, 139, 145

Zahl, Simeon, 5n, 37, 55, 58, 87
Zizioulas, John D., 41, 42

www.ingramcontent.com/pod-product-compliance
Lightning Source LLC
Chambersburg PA
CBHW031429150426
43191CB00006B/458